# TAFF'S ACRE
## —A History and Celebration—
## of Cardiff Arms Park

# TAFF'S ACRE

## —A History and Celebration— of Cardiff Arms Park

## Edited by David Parry-Jones

WILLOW BOOKS
Collins
8 Grafton Street, London
1984

Willow Books
William Collins Sons & Co Ltd
London · Glasgow · Sydney · Auckland
Toronto · Johannesburg

First published 1984
© David Parry-Jones 1984

British Library Cataloguing in Publication Data

Parry-Jones, David
Taff's Acre: A celebration of Cardiff Arms Park.
1. Cardiff Arms Park—History
I. Title
796.33′06842987     GV945.9.G7

ISBN 0-00-218097-9

Set in Monophoto Plantin by
Ace Filmsetting Ltd, Frome
Printed and bound in Great Britain by
William Collins Sons & Co Ltd, Glasgow

ILLUSTRATION CREDITS

Thanks are due to the following individuals and organisations for allowing their
photographs to be reproduced in this book: Associated Sports Photography;
BBC Hulton Picture Library; Colorsport; County of South Glamorgan Libraries;
Express Newspapers; John Harris, Swansea; Hill's Welsh Press, Cardiff; George
Herringshaw, Leicester; Illustrated London News; New Zealand Rugby
Museum; Terence Soames, Cardiff; South Wales Argus; Sport & General;
Welsh Folk Museum, St Fagan's; Western Mail & Echo Ltd; David Williams
Photography, Cardiff.

# CONTENTS

# FOREWORD

For a twelve-year-old to choose Boxing Day 1945 – and what was to prove one of the outstanding rugby matches of the decade – for his first visit to Cardiff Arms Park's north terrace was, with hindsight, a daring move. Starved of rugby by the Second World War a hundred thousand Welshmen would dearly have loved to watch unbeaten Cardiff RFC meet the undefeated New Zealand Army touring XV, the Kiwis, but bomb damage had limited the ground's capacity to 27,000. Even so, as Bleddyn Williams and Billy Cleaver attacked and Ike Proctor or Bob Scott hit back, powerful undercurrents of excitement and involvement flowed through the huge throng causing it to lean and sway and press upon itself alarmingly; and I neither felt secure nor saw any of the game until some cheery-voiced grown-ups who declared that they were miners from a place called Treorchy lifted me with strong, kind hands onto a crush barrier. Perched there I saw Jim Kearney score the single try that beat Cardiff, and blinked back tears.

But since that day I remember only joy, laughter, excitement and exhilaration at Cardiff Arms Park. I have swallowed its mud, barked my knees on its April sandpaper surface. I have stood spellbound to acclaim magnificent deeds by the brightest stars in world rugby; lost a hat when Jarrett or Edwards scored; ducked as half-time urine emptied onto the terrace from rusted pipes high in the old North Stand; stood through three hours' torrential rain while Wales failed to beat South Africa; broken pressbox discipline by cheering a Barry John burst; lost my microphone cool as Holmes scored a winning try. Cardiff Arms Park has consistently staged the Greatest Rugby Shows on Earth.

As a Welshman and a citizen of Cardiff one is grateful to the players – both club and International – who have given such pleasure and pride of identity down the years; while as a devotee of the Rugby game one salutes the administrators responsible for the twin-theatre complex which Wales's capital city now boasts. And presumably, in the main, these are also the considerations which have motivated others whose contributions comprise what the publishers describe as a Celebration of Cardiff Arms Park. For their willingness to put pen to paper I thank:

GARETH WILLIAMS, lecturer in History at the University College of Wales, Aberystwyth; co-author of *Fields of Praise*, the widely-acclaimed history of the Welsh Rugby Union which won the Welsh Arts Council's 1981 Prize for Literature;
J. B. G. THOMAS, an elder among rugby writers. Author of thirty books, sometime Sports Editor and Chief Rugby Writer of the *Western Mail*;

H. M. BOWCOTT, eight times capped for Wales and a member of the British Isles party to New Zealand in 1930; subsequently a Welsh selector and President of the WRU;

WILFRED WOOLLER, like Harry Bowcott a one-time Cardiff RFC player who won 18 caps for Wales; as a cricketer he captained Glamorgan and was later an England Test selector;

BLEDDYN WILLIAMS, prince of post-war midfield players, a highly successful captain of Cardiff and Wales who won 22 caps;

JOHN BILLOT, succeeded J. B. G. Thomas as Sports Editor and Chief Rugby Writer of the *Western Mail*; distinguished rugby historian and statistician;

DAVID HAYWARD, 325 appearances for Cardiff (captain 1962–64), six Welsh caps; humorist and programme-editor supreme;

and RAY WILLIAMS, the Welsh Rugby Union's first Coaching Organiser who became its Secretary in 1981.

Several contributors, including the Editor, acknowledge the debt owed to C. S. Arthur's *Cardiff Rugby Club: History and Statistics 1876–1906* and to Danny Davies's immense work *Cardiff Rugby Club, 1876–1975*. Another valuable source has been *Fields of Praise* by Gareth Williams and David Smith (University of Wales Press, 1980).

Thanks are also due to a host of other contributors for shorter but no less vivid personal memoranda.

DAVID PARRY-JONES
Llandaff, Cardiff, 1984

# PROLOGUE

It might have been called Butefield, after the Marquess who lived in the castle and once owned the land. Or Victoria Gardens, to commemorate the monarch of the day. Or even, simply, Riverside Stadium. Instead it immortalised a nearby coaching inn and became 'Cardiff Arms Park'. Thus, by chance, was bequeathed to Wales's colosseum one of its greatest attributes.

To be sure, no latter-day image-maker could have dreamed up a name which so ringingly suggests challenge and chivalry together with the open space required for a volatile, fast-moving sport. From the start, it struck an answering chord among rugby footballers everywhere. Slowly and steadily during the twentieth century clubs and countries came to accept that an appearance at Cardiff amounted to a winning of spurs in the game.

For Frenchmen, New Zealanders, South Africans, Australians and members of nations newer to the game, visits have necessarily been rare, and hence more precious. But equally, to the Welsh themselves and to their near neigh-

*The Cardiff Arms hotel, demolished in the nineteenth century but immortalised by the nearby Park which took its name. Above the window, top centre, are mounted the arms of the city of Cardiff, or township as it then was: red chevrons on a yellow shield.*

9

bours from England, Scotland and Ireland, to play at Cardiff is and always will be something special and out of the ordinary.

The communications revolution of the seventies meant that the ground went global, with television viewers in five continents enabled to enjoy the action as it happened and share the magic of the place. But to be brought wholly under its spell demands not pictures, however brilliant, but actuality: the feel of a match ticket, floppy-edged from constant fingering; the bright and beery breeze down Quay Street; scarlet dragons beside the Angel Hotel, swirling above anoraks, bobble hats and duffel coats; the huge human embrace within the stadium; the torrent of sound with which the Thirty are greeted by the Sixty Three Thousand . . . Cardiff Arms Park is as much sensation as spectacle.

Wait, though: there are terms which have to be defined.

What Cardiff Arms Park, precisely, are we talking about?

A question which is more meaningful than it sounds, as a first-time visitor passing from Westgate Street through the Gwyn Nicholls gates swiftly discovers. He is immediately confronted by a choice: to proceed down the ramp on his right, or to walk upwards and to his left. Either way he then arrives at a rugby football ground – a trim, compact and homely enclosure with royal-blue seating in grandstands set off by a distant line of conifers; or

*Exuberance and hyperbole on the terraces.*

a massive U-shape serried round with a myriad scarlet seats, a soaring state-ment in concrete.

In other words, he has entered a single park divided by its central grand-stand structure into two exclusive semi-detached properties. They are respectively the home of Cardiff Rugby Football Club, and the national rugby ground of Wales owned and administered by the Welsh Rugby Union, with 33,000 seats and 29,500 standing places, completed – with a special match to mark the achievement – on 7 April 1984.

The complex represents the realisation of a magnificent dream – and yet one which so nearly remained unfulfilled.

In July 1958 Wales played host nation to the Sixth British Empire and Commonwealth Games. Beautiful Llyn Padarn staged rowing events. Featherweight boxer Howard Winstone won a gold medal for the home country at Sophia Gardens Pavilion across the river from Cardiff Arms Park. Swimming and diving events were held in a purpose-built pool nearby.

But the centrepiece of everything, the athletics meeting, took place in the heart of the city on the rugby football field where Cardiff and Wales had played matches since the previous century. Owned by the Cardiff Arms Park Company, in which the Welsh Rugby Union held a controlling interest, the stadium's facilities were leased to the Cardiff Athletic Club with its several Sections, including Rugby, and also for certain periods each week to a grey-hound racing company. It was the two lessees who stepped aside to make room for the athletes.

On top of the perimeter dog track was laid a racing circuit for human sprinters, field events being mounted between the goal-lines. Behind the existing north stand leading athletes of the day could limber up in the club and county cricket enclosure fringed by bowling greens and tennis courts. The setting proved admirable, the weather was fine, competitors showed their satisfaction with the organisation by cracking records every day, and although illness prevented the Queen's attendance her tape-recorded voice was broadcast on the public address system announcing that she would create her eldest son Charles Prince of Wales. There was widespread agree-ment that the whole event had been a stunning success.

It was, however, to have far-reaching and decisive effects on the future of rugby in Wales. Hardly had the Duke of Edinburgh completed the closing ceremony and the athletes left for home than work-parties came bustling in to restore the ground to its normal condition. In September the national XV of Germany were to be Cardiff RFC's first opponents of the new season, while the greyhound company's wish to resume meetings was even more pressing. As a first priority the running track was torn up for removal to another part of the city and turf re-laid for the dogs.

In their haste, however, the gangs failed to fork and break up the sub-soil which had been intensively packed and rolled some inches below ground-level

*Curtain down on the Sixth British Empire and Commonwealth Games. Hardly was the closing ceremony complete – see athlete with national flag – than workmen moved in to refurbish the stadium for greyhound racing and rugby. Their haste seemed almost indecent.*

to provide a sure foundation for the six lanes. Henceforth it would act as a barrier to effective drainage, so that rain falling on the perimeter of the rugby pitch would collect and seep with dire results on to a playing surface which, formed of silt and lying beneath the level of the adjoining Taff estuary at high tide, had always been heavy and glutinous.

The problem was exacerbated by a succession of wet winters; but whereas, when the ground was unplayable, the Cardiff club could, reluctantly, move, postpone or cancel fixtures, International matches had perforce to be played. Hence the Welsh Rugby Union began to be embarrassed by an ever-increasing volume of criticism from other Unions, whose headquarters boasted excellent playing surfaces. Their administrators viewed with understandable distaste the reptilian conditions into which their select XVs were regularly plunged on visits to the Principality.

To its chagrin the Union was powerless to act. For years it had paid the major part of bills connected with the ground – rates, repairs, insurances and the periodic improvements carried out. Yet all it possessed in exchange was the right to use Cardiff Arms Park six times a year. Further, because of leases drawn up nearly four decades earlier it could not prevent the pitch being used as often as Cardiff RFC required it. Welsh rugby's theatre of action was therefore without a satisfactory stage.

The situation was unsatisfactory for numerous other reasons. The WRU had never owned offices at the stadium and carried on its day-to-day business at a rented and rather antiquated suite several hundred yards away. There were no rooms at hand where visiting officials and VIPs could be received and entertained. The bench-style seating accommodation in the stands was cramped compared with that provided at grounds such as Twickenham and Murrayfield, while the terracing and enclosures lay in need of refurbishment. There were even murmurs that sections of the superstructures were unsafe and moreover, being largely of wood, constituted a fire risk (though any blaze would surely have been extinguished at half-time by the nauseous and widespread leakage from ancient urinals).

Thus in these many respects the proud Welsh came a poor fourth behind England, Scotland and Ireland.

Although the impact of television (and, in particular, of representative rugby screened live) was already eating into attendances at all kinds of sporting contests, Cardiff RFC were still used to gates averaging around 10,000 at this time and thus not discontented with the status quo. Their first, second and youth XVs used the Park at least once a week, and they were generous in the granting of permission for the staging of county, district and charity matches. Yet despite the inevitable deterioration in the condition of their pitch the club politely but firmly turned down requests from the WRU to limit its use. A scheme for underground heating, which might have helped dry the turf and encourage the growth of grass, was briefly considered before being rejected as too expensive.

Some people wonder why in the broader interest of the game in the Principality the Cardiff Athletic Club – in particular Cardiff RFC – were not prepared to play at home less frequently, especially in December and January. It needs to be remembered, however, that Cardiff were the ground's senior users and had played on it since 1876; International games were not held there by the WRU until 1884 and then only occasionally. The Cardiff membership, vociferous and powerful, wished to play and watch rugby as regularly as possible, while the large casual following which paid at the turnstiles also needed encouraging. For the time being, therefore, no radical proposals for upgrading the stadium could be expected from this direction.

The WRU, however, had enjoyed an infusion during the fifties of new men with energy and vision who were to effect a transformation of the situation. There was W. H. 'Bill' Clement who became its Secretary in 1956, turning his back on a promising career in local government. Endowed with an impeccable rugby pedigree he had been a wing for Llanelli, Wales and the British Isles in the years just before the Second World War. There was Cliff Jones – C. W. Jones (Cambs U & Cardiff) in the archives – who had established a reputation in the thirties as one of the all-time-great stand-off halves and now returned to the game as a member of the Union's thirty-strong general committee with ideas to contribute.

And, above all, there was Kenneth Harris, by his own admission never a player of great distinction but a rugby administrator who was to prove himself one of the most influential and far-sighted of the twentieth century. Certainly Wales was lucky in being able to draw on his talents at so critical a period.

Banking had run in Harris's blood since his departure from Penarth Grammar School at fifteen, via technical college, to a junior post with Barclays at their Pontypridd branch. Promotion was steady but sure, so that by the time an invitation arrived from the WRU in 1952 to become its Honorary Treasurer he had just returned from the head office of his firm in London to a district managership in Cardiff, where he would later be local director. With his career so surely founded he was in an ideal position to accept a big outside challenge.

After a thorough-going scrutiny of the responsibilities attaching to the office the newcomer decided that the task of putting Welsh rugby on a firm business footing was well worth tackling, but that it would be Herculean. To achieve an immediate increase in his muscle-power, therefore, he brought about a change in the Union's constitution by which its treasurer gained a seat on the general committee with a voice and a vote. In this way the pressure he could exert on colleagues and the advice he could give would be more immediate and direct.

By 1960 and the inward tour of Britain by South Africa Harris had brought off several fiscal coups which stood the WRU and its member clubs in good stead and could turn his attention to the question of a national ground. His background and character probably meant that from the outset he viewed the project as a money-spinner which could eventually put amateur Rugby Union football in Wales on a sound basis and keep it there for good. But there is no doubt that he was also capable of taking a patriotic standpoint and setting his sights on a prestigious headquarters complex which would reflect creditably upon his countrymen and the game they loved. Further, since taking office he had visited changing rooms at the end of some weather-stricken midwinter International matches at Cardiff Arms Park and viewed with horror the wretched condition of the players: young men deserved better, he determined, especially in Wales.

One of the worst days of all had been 3 December 1960. When they left the field at the close of the Wales–South Africa Test the thirty players were scarcely recognisable as human beings. After an eighty-minute slog through shin-deep mud and sheets of rain that beat in endlessly above the Taff they were plastered with filth, every orifice clogged with slime. If Harris and his fellow officers had any lingering doubts that something must be done they were finally swept into limbo during the night when the river burst its banks under the weather's maniacal assault. By Sunday morning much of central Cardiff lay under five feet of water – including the famous pitch where the Springboks had hung on so gallantly for a 3-0 victory.

*Sunday 4 December 1960. On the previous afternoon South Africa beat Wales 3-0. During the night the Taff burst its banks and Cardiff Arms Park lay knee-deep in water.*

The WRU's Development Committee, formed a number of years previously to deal with particular issues affecting Cardiff Arms Park, was thus spurred to the task of identifying a suitable site for the sorely-needed national ground. Negative outcomes of previous negotiations with Cardiff Athletic Club persuaded its six members that Cardiff Arms Park must be dismissed as a possibility; and in any case the argument for a greenfield environment untrammelled by considerations of joint tenancies was now being advanced cogently by Kenneth Harris. After two areas of land within the capital had been ruled out – Leckwith Moors because of a flood danger from the River Ely and Pontcanna Fields because of the City Council's unwillingness – a consensus view began to emerge in favour of some ninety acres south of Bridgend, roughly halfway between Cardiff and Swansea and adjoining the main A48 road through Glamorgan.

Island Farm, as the bulk of the land was known, had undoubted appeal. Its geographic location would find acceptance with the powerful rugby lobbies in both east and west South Wales. It could be reached easily by road or rail. There was room to build a stadium for 80,000 and lay out appropriate car parks. By May 1962 the WRU Treasurer could tell the Development Committee with no little satisfaction that the owners, Dunraven Estates, were prepared to part with the site for £19,250 – or £350 an acre – subject to one or two easily met conditions. History was repeating itself, for Bridgend had been the choice of an earlier generation of administrators whose goal was never reached.

Under a cloak of secrecy remarkable in a nation where gossip and chit-chat are also national sports, an admirable eighteen months of progress had been charted in the annals of the Welsh Rugby Union. When firm recommendations were put forward by the Development Committee nearly all member clubs indicated eagerness for the signing of a contract to buy Island Farm. At this juncture Kenneth Harris was convinced that no insuperable obstacle stood in the way of the construction of a national rugby ground there and that the project would proceed without ado. Declarations of intent quickly followed.

To Cardiff RFC, however (notwithstanding the existence of senior officers privy to the planning process of the WRU) and to the city council, the news came as a bombshell. The plan disclosed by the Welsh Rugby Union presaged a catastrophic loss of prestige to Cardiff, which would become the only capital in the northern hemisphere not to stage its country's home rugby International fixtures. Its shopping centre would be poorer by the thousands of pounds normally spent on match day by the Welsh from outlying areas as well as visiting fans. Imponderables such as the city's unique International atmosphere and tradition seemed doomed.

No wonder, then, that the Lord Mayor of the day, Alderman Clifford Bence, demanded the urgent presence at his Parlour of the Cardiff Athletic

Club's top officials. There were crucial questions to be answered: What exactly was going on? Why were the WRU threatening to deprive the city of International rugby? And should not some constructive counter-proposal be formulated in double-quick time?

For the second time in a decade Wales was lucky with her man of the moment. Heading the visiting delegation was a certain Hubert Johnson.

'Uncle Hubert', as he enjoyed styling himself, had come to Cardiff RFC from Llandaff as a bustling lock forward, appeared occasionally for the first team and for four seasons captained the 'Rags', or second, XV. Once his suburban confectionery business had been put on a sound footing this gregarious bachelor began devoting the bulk of his leisure-time to the affairs of the club, whose chairman and president he successively became. And though in later years other officials liked to say boldly, 'We could have managed without the WRU,' Johnson recognised that if the Union went through with its move to Bridgend, Cardiff would be left with an enormous millstone around their neck in the shape of a vast, ageing expensive-to-run stadium which no longer enjoyed the privilege of staging representative rugby football. He began burning the midnight oil and to his eternal credit came up with an outline scheme which, against the odds, seemed capable of meeting the rights and requirements of a variety of interested parties. By October 1962 its essence had been captured in an architect's drawing and could be put before the WRU.

Although differing in many respects from the complex which finally materialised, its two-stadium concept was to prove definitive. Grandstands were proposed for the east and west ends of the rugby ground, which would become the property and headquarters of the Union (the original sketch includes a tower block of administrative offices beside the river), stage International matches, and accommodate 75,000 spectators. Cardiff RFC would play next-door on a pitch running parallel to the existing one and flanked by purpose-built grandstands. The club and county cricketers of Cardiff and Glamorgan would move to a ten-acre expanse of meadowland, which the City Council was quick to make available, at Sophia Gardens. The requirements of the bowls, tennis and hockey enthusiasts within the Cardiff Athletic Club were also to be catered for. A bold and above all feasible vision, it received a warm welcome in most quarters.

During the months that followed anyone looking closely might have detected a gleam in the eye of Kenneth Harris. The Hubert Johnson plan contained many snags, but it possessed one signal merit: it was highly unlikely to meet local authority opposition. Conversely, despite the formal application for planning permission to build a national ground at Bridgend, Glamorgan County Council (as it then was) had been slow to respond. The issue of planning permission, as it turned out, was the stumbling-block which led to the eventual abandonment in 1964 of Island Farm as a possible site: the Ministry of Transport had said that flyovers would have to be built to give access to the proposed stadium so that match traffic would not cause congestion on the Bridgend bypass. For these, it added, the WRU would have to foot a bill of perhaps £400,000.

Reluctantly, and with a feeling that various public bodies had been less than co-operative, the Union backed off to focus its full attention upon Cardiff Arms Park, announcing its willingness to co-operate on the Hubert Johnson proposals. It was, no doubt, with a sense of relief that its Treasurer began to set the wheels in motion.

First, the various parties had to know where they would stand after the impending upheaval. The WRU's objective was nothing less than the un-fettered freehold of that section of Cardiff Arms Park which it was to occupy. Its officers also understood perfectly the Cardiff club's wish for absolute security of tenure in their territory. Control of the land involved, still the property of the Cardiff Arms Park Company, was required.

A holding company was formed with the object of buying in the equity. Although sixty per cent of the shareholders agreed to sell, this was not satis-

*Under the watchful scrutiny of senior colleagues, Kenneth Harris and Hubert Johnson sign the momentous agreement whereby the WRU acquires control of the freehold of Cardiff Arms Park. The date is 13 October 1970. Johnson's plan, advanced in 1962, for a two-stadium complex had proved decisive in the reconstruction project.*

factory. Under Kenneth Harris's guidance, the WRU put both companies into liquidation, obtained two professional valuations and then used its majority control of the Cardiff Arms Park Company to sell at the higher figure. In the final liquidation shareholders who had turned down the initial offer of £1 for each share received half-a-crown (12½p).

At last the Welsh Rugby Union owned an asset worth developing and putting money into. A chill might have gripped the hearts of its general committee had members known the havoc inflation was to wreak upon budgets and forward planning in the coming years. If their confidence ever flagged, however, the Honorary Treasurer had only to repeat the under-statement of which he was so fond about the appeal of the product: 'The demand for tickets at Cardiff Arms Park, particularly for seats, is always far in excess of the facilities available.'

If the Union now enjoyed a sense of swimming with the current Cardiff Athletic Club were positively buoyant. There were still traditionalists who talked of the 'sacrifice of a birthright' but realists knew that the deal was fair and even generous. The WRU was paying not only for the creation of a cricket ground at Sophia Gardens, to county championship standards, but also for the construction of a superb new club rugby ground to accommodate 18,000 spectators, 5000 of whom would be seated. There was a feeling that the club's main negotiators, Frank Trott and David Grant, had done a good job in persuading the WRU to commit itself to expenditure of £180,000.

Kenneth Harris would later be unstinting in his praise of the WRU member clubs' patience during the protracted in-fighting, particularly at the 1964 juncture when he had to cast cold water on the manifest enthusiasm for Island Farm and ask them to back the Cardiff project. For a time there were glum faces to be seen again when architects Osborne V. Webb and Partners (John Webb was a senior and highly respected member of the Athletic Club) and the engineers, G. A. Williamson and Partners, calculated that Hubert Johnson's scheme for two grandstands standing back to back between the grounds would not work since the space simply did not exist. But out of this apparent set-back sprang the elegant solution of a double-sided structure to overlook both pitches, with a most unusual 'flying freehold' relating not to a boundary along the ground but rather to the common profile of the two stands. For complex financial reasons arising out of the agreement reached with Cardiff, however, the modification cost the Union £100,000 more than it had bargained for.

There was a last hurdle to be overcome, in the shape of the totalisator used twice a week by the greyhound company and housed in the north stand. Not until this had been transferred to the southern side of Cardiff Arms Park – with the accompaniment of £15,000 compensation – could tenders be ob-tained and a contract awarded to the Andrew Scott civil engineering concern of Margam to build a new north stand. In this first stage of the WRU's plan to reconstruct the main stadium in its entirety it had been the intention to include a west stand, but when the estimated cost soared by more than one third from £1 million to £1,300,000 between June 1966 and October 1967 this and some other features were postponed.

Such expenditure, even after a little judicious pruning, was still staggering to contemplate for an amateur organisation whose receipts – not profit – from International matches twice each winter amounted to no more than £60,000 and which had no further dependable source of income. Was there the remotest chance that the money could be raised? And if it were, could it ever be repaid?

Again the Honorary Treasurer remained sanguine and suggested answers. Good husbandry, Kenneth Harris predicted, would mean that in 1969 when the bills had to be paid the WRU might expect to have accumulated from its own resources some £400,000. A bank loan, plus the proceeds from special celebration matches and other commercial enterprises, could yield £200,000. Much of the remainder, proposed the Treasurer, could be raised by the sale of debentures, a £50 subscription guaranteeing the right to buy a grandstand seat for all International matches in the next fifty years. For £100 purchasers could secure a pair of adjoining seats.

The offer brought in £365,000 – but only after a period when, with the public's willingness to spend apparently exhausted, it was feared that the promised erection of a north stand for the Cardiff RFC ground might have to be postponed. The final £100,000 was attracted through the imaginative scheme suggested by a Pontypridd accountant, Alfred John, whereby the Pearl Assurance Company agreed to buy debentures to this value and re-sell them linked to policies paid for over ten years. Ultimately this part of the issue was over-subscribed.

Criticism was encountered by the Union on the grounds that too high a proportion of its debentures was taken up by commercial interests and by wealthy folk for whom attendance at an International match was merely part of the social round. Kenneth Harris and his colleagues defended themselves by pointing out that strict priorities were observed, with clubs, club members and the public being first invited to back the scheme. Only when their interest and purchasing power waned were advances made to big concerns, who picked up the final five per cent of the issue and in effect clinched the project's success.

An unexpected phenomenon in the succeeding years was the brisk market in debentures, which came to command hugely inflated sums. In the era now dawning – of Edwards, John, J. P. R. Williams, Bennett, Gerald Davies and the rest – possession of a Cardiff match ticket guaranteed fantastic entertainment and a heady patriotic fix. Even so, the record sum known to have changed hands – for four well-sited and adjacent debenture seats – is still stupendous: £16,000.

The WRU had no means either of halting such transactions or securing some of the profit for itself, though the sale and re-sale of subsequent deben-

*The date is 1933 and rising above the covered terrace is the WRU's giant new north stand, with a planned capacity of 5242 seats.*

ture issues was strictly limited to member clubs. Despite imperfections, however, the scheme had served its purpose triumphantly; the grand project could go ahead. With customary prudence the Honorary Treasurer was quick to establish a sinking fund to accumulate the funds which would be needed for the debentures' redemption half a century on.

And so to work, at long long last. On 18 September 1966 Cardiff cricket club played its last match on the smooth sward beneath the Westgate Street flats, packed its bags and moved across the River Taff to begin its hundredth year at Sophia Gardens, thus clearing the way for Cardiff Arms Park's transformation. In 1968 the contractors moved in to do the job which a Nazi land-mine had failed to complete in 1941, toppling the gaunt but gracious old north stand and sinking foundations for its replacement. Wrote the Cardiff RFC historian sadly, 'For months the site resembled a blitzed area of broken, tangled structure, a desolate sight . . . Our players would not again hear the cheering and acclaim of the crowd from this side of the ground in future club matches.' The Welsh XV too, with its many promising youngsters, gave memorable performances to half-full houses especially during the spectacular Championship season of 1968–69. When left wing Maurice Richards crossed for four tries against England that April, it was helmeted site-workers who got the best view of his record-equalling feat.

To the contractors' credit the new north stand and terracing were completed on time and the WRU's new stadium had begun to take shape – with a capacity reduced from its pre-demolition total by 3000 places. The difference was that now there were 12,000 more seats, and potential revenue from representative fixtures had been increased to close on £44,000. This was impressively demonstrated at the official opening of the National Ground on 17 October 1970, when 40,000 spectators saw a Welsh XV under John Dawes matched with a side selected by the Rugby Football Union's president W. C. (later Sir William) Ramsay. To Gareth Edwards fell the honour of obtaining the first score there, one of a six-try spectacular from which Wales emerged 26-11 victors. The teams, in a match refereed by Meirion Joseph, were:

WALES   J. P. R. Williams (London Welsh), A. Hill (Llanelli), S. J. Dawes (London Welsh, capt.), A. Lewis (Ebbw Vale), R. Mathias (Llanelli), B. John (Cardiff), G. Edwards (Cardiff), J. Lloyd (Bridgend), J. Young (Harrogate), B. Llewelyn (Llanelli), W. D. Thomas (Llanelli), D. Quinnell (Llanelli), D. Morris (Neath), M. Davies (London Welsh), J. Taylor (London Welsh).

RFU PRESIDENT'S XV   T. Kiernan (Cork Constitution & Ireland, capt.), K. Fielding (Moseley & England), J. Spencer (Headingley & England), D. Duckham (Coventry & England), R. E. Webb (Coventry & England), J-L. Berot (Toulouse & France), M. Pebeyre (Vichy & France), N. Suddon (Hawick & Scotland), F. Laidlaw (Melrose & Scotland), P. J. O'Callaghan (Dolphin & Ireland), M. Davis (Harlequins & England), J. Le Droff (Auch & France), R. Arneil (Leicester & Scotland), B. Dauga (Mont-de-Marsan & France), F. Slattery (UC Dublin & Ireland).

By a happy coincidence Kenneth Harris's seniority meant that he was the WRU president in this momentous year. 'At last,' he wrote in the match programme, 'the day has come when we can say, surely with some pride, that Wales has a National Rugby Ground of its own.' It fell to this past-master of understatement to select the side which opposed Cardiff RFC a fortnight later when the smaller adjoining stadium was opened. A parade of seventeen past captains before the kick-off must have inspired the club, which romped to victory by 17 points to 8. In the evening a celebration ball was held.

Well might Cardiff make merry. They had no debts to speak of and a magnificent new ground worthy of comparison with any in the world. Though their pitch would before long require expert attention to improve its texture, facilities generally were of an immensely high standard. Occasionally in the years to come there would be sharp exchanges with the folk next door about rights of way on International match days, car parking and similar details, but on the whole the club could look forward to an enhanced future. And they had been expressly granted permission to play showpiece matches against, for example, touring sides from New Zealand, Australia and South Africa on the National Ground.

For its part the WRU had momentum to keep up. Spectacular rugby football, with regular Welsh victories, ensured that the National Ground was a sell-out for major International matches and well-filled for representative fixtures featuring novel and exotic touring sides like Fiji, Tonga and Japan so that to Kenneth Harris's pleasure bank borrowing was eliminated by 1976. Now the Union installed offices at the ground's north east corner and reception rooms in the north stand, the existing suite being converted to a bar and writing-room for the press. The new premises included a board room, where the general committee could contemplate its next major step – building a west stand with 4300 seats and 1000 standing places. To clear the way for its construction the greyhound company was bought out for £12,000, some six years before their licence was due to expire.

Now began a period when nerves needed to be at their steadiest, for between March and June of 1976 the estimated cost of the structure shot from £610,000 to £700,000. Moreover controversy revolved around Kenneth Harris's latest money-raising scheme which proposed a bank loan of £350,000

*Painter Thomas Rathmell shows WRU Treasurer Kenneth Harris the mural chosen as a result of a competition sponsored by British Petroleum to decorate the reception rooms at the stadium.*

*The cantilever solution to the main grandstand, here shown at the western end of the ground, provided maximum spectator capacity and uninterrupted views of the whole field.*

and a debenture borrowing of another £350,000 from clubs. The latter stratagem, however, involved installing 4000 seats along the north terrace where hitherto 7000 had been able to stand, sing, barrack, boo, shout, clap and generate the arguably unique 'atmosphere' for which Cardiff Arms Park was famous. Traditionalists shook their heads and warned that the price of progress was too great. However, the spectre of hyper-inflation caused this lobby to haul down its colours, and a convincing address by its Honorary Treasurer at the WRU annual general meeting of 1976 won a vote of confidence from the membership. By February 1977 the lowest west stand tender had risen to £993,000; but emboldened by the preparedness of Barclays Bank to raise its overdraft to £500,000 and by a £1,048,000 response to its latest debenture offer (which was thus oversubscribed three times) the Union soldiered on, awarding a contract to the Sir Robert McAlpine concern.

Because the dog track and its overhead lighting had been removed it was possible at the same time to re-site the pitch five yards to the north – thus creating space for the eventual erection of a south stand – and fifteen yards west so that an enlarged and streamlined east terrace could be built at the city end of the stadium. Some north stand debenture holders grumbled that their seats as a result enjoyed a less advantageous position – complaints that were, naturally, balanced by expressions of satisfaction at the stand's other extreme.

This move was not before time, since late in 1976 it became apparent that the existing east terrace was in so appalling a state of repair that the WRU might be barred from using it at all. Some £900,000 was allocated to its reconstruction, also by McAlpine, and a double-tiered, uncovered structure stood complete by March 1980 in time for the Centenary season. Beneath it was laid out a snug banqueting suite where it soon became a tradition for incoming tourists to be received; above was sited an electronic scoreboard in keeping with contemporary trends: besides showing the state of play it could print out messages such as, 'Cardiff Arms Park welcomes the Scottish XV.'

Why was the eastern end of the ground not capped with a grandstand, so that a bowl rather than a U would be the final shape? With a twinkle in his eye Kenneth Harris enjoyed replying that he found the Parc des Princes in Paris – a complete oval – too noisy! He always added quickly that had the stadium been enclosed by tall stands it could have run into a serious light

*'Well, what did you expect for a quid – front row of the north stand?'*
South Wales Echo *cartoonist Gren's view of Irish supporters hoodwinked by ticket touts.*

problem, and those who saw the Wales–Maoris match of 13 November 1982, played in near darkness, appreciated the treasurer's caution. It was also thought desirable to keep one end of the ground open to drying winds – the bad days of the fifties and sixties were not being forgotten. Considerations of cost ruled out other adjuncts of modern sportsdromes such as under-turf electric heating and floodlights.

The prologue is nearly written, since the Centenary celebrations of 1980–81 produced a profit which made the completion of the national ground a realistic proposition. Nonetheless the financial requirements for the building of the

*A near-complete colosseum: a view of Cardiff Arms Park on 29 September 1983 with the gap between west and south stands about to be closed by the builders, Wimpey. Due north of the two rugby stadia can be seen the Castle restored for the Bute family by William Burges in the nineteenth century and, beyond, the national and civic buildings of Cathays Park.*

south stand were still chilling: not only would the WRU have to borrow £2.5 million from its bankers, it would also need £1.8 million through another debenture issue. Happily the success of the second issue was borne in mind and although the price per subscription was now £500 applications well in excess of the amount required still came in. Enterprising clubs used their debentures to secure monetary gain for themselves and, more to the point, Wimpey Construction was awarded a £4.3 million contract to build the stand with new changing rooms, a reception suite and dining facilities for players.

Rome had by no means been built in a day, and the 1967 prediction that reconstruction would be complete by 1982 proved optimistic by two years. But ultimately, when Scotland came to Wales in January 1984 for the opening match of the Championship season, it was to a reborn and perfectly formed Cardiff Arms Park which nevertheless enshrined within its new concrete ramparts the racial memory of a nation at play. In April 1984 the WRU staged a special match to mark the project's fulfilment – a hundred years to the week since the first international match staged at the ground.

It was only sad that Hubert Johnson, who had envisaged the whole mighty complex two decades earlier, was not there to witness its consummation. After a lingering illness he died on 5 June 1978 – having seen his beloved Cardiff RFC play many times on their new ground, and having planted a row of conifers which now flourish and commemorate 'Uncle Hubert' at the Taff end of the club ground.

Kenneth Harris never tired of saying, 'This has been the work of the whole fraternity of Welsh Rugby.' Certainly the achievement owed little to outside aid, for of the £8,794,500 total outlay only £160,000 came from public funds in the shape of a Sports Council grant. If as the years went by an apparently perverse determination manifested itself from time to time in the WRU to swim against tides of opinion and, for example, preserve links with South Africa, its origins may well lie in the disappointments experienced when it cast around for financial help from the Welsh Office, central Government, and the European Economic Community, only to find doors slammed in its face. Happily this mattered less because of the good counsel and financial acumen available within the Union's own ranks.

And no doubt the Honorary Treasurer allowed himself a rare glow of satisfaction as he surveyed the finished arena – an astonishing achievement for an amateur organisation hard pressed in turn by galloping inflation and then confidence-sapping recession. As a capital programme undertaken by a sporting organisation it is unsurpassed; as an act of faith it is unique.

Kenneth Harris was chairman of the WRU's Development Committee for all the twenty years in which Cardiff Arms Park was reborn as Wales's National Rugby Ground. He would wish his blushes to be spared.

But his midwifery cannot be denied. And our marvelling visitor to the stadium can be told, If you would see his achievement, Look around you.

## THE ARCHITECTS

### David Parry-Jones

Having been fellow students at the Welsh School of Architecture it was not altogether surprising that Ted Williams and John Webb subsequently elected to practise together, founding a partnership in 1952. Their experience widened and their professional reputation grew. Outside office hours they found time for active involvement in the social and sporting life of Cardiff – notably the Cardiff Athletic Club for whom they produced an imaginative drawing in 1962 to illustrate how Cardiff Arms Park might be developed as a two-stadium complex where the Welsh Rugby Union and Cardiff RFC could live as neighbours. But it still took their breath away when in 1964 they were briefed by the Welsh Rugby Union to proceed with the realisation of the scheme.

At the time there were very few points of reference. Most British football stadia had originated early in the century, but spectator sports had been in a sellers' market since the Second World War, with small need to persuade fans to flock in and still less to cater for their needs in a modern way. Hence little new construction or even rebuilding had taken place which might have repaid study. So after rapid visits to Wembley and to Sheffield Wednesday's Hillsborough ground, which boasted a rare new stand, the Osborne V. Webb Partnership set to work mainly sustained by confidence in their own ability to do the job.

*The drawing produced in October 1962 by architects Osborne V. Webb and Partners for the retention of international rugby football at Cardiff Arms Park. Though differing in many respects from the final complex its two-stadium concept was definitive.*

Several crucial and original decisions made along the way have drawn praise from professional critics and yielded great practical benefits. On discovering, for example, that the site scarcely afforded room for two distinct grandstands to be put up back-to-back for the WRU ground and Cardiff RFC, it was the Partnership which advocated a sharing of 'air-space' and the integration of the two stands – an ingenious concept, and one which improved spectator safety in the national ground by permitting a gentler rake to the tiers.

A cantilever solution for the main grandstand structure was the one adopted, since it provided maximum spectator capacity and uninterrupted views of the whole field. The roof structure is of mild steel, and is characterised by a simple but unusual arrangement of gutters which makes for effective, non-drip drainage. Beneath the roof is a facility for slung gantries so that maintenance work can be carried out without the erection of forests of expensive scaffolding.

The evident satisfaction of the main parties to whom the redevelopment mattered most, the Welsh Rugby Union and Cardiff Athletic Club, gave the Partnership a warm glow. Equally they were delighted to welcome and confide in visiting consultants from other bodies building or rebuilding major stadia. In the seventies Glasgow Celtic and Newcastle United soccer clubs sent delegations, as did the city of Paris – busy planning the Parc des Princes – and the Scottish, Irish and South African Rugby Unions who had plans for Murrayfield, Lansdowne Road and Ellis Park.

PHASE 1 Transfer of cricket ground to Sophia Gardens; conversion of existing ground to rugby enclosure for Cardiff RFC. 1966–67, cost £150,000.

PHASE 2. Demolition of north stand, construction of a stadium for Cardiff RFC and a new north stand and enclosure for WRU. Carried out by Andrew Scott Ltd, 1968–71, cost £1,100,000.

PHASE 3. Construction of WRU offices and Cardiff reception rooms. Carried out by Hinkins & Frewin, 1972–73, cost £250,000.

PHASE 4 Demolition of west terrace, construction of a new west stand for the WRU, and conversion of the north enclosure into a seating area. Carried out by Sir Robert McAlpine & Sons Ltd, 1977–78, cost £1,100,000.

PHASE 5 Demolition of east terrace, construction of new two-tier east terrace with reception rooms beneath. Carried out by McAlpines, 1979–80, cost £800,000.

PHASE 6 Demolition of south enclosure and stands, construction of new south stand, south enclosure, television and radio accommodation and dressing-rooms. Carried out by Wimpey Construction (UK) Ltd, 1982–83, cost £4,500,000.

Engineers: G. A. Williamson & Partners (Porthcawl) and James & Nicholas (Port Talbot). Quantity surveyors: Patterson, Seaton & Co (Cardiff).

# TAFF'S ACRE
## ——— *The pre-1900 Years* ———
### GARETH WILLIAMS

'The River *Taff*, sliding downe from the Hilles, runneth toward the Sea . . .
to Caerdiff, called of the Britains *Caerdid*, a proper fine Towne (as Townes
goe in this Country) and a very commodious Haven.'

William Camden, *Britannia*, 1610.

To begin at the end, a 63,000 capacity crowd at the completed National
Ground now generates £300,000 in International ticket receipts. This is quite
an advance on the situation of ninety years ago.

On 18 March 1899 a world record attendance for rugby of 40,000 at Cardiff
Arms Park paid record receipts of £1700 – though not all of them did – to see
whether Ireland could snatch their second Triple Crown of the decade at
Wales's expense. The 0-3 final score indicated that Ireland could, denting
Welsh pride and, in the process, two of full-back Billy Bancroft's ribs, fractured in the over-affectionate embrace of a whole seminary of green-shirted
forwards. We can be sure there were some bruised ribs among the spectators
too, for there were at least 10,000 more of them inside the ground that afternoon than it could comfortably or safely accommodate.

Admission in that relatively inflation-free era was what it had been for the
previous fifteen years and would be for another ten: field, one shilling (5p),
enclosure, two shillings (10p) and three shillings (15p) according to location.
Reserved but not numbered ringside seats 'inside the ropes' (some ropes –
either steel fencing ot strong iron-bound wood palings!) cost three shillings
too, while the 1200 reserved and numbered grandstand seats cost five shillings
(25p). Until the rotation of International fixtures was introduced in 1973–74
the Irish match was often the Triple Crown decider and attracted massive
crowds. 1899 did not see quite the chaotic scenes attending the corresponding
fixture in 1936, when 70,000 defied hell and high water (from the hoses of the
local fire brigade) to get into the ground, but graphic eye-witness accounts
make it plain that the events of 1899 were the most turbulent yet seen at an
International match. They also give us an indication of the physical appearance of Cardiff Arms Park at the end of the nineteenth century.

Within an hour of opening the gates at 1 p.m. there were 20,000 inside the
ground, many by rushing the pay boxes and scaling the walls. There were two
official entrances in those days – opposite the Angel Hotel (today's entrance
number 5) where the path curved around the old cricket ground to the river
end, and by the Glamorgan County Club (today's Guildhall Place entrance

number 3). Tickets were sold at pay boxes in Westgate Street, and with such unexpectedly large crowds milling about, the sixty uniformed policemen on duty were hard pushed to keep order. From the Angel Hotel entrance to the Post Office ran a fifteen-foot wall, later demolished to make way for the Westgate Street flats. As the impatient multitude surged and jostled around the pay boxes, a 'terrific rush' was made for the wall. 'First of all they were small boys who went over, then the everyday respectable wearer of a bowler hat went over, and finally the high hat and frock-coated gentlemen went over . . . By the gates and pay boxes was a mounted constable but he was more than useless. As the crowd clambered the wall he turned his animal around, which only served as a sign for the dozens behind him to go for the wall . . . the big drop of some fifteen feet from the top of the wall to the ground between the Post Office and the County Club was deemed mere child's play.' According to another account, the crowd swarmed over the pay boxes 'like so many ants on an anthill' and using them as a leg-up 'went for the wall that stood between them and the game in their hundreds . . . altogether it was a most entertaining sight viewed from the street but it must prove a costly experience for the Union.'

Once inside the ground many climbed into the forks and branches of the trees which surrounded it. 'Every tree that was at all possible was thus requisitioned and frequently half a dozen men and youths, one above the other, clung with hands and knees in all sorts of awkward and angular shapes.' Even the distant tower of St John's Church was 'alive with moving pygmies' – presumably pygmies with telescopic eyesight.

Meanwhile those at ground level were in no mood to respect the temporary fencing marking off the variously priced sections of the enclosure. Sheer weight of numbers on the north side caused it to give way 'and the reserved seats in the enclosure were quickly occupied by non-ticket holders who rushed pell-mell for them . . . Hoardings topped with barbed wire were unflinchingly scaled, utterly regardless of sartorial disasters and epidermis wounds.' On the south side, others took up the challenge presented by the heavy square-timbered supports of the grandstand. Though again barbed with wire, these vantage points too were soon commandeered, while the most resourceful actually got up on to the corrugated roof. 'That football enthusiasm will induce usually cautious men to risk life and limb has often been demonstrated at Cardiff, but rash daring was never so amazingly exemplified as on this occasion,' mused one eye-witness, mindful that some blithe spirits had actually crossed the Taff to gain entrance on the west side of the ground.

And of course there were good precedents for this, since the ground itself in a very real sense had come from the river. The landmarks by which the Park is still identified – the Taff, Quay Street, the very name Cardiff Arms – are reminders of an earlier, more tranquil era before Cardiff became the coal metropolis of the world and rugby football captured the imagination of its teeming thousands.

*Buck's drawing of Cardiff from the West, published in 1748. Ships can be discerned at the Old town quay where two centuries later important tries were being scored.*

At the beginning of the nineteenth century, it was still a small market town of less than two thousand souls huddled around its castle, an edifice that had seen more centuries borne away by the Taff than changes taking place on its banks. Although the castle was a legacy of their occupation, the Romans were not the first settlers in south Wales. That distinction belongs to the early bronze-age Beaker people, broad-headed, muscular and thirsty. But it was the Romans driving on from their legionary fortress at Caerleon who recognised the strategic potential of a fortification on the Taff, commanding a fordable river and with access to the sea for supplying their fleet. The invaders, moreover, were shrewd tacticians. They made a ball-game and called it *harpastum* and were sufficiently endowed with what certificated rugby coaches would later call 'peripheral vision' to subdue – but only just, as Tacitus confirms – the local Silures, bellicose boyos who had acquired stamina and a side-step among the wooded hills to the north.

It was this fort on the Taff that became the nucleus of the first settlement at Cardiff. What happened between the Roman withdrawal in the late fourth century and the coming of the Normans in the eleventh is unclear, though one of the changes to occur was a shift from a loosely organised tribal society to the creation of a new kingdom extending from the Usk to the Tawe. This was Morgan's land, Morgannwg, and the erratic imprints of Morgan and his descendants lie all over south Wales and not least on the Arms Park. But even

Morgan's furious energies were no match for the marauding Norsemen who pillaged the coasts of west Britain from their bases in Dublin, Wexford and Cork Constitution. Liking and settling down in Cardiff they left their mark in places like Womanby (Hundemanby) Street, an axe-throw, or drop-kick, from the Quay Street entrance to the Valhalla of Welsh rugby.

It was left to the Normans, flushed by their 10-66 away victory at Hastings, to revive the neglected Roman fort on the Taff, and Robert Fitzhamon, lord of Glamorgan, acquired control of the settlement that had grown up around it. For the next few centuries south Wales was a cockpit of rebellion and resistance, and its history is illumined by the colourful exploits of various de Clares and Despensers, of Gilbert the Red, first of the men in scarlet, and of Ifor.Bach who in 1158 made a daring attack on Cardiff Castle and snatched away to his Senghennydd hideaway Fitzhamon's grandson and all his family. 'Yvor was a man little of stature yet bigg and mighty of heart,' wrote Rice Merrick of him four centuries later, for all the world as if describing the classic Welsh half-back. Ifor, with his bandy legs and evident speed off the mark, was clearly a son of Morgan and forerunner of many subsequent Morgans.

By the end of the thirteenth century Cardiff had become the largest of the Welsh boroughs, with an estimated population of more than two thousand. So it is a remarkable fact that its population was even less – 1870 in 1801 – at the beginning of the century which would transform it into the greatest coal exporting port in the world than it had been five centuries earlier. Yet it would be premature to conclude that the only thing moving in Cardiff in the intervening centuries was the Taff. A French roll of 1460 refers to one 'John Derell of Cerdyf in Wales, merchant' taken prisoner in Britanny while forging those Cambro–French links that would be strengthened by the activities of Percy Bush, vice-consul at Nantes from 1910, and Owen Roe, pirated out of Penarth about the same time to teach rugby to the Bayonnais.

Piracy has long been a Cardiff speciality. Not for nothing did the infant Cardiff RFC sport the skull and crossbones on its jersey, and rejoice in the nickname of 'the Pirates': from the thirteenth to the eighteenth centuries its havens and creeks were the haunts of smugglers, wreckers and illegitimate traders who handled rum, tea and tobacco with all the fingertip rapid-transfer skills of later coaching manuals. There is abundant testimony that infamous freebooters like John Callice (a 'notorious malefactor who hath committed sundry great piracies'), William Herbert, John ap John, John Robert ap Ieuan, John Thomas, Robert Adams, Nicholas Herbert and, inevitably, Morgan the Pirate – a formidable eight by any standards – gave the town's more lawful citizens such a bad name 'that they dare not avow abroad the place of their dwelling at Cardiff lest they be discredited'.

Whether the Tudor peace ever made it a more law-abiding place is an open question: in 1595 one Llewellyn David 'did with his sword very cruelly cut and split the nose of [a] woman in such sort as the same hung down over her lip'. Perhaps this was how Elizabethan Welshmen motivated themselves for a brisk bout of *cnappan*, the Tudor ball game alleged by some earnest scholars to be the missing link between *harpastum* and rugby. What is clear from this period is that the material life of at least the town's leading citizens improved. The century after the Act of Union (1536) saw a revolution in housebuilding, and Cardiff's 'many fair houses and large streets' owed much to the activities of gentlemen like Sir Thomas Morgan who in the early seventeenth century built Ruperra Castle (1626) and what was at one time the best known of Cardiff's stately homes, the Red House. In the next century this became the Cardiff Arms Hotel.

In view of the direction which rugby football would follow in the late twentieth century, it is entirely fitting that the Cardiff Arms Park should have taken its name from a coaching inn. The establishment came to prominence with the improved travel facilities of the eighteenth century and the evolution of the mail service and turnpike system, so that 'instead of the quiet of thirty years ago an eternal racket has succeeded at this [summer] season, every bed of this [the Cardiff Arms] Inn being filled and many travellers obliged to go on with tired horses'. The Cardiff Arms was one of several Glamorgan hostelries whose mere names – the Beaufort Arms at Chepstow, the King's Head at Newport, the Angel at Cardiff, the White Hart at Cowbridge, the Mackworth at Swansea – conjure up Christmas-card visions of bustling red-faced porters clumping over cobbled yards, cheery Pickwickian travellers and the aroma of port and brandy.

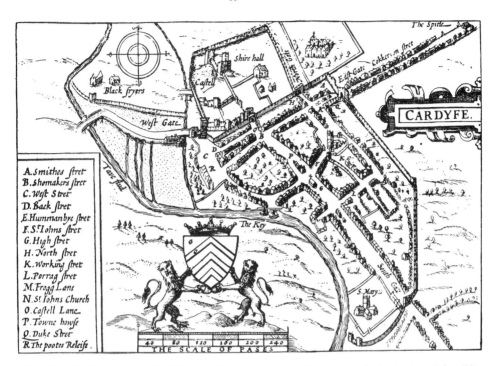

A. Smithes *ftret*
B. Shomakers *ftret*
C. Weft S *tret*
D. Back *ftret*
E. Hunmanbye *ftret*
F. S.<sup>t</sup> Iohns *ftret*
G. High *ftret*
H. North *ftret*
K. Working *ftret*
L. Porrag *ftret*
M. Frogg Lane
N. St Iohns Church
O. Caftell Lane
P. Towne howfe
Q. Duke Stret
R. The pootes Releife.

*John Speed's 1610 map of Cardiff, containing the key – and quay – to the beginning of Cardiff Arms Park. Today's complex lies on land reclaimed as a result of the straightening of the River Taff.*

Whether or not it ever looked quite like that – and probably not – the Cardiff Arms Inn, demolished for good in 1882, bequeathed to Welsh and world rugby a name as indelible as a watermark. In fact at high water mark its yard flooded over, and coaches and chaises floated out to sea: for the Cardiff Arms stood in Broad Street, a short thoroughfare running at right angles to Angel Street and Castle Street, and the Taff ran behind it. Yet were it possible today to deposit the Cardiff Arms, like Dr Who's police kiosk, magically in its old position, we would find that the Taff was running elsewhere. This is the key to the beginning of the Cardiff Arms Park.

Key, and quay, for as Speed's map of 1610 shows, Cardiff's quay was of ancient origin. Already by mid-sixteenth century the town corporation was complaining that it had borne the costs of maintaining it 'tyme out of mynde', for it was being constantly eroded by the river's floods and currents. At the beginning of the nineteenth century the Taff flowed past the ruins of the old Cardiff bridge that had collapsed in the floods of 1792, under the later Canton bridge (completed in 1796 though rebuilt in 1859 and widened subsequently) and then, as it had always done since time immemorial, continued along its north to south course for about four hundred yards before curving sharply east to join the Town Quay. It there ran along the line of modern Westgate Street, with private wharves like the Golate on its eastern bank and the

35

gardens behind St Mary Street sloping down to the riverside. Then it turned off under the site of what is now the general station to rejoin the present river just above Penarth Road bridge.

The Taff had always been an unpredictable creature. In 1614 thirteen people had drowned while crossing it in an open boat and there were plenty of later examples of drownings occurring in the course of fording it. At one time 'a faire Key and a safe harborowe for shippinge' (Rice Lewis, 1596), by the nineteenth century it had fallen into virtual disuse, though small vessels still came up at high tide – the same tide that flooded the yard of the Cardiff Arms.

Indeed, as the century opened it seemed that Cardiff itself was in disuse. Its physical shape was hardly different from what it appeared to William Camden and John Speed. Even by 1821, when it had a population of three and a half thousand, it ranked only twenty-seventh among the towns of Wales, smaller than Llanelli and Pembroke let alone Merthyr Tydfil. It was still largely unpaved and unlighted and its sanitation little better than in 1750 when a woman drowned falling into the privy of the King David Inn. Although in 1774 it had been the first Welsh town to obtain an Improvement Act, the seriousness with which the Commissioners viewed their responsibility may be gauged from the fact that for many years the venue for their meetings was the Cardiff Arms Hotel.

But after centuries of stagnation, frantic change was imminent, as Cardiff became rapidly transformed from a sleepy market town to a major port with worldwide ramifications. The engine of change proved to be the building, in the revolutionary decade of the 1790s, of the Glamorgan Canal, with a sea-lock at Cardiff, to provide an outlet for the great Merthyr ironworks. By the 1830s the canal was handling annually such a large volume of iron and coal that it was becoming inadequate. The basic problem was that the sea-lock was two and a half miles from low water mark and the canal could not be widened. The second Marquess of Bute, who owned all the land between the town of Cardiff and the sea and enjoyed manorial rights over the River Taff and the foreshore, saw in the predicament of the canal company his own opportunity: a new and wider ship canal parallel to the existing sea-lock and further east. The Bute Ship Canal, or West Docks, opened in 1839, and with the opening in 1841 of the Taff Vale Railway linking Merthyr and Cardiff with connections to the Cynon (Aberdare) valley in 1846 (and the two Rhondda valleys a decade later), by 1850 the trade of the Bute Docks had not only overhauled but doubled that of the canal.

The West Docks cost £350,000 and only the Butes could have afforded it, just as only the Butes could raise enough coal from their lands to keep a whole docks supplied and require even more to be built. For not only was Cardiff 'Lord Bute's own town', his estate encompassed its industrial hinterland: in all, 22,000 acres of Glamorgan. The Butes were landlords of the Dowlais ironworks, in the 1840s the greatest in the world; they constructed and owned the Bute Docks, soon to become the greatest coal port in the world; they promoted the mineral exploration of the Rhondda, the greatest coal valley in the world – and if all that were not enough, they also owned the Cardiff Arms Park, before long the greatest rugby ground in the world. For the Cardiff Arms was a Bute hotel and just as the foundation of modern Cardiff can be laid at the door of the second Marquess, so it is to him that the Cardiff Arms Park owes its existence, for it was he who was responsible for the diversion of the Taff, and at his prompting Isambard Kingdom Brunel undertook it.

Brunel was in the 1840s an engineer with the South Wales Railway Company, and it was to the advantage of the emerging commercial centre of Cardiff to be linked to the line from London to Swansea and beyond. So between 1848 and 1853, to facilitate the entry of the railway, the Taff was diverted into a 'new cut' between Canton bridge and Penarth Road bridge. This amputated the eastward loop sweeping around to run alongside St Mary Street, and left the old quay, at the point where modern Quay Street meets Westgate Street, high and dry, as well as a health hazard in the form of a stagnant channel of foetid water which was not filled in till 1865.

*The view south from Cardiff Castle around 1890 showing Westgate Street and the section of Cardiff Arms Park which refused to drain.*

The consequences that followed from the diverting of the Taff were profound. It provided a site for the railway station, removed the recurrent danger of flooding in the town centre, made new land available for redevelopment, and enlarged the meadowland that had existed north of the old loop known as the Great Park. More precisely, the reclaimed land near the old quay, and behind the Cardiff Arms, became the site of Westgate Street – and of the Cardiff Arms Park.

The Great Park was already a favourite recreation area for the citizens of Cardiff and for military and civil celebrations. The eighteenth birthday of Princess Victoria in 1837 was the occasion for a fireworks display on 'the park behind the Cardiff Arms' and in 1856 the ending of the Crimean War was celebrated there with processions, bands, flags and enough spectacle generally that one eavesdropper could not but overhear one wide-eyed bystander remark to another 'Dear, dear, did you ever see such a thing in Aberdare?'

Ten years later a long discussion took place in the town council as to whether the Park should be converted into a cattle market. This in turn hinged on who owned it. The land did not formally pass out of Bute hands until 1922, but the third Marquess had already virtually conferred it on the town by charging the most nominal rent for its use. The decision not to go ahead with the cattle market was a great relief to the Cardiff Cricket Club, established in 1845, whose members had been playing there since 1848. It has to be admitted that there would be occasions in the next century when intensive usage, allied to deep-seated drainage problems, would churn up the playing area of the Park so badly that it looked as if the cattle market had won after all.

It was the Cardiff Football Club, formed in 1876, that set about the development of the area now reclaimed from the river. Its origins can be traced to the autumn of 1874 when sixty-six members paid a half-crown subscription (12½p) to join the Glamorgan Football Club, and their first practice was held in front of the cricket pavilion on the Arms Park. A number of them were old boys of Cheltenham College who were not above, or below, playing in evening dress, 'and some did not discard their bowler hats'. Several were already members of the Cardiff Cricket Club who had long been playing on the Park, and so a football club was a convenient way of extending their association into the winter months. In 1875 the Glamorgan FC held a sports meeting on the Arms Park, and as well as the usual events there was a prize for the longest drop-kick. The winner was credited with an incredible 145 yards, which reduces acknowledged siege-gun kickers of later years – Brand, Wooller, Bob Scott and Don Clarke – to the level of blow-footballers.

The Cardiff Rugby Club grew out of an amalgam in 1876 of the Glamorgan FC and two local organisations, Wanderers and Tredegarville, whose founder was James Bush, father of the celebrated and irrepressible Percy. It was symbolic that the prime movers in the new combination were W. H. and S. C.

*The first-ever grandstand at Cardiff Arms Park, opened on Boxing Day 1885 for a match in which Cardiff, under F. E. Hancock, beat Liverpool 3-0. The new structure cost £362.*

Cory, for if any name connoted the bustling world of Cardiff's now booming export and shipping business it was Cory.

As yet the football area of the Park was not enclosed. Its sole facility was the cricket pavilion, and beyond it, for candidates for an early bath, the river. There was no charge for spectators; Newport's Rodney Parade was the first Welsh ground to charge admission and it was an unpopular innovation. When in 1879 the South Wales Challenge Cup Final was played at Sophia Gardens – another Bute bequest – it was because Cardiff Arms Park was not as yet roped off, and unable conveniently to accommodate the expected 3000 to 4000 spectators who duly turned up and paid sixpence (2½p) for the privilege. It soon could. During the summer of 1881, on the strength of the previous season's income of £130, the ground was levelled and re-turfed, and its first grandstand built at a cost of fifty pounds, on the north side towards the Taff end 'for the convenience of the spectators and the ladies in particular'. Cardiff were drawing up to 4000 spectators a game. In 1885–86 there would be still more.

By now the whole town had undergone colossal change quite beyond the control of the Butes who had initiated it. The third Marquess (1847–1900) rebuilt Cardiff Castle and Castell Coch, donated large sums to various charitable and educational institutions, and preserved for the town its many splen-

## THE FIRST LAWS

*Rugby football's Laws have experienced a multitude of changes since Cardiff Arms Park first staged the pick-up games of the local young bloods. In his Cardiff RFC history published in 1906 Charles Arthur summarised the rules that governed play in the pioneering days of the 1870s :*

There were twenty players a side;

The ball was round, not oval, and was never to be picked up off the ground but must be dapping, if only a few inches;

The ball when caught on the full, or on any hop, was carried by the player, who made a run for a try – passing was unknown;

A player, when collared, sometimes handed the ball to one of his own side, but never threw it, the usual thing being to put it on the ground and then form a scrum;

When the ball went into touch there was no line-out, but the forwards, twelve each side, formed a line with their heads down and the ball was thrown into the tunnel by a spectator. The object of the forwards was then to force the ball through, heeling out being unknown;

Punting was considered bad form and drop-kicking was cultivated;

Tripping was never considered etiquette but the scientific hacking over of a back who was running and could not be reached with the hands was sometimes employed;

There was no regulation costume worn then. Most of the players turned out in ordinary attire, just taking off their coats. One person even played on one occasion in evening dress, and some did not discard their hats.

did and centrally sited squares and open spaces. His stupendous wealth enabled him to indulge to the full his interest in the mediaeval, the occult and the oriental (hence Canton and Cathays) and he travelled widely in Italy, Greece and Palestine. To a man of his tastes and temperament, therefore, it is unsurprising that the pursuit by thirty vigorous young men of a pig's bladder encased in leather exerted as little appeal as the expanding docks and thrusting coal freighters which made his life-style possible. Though Cardiff Arms Park was one of his most famous benefactions, he chose to be buried not beneath it but on the Mount of Olives: less Taff than Acre, so to speak, for as he said, 'Athens and Assisi have spoilt me for anything else.'

Certainly spoilt him for late-nineteenth-century Cardiff. His desire to get away from 'coalopolis' became urgent as its population more than doubled from 39,000 to over 82,000 between 1871 and 1881; by 1901 it doubled again. This demographic explosion was matched by the doubling of coal exports in the same period to $7\frac{1}{2}$ million tons (from a mere 21,000 tons in 1839), which almost doubled again by 1913. Thousands of immigrants poured in annually to the docks, railways, shops and offices of this El Dorado on the Taff, creating a vibrant, energetic, increasingly self-confident community that took drink, religion and rugby in large draughts. Among the thousands of newcomers to arrive in 1883 were the Hancock family from Wiveliscombe in Somerset. The Hancocks were brewers and could recognise a thirst from the other side of the Bristol Channel. The Beaker people were back.

That the West Country was a rugby-playing area largely explains why adjacent, fixture-seeking South Wales adopted rugby rather than soccer in the crucial and explosive decades of the 1870s and 1880s. Some of the greatest players to achieve fame in the scarlet jersey – Arthur Boucher, Bobby Brice, Harry Packer, Dick Hellings, Wallace Watts, Jim Webb and the immortal Gwyn Nicholls – were West Countrymen by birth but Welsh by location, adoption and inclination. Hancock, chunky, skilful, unselfish, somewhat authoritarian, had already captained his club and county sides in Somerset; he was now ready to try his hand with Cardiff, where tradition and convention counted for less than innovation and enterprise and where styles and attitudes were being fashioned afresh in a buoyant environment whose chief characteristic was its novelty.

Charles Saxton's 1946 Kiwi dictum that the essence of rugby football is fourteen men putting the fifteenth clear had not yet been enunciated, but the Cardiff committee anticipated its spirit when in February 1884 they decided to rearrange the usual formation of nine forwards and three three-quarters to eight forwards and *four* three-quarters. This was to accommodate the go-getting Frank Hancock who, called up at the last moment to make his first team début in a tough away fixture against Cheltenham College the previous week, had scored the only two tries of the match. The committee, reluctant to drop him but equally unwilling to break up their regular three-quarters, included Hancock at centre in a four three-quarter line for the next match with Gloucester on 23 February 1884. It is an historic date.

Cardiff maintained the system till the end of the season but abandoned it for most of the next owing to prolonged injury to their regular full-back. But in 1885–86 Hancock captained the club to one of its greatest seasons when, playing four three-quarters throughout, 26 out of 27 fixtures were won and 131 tries scored to a mere 4 against. The Welsh XV soon adopted the same formation, as did all the other rugby-playing countries, and the four three-quarter system remains to this day Wales's greatest contribution to rugby.

The outstanding success of Hancock's side attracted a great influx of sensation-seeking spectators, and from that season's income of £900 – more than double the previous season's takings – the old grandstand was dismantled and a new one erected. It cost £362 and was first used for the 1885 Boxing Day fixture with Liverpool. A steel rope was put around the ground in place of the previous hempen one, and duckboards put down for the first time to save spectators having to stand ankle-deep in mud. A further temporary stand went up in 1886–87 'to accommodate the ever increasing number of spectators'.

By the early 1890s there were stands on both sides of Cardiff Arms Park as, in common with many football grounds throughout Britain, it began to acquire the corrugated characteristics and appurtenances of a stadium – though not without expenditure. In 1891 platforms were laid around the ground at a cost of £21, while more steel fencing cost nearly £150 although 'the purpose for which it was erected, viz. to keep the street urchins from getting into the ground, proved a failure'. Of more value was the provision of a space under the grandstand for the players to hang their sweaters and wraps, a kind of temporary dressing-room. However, until the erection of a new pavilion in 1904, it was the Grand Hotel in Westgate Street that fulfilled that function, and on International days, the Angel.

The first International match played on the Cardiff Arms Park was against Ireland on 12 April 1884 when Wales won by a dropped goal and two tries to nil and supplied their opponents with a couple of players into the bargain. The pride of Erin had arrived two men short, highlighting even then the problem that has wondrously plagued the Irish selectors ever since, of having to choose a team of fifteen from a squad of thirteen. It is a minor curiosity, too, that while Ireland and Scotland played three times at Cardiff before the nineteenth century ran out, England, Wales's first International opponents in 1881, got to play there only once. That was in 1893 and it could hardly have been a more dramatic occasion.

By then Cardiff was a major town with a population of 130,000. The basic problems of water supply, sanitation and drainage had been met. All-night street lamps were in operation. Gas and electricity systems had been installed in the 1870s. Its main streets had long since been laid and paved and were already congested with horse-drawn trams and buses. Imposing buildings designed and constructed in the grand manner were shooting up. Public and private offices, palatial hotels and banks and enticing shopping arcades all proclaimed Cardiff's swelling importance. The 1880s and 1890s saw between them the building of the arcades, the Central Library in the Hayes, the Royal Infirmary, St David's Hospital, the University College, the Cory Hall, the Empire and Grand Theatres and the Theatre Royal (later the Prince of Wales) in Wood Street. It was in 1881, foundation-year of the Welsh Rugby Union, that the merchant palace of a Coal Exchange went up in Mountstuart Square, and the two institutions symbolised the same headlong growth of industrial South Wales.

A native of Cardiff noted with wide-eyed wonderment in 1884 that its rise 'more nearly resembles that of an American city, of Cincinatti, St Louis or Chicago'. In the momentous year 1905 – when Cardiff was granted the status of a city and Wales celebrated by alone defeating New Zealand on the Arms Park – Cardiff was acclaimed for its 'impression of modernity and progressiveness, of spacious streets and buildings, of docks and ships and of great commercial activity, which well merit the epithet "the Chicago of Wales"'. In 1893 Chicago staged a World's Fair, where Ben Davies, the Welsh tenor, brought the house down. What meat was to Chicago, coal was to Cardiff, and was itself a spectacle that year, when eighteen tons of it were burnt on the Arms Park to save an International match.

The winter weather of the first week of January 1893 had been severe all over South Wales. There were ice floes on the Taff, the River Rhondda had frozen over, there was even curling in Llwynypia. Cardiff Arms Park was 'as hard as a brickbat' to the *South Wales News*'s 'Old Stager' (who was well accustomed to throwing them). With Saturday's game against England in mind, on the Thursday it was decided to employ 'fire-devils', coal-filled buckets pierced with holes and mounted on bricks to help thaw out the ground. For twenty-seven hours up to 11 a.m. on the morning of the match five hundred 'devils' along with thirty to forty large hot boiler plates were spread over the Arms Park.

So when the correspondent of the London *Morning Leader* arrived in Cardiff with the English team on Friday night, he saw 'a strange, weird, uncanny sight . . . like a scene from Dante's *Inferno*. Imagine if you can an acre or more of ground heaped several feet high with live coal from five hundred fires blazing far up into the dark night. Dozens of dark, ghoul-like figures were threading their way about the fires, heaping on fresh fuel, while the falling snow rendered the scene one of the most unique and romantic ever seen on a football field. Like Wellington at Waterloo your reporter walked over the field at midnight, and found it in a fairly good condition.'

The following day, 7 January 1893, found the Welsh XV in good condition too, and it was England's Waterloo as Wales, spearheaded by the incomparable Arthur Gould and propelled to a 12-11 victory by the unerring boot of Billy Bancroft, laid the foundations for the first-ever Welsh Triple Crown, a triumph that 'sent the population of Cardiff plus the thousands of visitors off their blessed chumps'. In fact it was Wales's only Triple Crown of the nineteenth century, though they would win another six during the first decade of the twentieth.

With rugby now a mass spectator sport in South Wales, it was difficult for Welsh soccer to mount a serious challenge before the turn of the century. At representative level a bridgehead was established in 1894 when the first soccer International to be held in South Wales was staged at St Helen's, Swansea's rugby and cricket ground. It is often forgotten that Cardiff Arms Park, too, was the venue for a variety of South Wales League, Cup and International association football matches between 1891 and the opening of Ninian Park in 1910, about a dozen games in all. The six International matches were, with one exception, played on a Monday. The first was against England in March 1896, and though the occasion was graced by the matchless skills of the mercurial toothpick-chewing Billy Meredith, Wales suffered a 9-1 drubbing. Things would improve, and so would attendances, but the very modest 'gate' of £245 taken at that pioneer event of 1896 confirmed that it was rugby that still enjoyed the majority popular support in Cardiff as in

South Wales generally at this time. Crowds of 12,000 regularly attended club matches at Cardiff, and there was plenty worth watching – apart from a period of five weeks early in 1897 when the ground was suspended because of the rough handling of the referee in a needle match with old rivals Newport. On 4 February 1893 the great Gwyn Nicholls played his first game for Cardiff, and within eighteen months two wings had to be added to the grandstand, increasing its capacity to 1200.

Already, though, the excellence of the rugby served up was not always matched by the quality of the playing surface. When Cardiff played the Maoris in December 1888 the ground was 'in a deplorable state, wet, muddy, with pools of water on the pitch'. It was not the first or last time that it would resemble a tributary of the adjoining Taff. The problem was a section of the field on the south side which refused to drain: it was as if the ancient bed of the old river would not lie down. In the summer of 1895 the entire surface

*The Maori tourists of 1888. When they played at Cardiff the pitch was 'in a deplorable state, wet, muddy, with pools of water on the pitch.'*

was taken up and a network of drainpipes, a layer of ashes and a thin covering of new soil put down, and the whole area re-turfed at a total cost of over a thousand pounds. Drainage cost the club another £100 in 1896. Not until the massive rebuilding programme begun in the 1960s would the ghost of the old River Taff finally be laid to rest.

By then Wales was about to enter a second golden era. In 1900 it was on the threshold of its first. As if in anticipation of the momentous decade in prospect, in 1900–01 the Welsh Football Union agreed with the Cardiff club, who were themselves anxious to retain International matches at Cardiff, to shoulder three-quarters of the costs of ground improvement. That season, with the great crowd of the Irish match of 1899 fresh in its mind, and a second Triple Crown won in 1900, the Union contributed substantially to a £2000 project for increasing the grandstand accommodation to 1800, and the over-all capacity of the ground to 35,000.

Every inch, every vantage point would be needed during the next decade, when the acre on the Taff staged some of the greatest rugby football ever seen.

# GOLDEN ERA
## 1900 to 1919
### J. B. G. THOMAS

Having watched all the International matches played at Cardiff Arms Park in the second half of the Welsh Rugby Union's century of existence, one has grown accustomed to its atmosphere. Yet as a citadel of rugby, a place for hero-worship of the leading performers in the chase after the leather, it never ceases to thrill; no other ground has quite the same fascination for a Welshman. But its present capacity is well in advance of what it was at the turn of the century, when Welsh rugby was just beginning to establish itself as the equal of that played anywhere in the world.

In the early days it suited the infant Welsh Football Union to make use of club facilities. Newport, who boasted a well accommodated ground at Rodney Parade, had staged International matches as had Llanelli. But from 1898 Wales's home games took place only at Cardiff Arms Park and St Helen's in Swansea. Given the prevailing atmosphere of rivalry between the two towns and their clubs it was only natural that argument and discussion arose between supporters as to which of the two best deserved the honour of International matches. The respective followers though hoping that one day a decision would be taken to use only one of the grounds, yet believed it unlikely – 'never the twain shall meet'.

So although an International venue, Cardiff Arms Park was the property of the Cardiff Football Club to whom (along with the cricket club) it had been leased by the Bute estate. Thus the development of the ground was in the main the responsibility of the club which, since it was flourishing, could afford to shoulder it – at the turn of the century membership was one thousand, income reached £2742 and bank deposits stood at £1700. As the 1899–1900 season closed contractors moved in to prepare additional accommodation which would lift overall capacity at the rugby enclosure to 35,000. This rather detracts, incidentally, from attendance estimates of 40,000 which had accompanied the Wales–Ireland game of 1899; but it was both indicative of the enthusiasm for the game in the Principality and prophetic concerning what was to happen in the years ahead.

The expansion owes much to the intervention of one W. D. Phillips who, besides being belonging to the Cardiff Match Committee, was also a member of the WFU and Chairman of its International Grounds Committee. He it was who warned Cardiff that if they wished to retain representative rugby they had to make provision for its growing number of followers. Thus the grandstand accommodation was trebled from 600 seats to 1800 and terraces of twenty-five tiers were constructed round touch-lines and dead-ball areas. The work was carried out by a Mr Harry Gibbon for £1926.

Phillips's wisdom at negotiating, however, meant that the WFU agreed to pay 75 per cent of the bill, or £1445, Cardiff finding the balance and undertaking responsibility for the care and maintenance of the new structures for five years. The club benefited greatly, its members appreciating improved facilities fit for a club whose fame and strength was spreading through the rugby world with an impact almost equal to that of the national XV. Gwyn Nicholls was captain of Cardiff in 1900–01; this was his third successive year in control, suggesting that he was a true torch-bearer along the road to greatness in the game.

In the scarlet of Wales the same Nicholls played in the first International match staged in the enlarged arena – and scored a superb try as England went down to defeat by two goals and a try (13) to nil. It is reported, however, that Wales did not play well, with an unfit Billy Bancroft a mere shadow of his true self. As it turned out this season·marked the end of the Swansea full-back's illustrious career after thirty-three appearances for his country.

Scotland it was who carried off the Triple Crown; but the Welsh were not to lose a match at Cardiff Arms Park until the South African visit of 1912. It became the most feared and respected of grounds in the minds of visiting sides – and more: as it grew in stature, so it matured into a symbol of con-

*Committee members watching a match at Cardiff Arms Park in 1908. The man with the cigarette is Lord Ninian Creighton Stuart, second son of the Third Marquess of Bute.*

temporary Welsh supremacy in the game with, perhaps, a touch of arrogance, something that has never quite left it and remains an ethereal part of the atmosphere which has engulfed so many challengers. The long years of invincibility seem to be a very part of the turf itself.

In those days Cardiff's rugby men were often generous to charities, while in 1903 they presented Lord Bute with an illuminated address on the attainment of his majority plus the sum of '£500 to devote to any charity he wished to choose'. It was the club's way of expressing thanks to the Bute family for being allowed the use of Cardiff Arms Park for just one shilling's rent per year (provided that it was kept for amateur sport).

The season 1902–03 produced another good profit for the club, some of which was put to a most constructive purpose with the launch of a Cardiff and District Schools Rugby Union. Cardiff met the expense of kitting out 600 young enthusiasts in full gear for £289. They also issued free tickets for members of school teams – a privilege I was to enjoy as a high school player in the early thirties.

At this time, too, the cricket and rugby clubs joined forces (thereby conceiving what is now the thriving Athletic Club) to plan the construction of a pavilion, dressing-room and training quarters for both clubs. Building started in the spring of 1904, the rugby club having agreed to provide 54 per cent of

*Full of warmth and character, the pavilion erected in 1904 backed onto the River Taff, serving rugby and cricket enclosures.*

*Snow at Cardiff in 1901. The south stand had just been extended, raising its capacity from 600 seats to 1800.*

the cost (£2500), the cricketers the rest. It was in use during the 1904–05 season, and Charles Arthur commented: 'The new pavilion proved of considerable value in the training of players and their comfort generally and the wonder is how the club did without one for so long.'

One of its earliest functions was in October 1904 when a smoking concert (the contemporary term for a friendly drinking party with entertainment) was held to welcome back Welsh members of the British Isles team from a tour of the Antipodes, Arthur wrote: 'The room was decorated with flags and draperies, and a thousand faithful followers and rugby VIPs assembled to honour the Welshmen.'

Cardiff RFC's later historian, Danny Davies, also describes the pavilion in glowing terms as one of the first of its kind in British rugby. Situated in the south-west corner of the cricket field, it was an attractive building whose facilities welcomed players from all over the world for the next thirty years. Its front was used for cricket matches by the Cardiff and Glamorgan teams, and was an impressive back-drop as seen by spectators on the Westgate Street boundary seating. Its 'spacious and lofty' gymnasium helped considerably in ensuring the fitness of the rugby side. Training nights there were much enjoyed by the players for the kippers and buttered rolls served after their work-out! Often present was Rhys Gabe, who later told me of the place's happy atmosphere – adding how many a visiting International of the pre-World-War-One days hinted that there was something uncanny about the visitors' dressing-room, so rarely did it inspire any hope of victory.

## BOYHOOD MEMORIES OF CARDIFF ARMS PARK

### D. E. Davies

*A stand-off half, 'Danny' Davies made 192 appearances for Cardiff between 1921 and 1934, skippering them in 1925–26. He later became president of the Welsh Rugby Union. His magnum opus is the statistical history of Cardiff RFC published in 1976, from which this extract is reproduced with the author's permission.*

My boyhood memories of the Cardiff Arms Park arise from the earliest years of the century and are of sound – the sound of singing and cheering which could be heard from the area in which I lived, East Terrace, at the southern end of Churchill Way then known as Pembroke Terrace. Nearby was the Taff Valley Railway Station, Cardiff's Queen Street station of today. The flow of hundreds of ardent enthusiasts from the station was a most lively indication of an important rugby match. Hats and coat lapels were adorned with leeks of competitive size (many eaten in bravado) on big match days!

Westgate Street would be thronged. There was little or no horse-drawn traffic to hinder the crowds. The motorcar had not 'arrived' and police, some of them on horseback, ushered the fans towards the entrances to Cardiff Arms Park. Vendors were at large selling hot chestnuts and potatoes from smouldering coke fires, their stands magnets for urchins in winter. Others sold sweets, peppermints, bulls-eyes, brandy snaps and pasties from their baskets and even pepsin chewing gum. Their cries were well known in and around the ground.

A castellated wall about twelve feet high ran the length of Westgate Street from the Angel Hotel entrance to a point opposite Quay Street. It was often used on International day by clambering gate-crashers trying to gain entrance after the gates were closed (from the west side of the ground attempts to gain admittance were quite often made by bold spirits crossing the River Taff at low tide). Inside the cricket field, immediately below the wall, was a moat about eight to ten feet wide, probably the residue of an ancient stream which had its original source from some part of Cardiff Castle grounds. Weeds, reeds and wild flowers grew in it and occasionally a water rat might be seen scurrying through the scum. The moat was filled in for use as tennis courts by the Athletic Club and later disappeared with the building of the Westgate Street flats, as did most of the wall.

Tickets were sold from pay-boxes in the street and entry to the ground was through tall wooden barriers at whose openings gatemen would lustily cry out, 'Show your tickets *please!*' Inside the Angel entrance a pathway curved leftwards around the cricket field to the west entrances of the football enclosure where stood a splendid twin-turreted pavilion erected in 1904 for the use of Cardiff's cricket and football clubs. It was my privilege to use it when making my début for Cardiff on 2 April 1921.

Trees surrounded the whole perimeter of the football and cricket fields, besides lining the river bank, and there was a splendid clump with many beautiful old chestnuts stretching from the Angel entrance to Canton Bridge – but sad to relate most of them disappeared with the building of the modern hotel which now occupies the spot. Part of a low wall still fronts this area and against it stands a relic of the past, an old milestone from which I learned a little of my geography: 158 miles to London, 12 to Cowbridge and 12 to Newport. Passers-by were wont to sit and rest on the wall, or stand on it to try and glimpse a little play during a cricket match.

Before the new pavilion was fully utilised teams changed for matches at the Angel and Grand hotels outside the ground. Players walked down the Angel entrance pathway to the west corner of the football field. After the match they would have to mingle with the crowd making its exit. I remember one occasion, as a nervous young boy, slapping the back of one of the returning players and learning from the crowd close to him, 'It's Hinton!' It was indeed W. P. Hinton of the Old Wesley club who had just made his début as full-back for Ireland against Wales on that day, 9 March 1907. But it was a sad début for Hinton, as Wales beat Ireland 29-0, a brilliant triumph.

After International matches mourning cards were sold outside the ground. The verses extolled the glory of 'Gallant Little Wales' victorious over her English, Scottish or Irish opponents. I am not sure if alternative cards were simultaneously printed with a patriotic promise of future triumphs!

*Danny Davies scoring for Cardiff against the 1926–27 Maoris.*

In 1934, to make room for a new north stand overlooking the rugby pitch, this remarkable pavilion was dismantled and removed to a sports field in a Cardiff suburb. Undeniably part of the atmosphere and tradition of the famous ground went with it. Many famous teams were photographed in front of it before taking the field, so that its glorious facade was recorded for the gaze of those who were never privileged to see or visit it as a wonderful symbol of Welsh sport.

Gate receipts are always interesting, as an indication of prices at the time and the steady effect of inflation upon our sporting lives. In 1905 Cardiff RFC met the First All Blacks, losing an exciting match 10-8 through a mistake by the captain, Percy Bush. The New Zealanders attracted the largest crowd up to that time for a club match at the ground. Takings of £1862 proved to be more than the amount for any full season before 1892. For the first time the grandstand was reserved for 'members only' (though a long interval was to follow before matches became all-ticket affairs for touring teams). The official attendance for the International match ten days earlier was 35,000, though some estimates at the time suggest that far more squeezed their way

*With Scottish, Irish and English resistance upended, Wales prepares for a last-ditch defiance of the all-conquering New Zealanders. There seems, however, to have been some ethnic confusion in the mind of this* Western Mail *cartoonist, 1905 vintage!*

*Fashions change, but not the happy expressions. Fans at Cardiff cheer as Wales heads for victory over the 1905 All Blacks.*

in – judging by the number of sportsmen who claimed to have been present the 'gate' must have exceeded 100,000!

More words have been written, and certainly spoken, about the Wales v New Zealand match of 16 December 1905 than any other in history. It was something special. It remains something special. It was *the* match of the Golden Era, establishing Wales as the foremost country in the game. It contained only one dramatic score, the decisive try for Wales by Dr Teddy Morgan. The next day a member of the *Daily Mail* staff dreamed up a story suggesting that New Zealand had equalised – and the controversy still rages!

Events leading up to the meeting between the two countries created an atmosphere of incredible expectancy. In March Wales had won the Triple Crown and the Home Championship, while under the leadership of 'rover' forward Dave Gallaher New Zealand had gone through their autumn tour with 26 victories out of 26, including three International successes – Scotland, strong at the time, had given the visitors their closest match at 12-7. Yet everywhere they went the All Blacks were told, 'Wait until you get to Wales – they'll beat you!'

The Welsh XV included several men who had been on the recent British Isles tour and were thus aware of the tourists' tactics, especially the 2–3–2 scrum formation and the 'rover' – a loose forward and extra scrum half. They devised one plan to nullify this advantage – and one to produce a try.

The 2–3–2 formation (eventually banned in 1931 when a front row of three, no more and no less, was decreed) produced a remarkably quick heel. Wales placed four men standing ready to pack in the front row, leaving three to go down as the ball came in, always with the loose head. This confused the All Blacks and helped to disrupt their rhythm.

Added to this clever ploy, the fervour of the forwards, hard tackling by the backs and sound kicking to touch enabled the home team to hold its own. The bonus was the little wizard from Swansea, Dickie Owen at scrum half, who plotted the winning score – in which a Welsh 'rover', Cliff Pritchard of Pontypool, would play an important part.

Each player was acquainted with the move, practised in secret behind locked doors at Cardiff Arms Park. As skipper, Gwyn Nicholls was to give Owen the signal for its activation. Before a scrum inside the New Zealand half to the right of the posts Nicholls gave a nod, Owen put the ball in, and Wales won the heel. Owen gathered and moved right, taking outside-half Bush with him, Nicholls running outside Bush. The All Black defence moved across to cover, at which to their surprise Owen sent a reverse pass over the scrum to switch the movement.

Pritchard, now running at top speed to the left in anticipation, took the pass perfectly and handed on to the strong-running Gabe at left centre. The latter drew New Zealand's right wing McGregor before sending out a pass to Teddy Morgan who scuttled away to get round full-back Gillett and score in the corner. The crowd went mad, and though the try was not converted Wales had drawn blood. However, they remained content with the situation and Rhys Gabe once admitted to me, 'It was a mistake. We should have attempted more moves and scored more tries.'

In the second half, as the tourists strove to equalise against a rock-solid defence, came the controversial incident. W. J. Wallace, probably the greatest All Black, playing on the wing instead of at full-back in this match, turned infield suddenly to deceive the defenders. Centre Bob Deans was up with him, taking a pass after Willie Llewellyn had challenged Wallace. Chasing Deans was Gabe, who brought him down a couple of feet short of the line. Deans struggled to manoeuvre the ball forward for a try, but when referee John Dallas of Scotland arrived he blew for a scrummage as Deans was still short of his target. It was no try!

At the post-match dinner following the deserved Welsh victory no mention was made of a New Zealand 'try' by Gallaher or any of his players. On the Sunday morning the *Daily Mail* reporter J. A. Buttery suggested to Deans that maybe he had scored. The All Black laughed and said, 'I thought I did!' On Monday the newspaper ran the story, 'Deans says he scored against Wales' – and thus was born controversy that would survive the test of time. Referee Dallas was later moved to write in a letter, 'Deans did not score.' As for poor Deans himself, he died at an early age and is reported to have uttered the words on his death-bed, 'I did score.' This is, sadly, folklore as he was in a coma for a long time before his death.

The match created the love-hate relationship which has made Wales and New Zealand rugby football's greatest rivals. While Welsh fathers have told their sons about Teddy Morgan and his try of tries, young Kiwis are told that Deans was robbed of his. So – 1905 and all that is more than just a part of Cardiff Arms Park's history: it belongs to the Game.

The supremacy of Wales, it has to be admitted, was short-lived as they went down to the touring South Africans at St Helen's. But Cardiff gained an historic victory over the Springboks in a match played in mud on New Year's Day, 1907. Charles Arthur wrote: 'It was most unfortunate that the ground was in such a terribly wet and sloppy condition, as outsiders believed that it was owing to the bad condition that our team was so successful; but in the opinion of the majority of those who saw the match our team would have won under any circumstances.' The match is very much a part of South African rugby history for come hail, snow or flood the Springboks were not to lose again on this ground.

Whatever the weather, spectators in their thousands were drawn irresistibly by such fixtures and Cardiff's resultant affluence was reflected in the £600 spent on repairs to their ground's surrounds and fencing. Donations to charity were resumed. There was tangible appreciation of players' efforts, too, such as the presentation of silver cigarette cases to the players who inflicted defeat on the First Springboks, while twenty-one eighteen carat gold watches costing no more than two guineas apiece (and sanctioned by the WFU) were also distributed. One of them is on display in the club's Hubert Johnson memorial room. The infant son of Gwyn Nicholls, Ivor – later to achieve fame in Welsh golfing circles – was presented with a silver knife, fork and spoon in appreciation of work done for the club.

Celebrities came frequently at this time to Cardiff Arms Park, sometimes to watch Wales, sometimes at Cardiff RFC's invitation. On 25 January 1908 a famous statesman, perhaps the most distinguished Welshman of the century, came to perform the kick-off for the club against Blackheath: David Lloyd George, then President of the Board of Trade and destined to be his country's leader in the First World War, whose ten-yard kick was fielded by the Wales and British Isles centre Rhys Gabe. Gabe immediately claimed a mark! A few weeks later on St Patrick's Day an Irish MP, John Redmond, kicked off in a special match between Billy Neill's XV and the Rest of Wales in aid of Roman Catholic schools in the city (as Cardiff had now become). Its large Catholic community have remained extremely loyal supporters of the club, supplying it with many talented players from those same schools.

During the early-twentieth-century period in Cardiff Arms Park's history the north terrace was uncovered and the unfortunate folk huddled there

*The north terrace (foreground) remained uncovered during the early twentieth century, spectators there suffering many a severe soaking. The east terrace has never been covered.*

suffered many a severe soaking (often leaving the ground at the end of a match wetter than the players, who could look forward to the pleasure of an immediate hot bath). However, Welshmen have always been able to sing to help dispel discomfort, and the pre-kick-off harmonising at big matches – club or country – became famous in the Golden Era when the gates were opened at noon and it was a case of first come, first served at the turnstiles. The hymns and arias of Wales were sung during the waiting hours before the teams took the field – sometimes the near-religious fervour must have put folk in mind of the 1905 Revivalist campaign of Evan Roberts. Except that he condemned rugby as a game for sinners!

And, admittedly, there were plenty of those around! On 12 February 1910 Cardiff Arms Park witnessed an extremely rough match before 20,000 spectators, a record crowd for an all-Welsh club game, in which Cardiff continued a long run of success over their great rivals Newport. Each side had a man sent off in an encounter 'that had not been equalled for ferocity and fouling since the game was introduced into Wales'. Strong words, and yet it has to be admitted that in rugby football the good, the bad and the ugly are always with us, their presence highlighted by occasional outbursts at the various grounds in the Principality.

In 1911 as the Golden Era neared its end Cardiff RFC played an important part in what proved Wales's last Grand Slam Championship season until 1950 by supplying the whole three-quarter line to the national XV – Gibbs, Spiller, Dykes and J. L. Williams. The final match was at Cardiff Arms Park against Ireland, Wales winning comfortably by two goals, a penalty and a try to nil. There were 40,000 present and, says the historian, 'every vantage point at the perimeter was employed by eager spectators'. It was 1899 all over again as hundreds of desperate enthusiasts had climbed over the stone surrounding wall and countless more were left in Westgate Street to follow the course of the match from the reaction of the over-capacity crowd inside.

At the end of the 1911–12 season the grandstand and temporary tiers were demolished and replaced by an imposing new structure along the ground's southern side. New terraces were erected on the other three sectors, the combined effect being to increase seating capacity to 3000 and standing room to 40,000. The bill just topped £8000, of which the WFU contributed £2500. The completion of work in time for the new season was marked by an official opening on 5 October 1912 – just two years, incidentally, after the RFU's new ground at Twickenham had begun its life.

Cardiff RFC could then boast the finest ground in Wales. Ironically, however, these years marked the close of a brilliant era for both club and country.

*Clearly the early twentieth century was a boom period for the hat industry.*

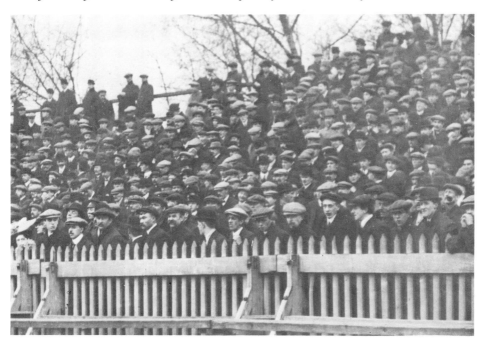

Soon, too, came an end to all organised rugby at Cardiff Arms Park and else-where, as the First World War engulfed Europe.

The Twickenham bogy denied Wales victory in England between 1910 and 1933, but even the citadel of the Rugby Football Union has never been feared as was the muddy turf of Cardiff Arms Park at the outset of the twentieth century, when it is quite remarkable how impregnable Wales were at home: in twelve glorious years there were only seven defeats in 43 matches – and just one at home, to South Africa at Swansea in 1906. The home countries were filled with dread from the moment they crossed the border; and the visits

*South Africa versus Cardiff, 1912. The Springboks' 7-6 win avenged a self-confessed 'humiliation' by 17-0 in 1906.*

were bleak for England from 1895 to 1913, for Scotland from 1892 to 1923, for Ireland from 1899 to 1928 and for France from their first Championship challenge at Cardiff in 1908 until 1948.

What was it, then, which somehow saturated Cardiff Arms Park with an atmosphere of Celtic defiance? Was it the magic of Merlin who made the young Wart a great warrior king? Was it a racial memory of the defiant Owain Glyndwr? Was it the inspiration of the first great Welsh captain, handsome Arthur Gould? Was it the technical perfection of Gwyn Nicholls or the jester's approach that hid Percy Bush's genius? Maybe all these factors contributed to the years of greatness; but there were important underlying trends that also have to be taken into account.

Throughout the formative years of the game and in International competition up to 1900 Welsh sides generally had skill and brains behind the pack and needed a steady supply of what is nowadays called 'quality possession'. At forward, however, they were neither as hard nor as strong as their opponents. The struggle was especially harsh once they had adopted the four three-quarter formation, which left eight forwards to deal with nine. It was in the last few years of the nineteenth century that this pattern began to change.

Now the selectors introduced a harder type of player in front whose prototype was known as the 'Rhondda Forward'. This did not mean that whole International packs came from the famous mining valley, but men like Dick Hellings (Llwynypia) and Penygraig's Dai Evans and Jack Rhapps provided a hard core of bone and muscle. Such men may not have been as clever or speedy as their predecessors but as W. J. T. Collins – 'Dromio' of the *South Wales Argus* – aptly put it, 'Welsh packs had been the anvil; now they were the hammer.' Full of aggression, they scrummaged low and hard, making sure opponents were held and tied down as they released the ball to their scrum half who thus had time and space to move in.

Many of these tough Valleys forwards migrated to the bigger clubs down on the coast and gradually became more skilful. But they were rarely allowed to participate in the open play as today. Whether leading Cardiff or Wales Gwyn Nicholls would tell his pack before taking the field, 'Give us the ball and we'll score the tries.'

In contrast to the 'Rhondda Forward' the typical three-quarter of the day was a professional man often with a college education – of the 1905 back division, for example, only R. M. 'Dickie' Owen was a manual worker. H. B. Winfield and Gwyn Nicholls were business partners, Gabe a Cardiff schoolmaster, Teddy Morgan a doctor and Willie Llewellyn a chemist. Percy Bush, then a long-serving student, would eventually enter the consular service at Nantes in France.

Cardiff Arms Park was within easy reach of several of these players, who often used it for lunch-hour training periods and achieved an almost uncanny understanding of each other's play. Nicholls and Bush were inventive leaders, thinkers with flair whose colleagues slipped easily into their plans with remarkable cohesion (fewer matches were played than in later years, but a great deal more practice took place at which novelty could be introduced and rehearsed).

There may, thus, have been a class demarcation line between backs and forwards at this time, both in representative rugby and in the Cardiff team; but nonetheless the Welsh XV became akin to a club (as it did in the seventies). As Willie Llewellyn, an outstanding right wing, once told me, 'We did not worry a great deal about the captaincy and virtually decided among ourselves which player would lead on the day. He would be the "boss". We knew each other's play intimately and chatted about our approach in the dressing-room beforehand. We remembered the players of other countries and how to deal with them. But there were no complicated preparations and we certainly did not get too excited before a match. Nor did we like selectors or WFU committeemen interfering or giving us advice on what we should do to win games.

'We possessed a quiet confidence; every player really knew his job.'

Strong words from a great player who scored seventeen tries in twenty appearances for his country in a Golden Era when the ratio was three to one in favour of Wales and penalty goals were rare indeed! But that is what success in rugby is all about: heavy scoring and men of character.

On 31 August 1914 the Cardiff RFC committee issued a statement: 'In view of the present crisis in the history of the British Empire the club will cancel all fixtures for the season 1914–15 . . . It urges all subscribing members to do everything in their power for the good of the Empire.' The tragic four years of war that were to follow cost the lives of millions of young sportsmen including some leading rugby personalities. One victim was Dave Gallaher, leader of the mighty 1905 All Blacks. Rhys Gabe, a gunner in Flanders, described to me with tears in his eyes how he came across the grave of this brave New Zealander shortly after his death in action.

But Cardiff Arms Park did not remain completely idle, a major rugby occasion taking place in April 1915 when for the first and only time Wales met the Barbarians for the purpose of encouraging recruitment and boosting war charities. The game was described as a 'military International' but is recorded neither in the WRU's official archives nor in those of the Barbarian FC.

Wales fielded thirteen Internationals among whom the Reverend Alban Davies and four of his great 1914 pack, the so-called 'terrible eight'. Edgar Mobbs was at centre for the Baa-Baas, another player soon to make the supreme sacrifice (and one whose memory is revered in the annual memorial match between the Barbarians and East Midlands). The visitors played five three-quarters and seven forwards, an unusual formation which yielded six tries against just two by Wales and a 26-10 victory. A sum of £200 was raised and 177 men enlisted in the newly formed Welsh Guards.

The following month a boxing tournament was staged and well supported for charity, with famous men topping the bill including the three legendary Welshmen Jimmy Wilde, Jim Driscoll and Freddie Welsh. Young Frank Moody fought as did J. T. Petersen, father of the illustrious Jack who became one of the most popular post-war British heavyweights. A sports meeting took place in August 1917 which featured wounded soldiers. December of that year witnessed a ladies' rugby match between Cardiff and Newport. A picture of the home team hangs in the Cardiff RFC museum and suggests that many years before the advent of 'women's lib', but possibly inspired by Mrs Pankhurst and her brave suffragettes, the ladies could have given their male counterparts a good game!

Since the Armistice marking the end of hostilities was not signed until 11 November 1918, the 1918–19 season was not an official one. However, it did contain an important match, that of 29 March 1919 when a New Zealand Army XV (the original 'Kiwis') played a scoreless draw with Cardiff. Perhaps the most significant aspect of the occasion was an attendance of 10,000.

It suggested that the appetite for excellent rugby football in South Wales had not been dulled by the four-year break in continuity and that Cardiff Arms Park could look ahead to more crowd-pulling afternoons when demand for seats in its stands or standing places on the terraces would outstrip supply many times over.

But the spell that brought success on the field was broken. Welsh supporters would wait long for the return of the rainbow to arc its brightness from the River Taff to Westgate Street and bring back with it the Crock of Gold.

# THE YEARS OF LEAST ACHIEVEMENT

## 1920 to 1929

## HARRY BOWCOTT

The decade began more than satisfactorily for Wales at Cardiff Arms Park. There were heavy wins at the ground in 1920 and 1922 over Ireland and England though critics said that a waterlogged pitch – its ill repute was already being spread about – had suited the fitter and more mobile home forwards. But then success dwindled away almost to nothing, so that in the end the twenties were the years of least performance. Defeats were frequent at English and Scottish hands, the record was more or less balanced against Ireland, and there was the humiliation of 1928 when France won a first-ever victory in Paris. Many Welsh XVs were certainly weakened by the unavailability of key men who had gone over to the professional game; but there was more to it than that.

As a player in those times one must first emphasise that Welsh Rugby Union members (the old title 'Welsh Football Union' seems to have lapsed during the war years) faced immense difficulties as they attempted to overcome the more tutored and sophisticated approach of teams from other home Unions. Traditionally the latters' players were taught basic skills – and encouraged to contemplate the whole concept of the game – during the formative years at public school before they went on to pursue maturity at university or in the Services. To counter such standards the Welsh had little to offer beyond courage, national enthusiasm and the ability occasionally to create openings (which tended at times to confuse their team-mates).

Such shortcomings were not helped by the existence within the WRU of a large, unwieldy Match Committee responsible for team selections. It was openly said, unfairly or more probably fairly, that in order to retain his seat on the Union each of its members had to obtain recognition for one or more players from his particular District either in a trial or, better still, in the national XV itself. Such a formula was unlikely to produce success.

As has always to be expected in Wales there was a ceaseless public outcry against the lack of team success, and most thoughtful onlookers agreed that little would change until the large Match Committee was replaced by a smaller panel of selectors. A sub-committee was set up and persuaded the WRU to accept its proposal that any future selection committee should comprise just five members. The decision was confirmed at the annual general meeting of June 1924 and the principle proved popular.

## MUDDY MEMORIES

*Writing of the Wales–England match of 1922 in his autobiography the great Wavell Wakefield had this to say about Cardiff Arms Park and its pitch, already becoming notorious :*

Although most of the successful English team of 1921 as well as several very promising young Varsity players were available that season we had a rude shock down at Cardiff when Wales beat us by six tries and two goals to two tries. The Cardiff ground has a reputation for muddiness but on that day it excelled itself. It was simply a squelching morass and football was impossible. It was most difficult to stand up at all, a difficulty which the Welshmen overcame by having phenomenally long studs in their boots, longer studs indeed than I have ever seen, and I imagine they had considerably outgrown the regulation size.

*Before the 1926 game 'Wakers' received a telegram from his friend C. A. Kershaw which said, 'Good luck to you all. Mind you wear your goloshes!'*

*An Englishman stems a Welsh rush in the drawn game of 1926. Despite the above-mentioned telegram warning the visiting team to wear goloshes, in the event the going was firm.*

There was dissent, however, over the lack of ex-player representation when the first 'Big Five' were appointed. This possible weakness had been removed by 1926 when Gwyn Nicholls (Cardiff) and Harry Packer (Newport), both Internationals, replaced two earlier members. And, in truth, it is doubtful whether a larger proportion of experienced players could have been achieved without going outside the Union itself. The rest of the general committee were simply executive or administrative, and certainly none was qualified to face the challenge of successive seasons of comparative failure.

If the Match Committee issue had focused people's gaze, it was only a symptom of the system's many imperfections. Policy, it was frequently argued, was negative if indeed it existed at all. The Union paid no regard to building a team, either in the short or long term. To outsiders it seemed that administration revolved around a handful of representatives under the direct control of the President and master-minded by Captain Walter E. Rees, who had been the WRU's Secretary for a quarter of a century by this time and dominated his rugby empire from a house in Victoria Gardens, Neath.

So much for a preamble which will indicate that the WRU was coming under sustained and general criticism by the mid-twenties. But running parallel with the demand for an improved performance from the governing body was pressure for a national ground. The RFU was steadily developing its imposing headquarters at Twickenham, Scotland had produced a Murrayfield and Ireland had opened an adequate ground, Ravenshill, in Belfast where Wales would play Championship matches for a number of years. Hence even if achievements on the field were mediocre and even embarrassing it was time to consider the advantages of premises which Wales would not have to share with Cardiff RFC, however congenial the relationship might be.

Cardiff was not yet the capital of Wales, but nevertheless it seemed to many objective onlookers that it should contain such a national ground. Swansea, where alternative International matches were staged, had its champions as did mid-Glamorgan. But Cardiff Arms Park looked an obvious choice with its tradition, amenities that could be easily developed, and its city-centre location – even the walk to Murrayfield from Princes Street or to Lansdowne Road from the Shelbourne hotel took the enthusiast forty-five minutes whereas in Westgate Street Wales had a site within minutes of the main-line station and the shopping centre.

There now began, however, a sequence of events which threw the WRU and Cardiff RFC even closer together than before. It was precipitated by the likelihood that the club's agreeable relationship with their landlords, the Bute family, would cease in 1922. The fourth Marquess informed the cricket and rugby representatives of his intention to realise that part of the estate known as Cardiff Arms Park; but he was also prepared to offer them the first opportunity of buying the existing cricket and rugby areas (excluding certain land on the perimeter which would later become the Westgate Street flats complex).

The price for this desirable, if not unique, site in central Cardiff was £30,000, indeed a lowly figure. It is important to realise that a refusal to seize this opportunity to buy the land would have meant, in due course, the end of amateur sport there. Terms were agreed, and the Cardiff Arms Park Company Ltd was formed to complete the transaction, with a nominal issue of £20,000 in £5 ordinary shares and £10,000 5 per cent debentures. It would lease the ground to the cricket and rugby interests, who now joined forces to become one Cardiff Athletic Club. From their revenue all debenture interest charges had to be met.

Unfortunately income from rugby football fell steeply at this time – the Cardiff RFC history by Danny Davies contains constant reference to the need for economy in the twenties – and the Athletic Club could not meet the whole financial burden. The Company therefore appealed to the WRU which agreed to put up £4000 in debentures. In return formal recognition was given to its right to mount International matches at the ground for another ten years.

Requests for money kept being made to the Union, persuading influential members like T. D. Schofield to keep up pressure for the creation of a national rugby headquarters. A ground committee was set up to appoint an architect who should design a stadium to hold 70,000 spectators, but the project seems to have lost momentum. The WRU paid for extensions to grandstand accommodation in 1926, but Cardiff Athletic Club continued to be hard up and in 1927 did a deal with a greyhound racing consortium to use the rugby stadium for seven years at an annual rent of £2000. When the decade ended the Cardiff Arms Park company was still in the throes of crisis, and the thirties would open to familiar cries for a national ground.

In South Wales during the early and mid-twenties Association Football was thriving with Cardiff City in particular enjoying their most successful period. Losing Cup finalists in 1926, Cup winners in 1927, creditably placed in Division One of the Football League, they demanded the support of sports-minded youngsters in Cardiff and its surrounds. As a player at elementary school level and later at Cardiff High School I followed these successes closely and attended home games at Ninian Park. The threat of soccer, an easier game for spectators to understand, remained (and in many ways still remains) until increasing failure on the field reduced its direct appeal.

But at that time the game was played in the majority of Welsh schools and its wide appeal, allied to poor International rugby performances by Wales, unemployment refusing to go away and unending poaching by Rugby League clubs, made action by the rugby authorities urgent. Then came the long-term answer – an important one and an attempt to reverse a trend – the founding of the Welsh Secondary Schools Rugby Union. Its Chairman was Dr R. D. Clarke from Porth Secondary School and its Honorary Secretary Eric Evans who had just joined the staff of Cardiff High School.

During the latter's twenty-five years in office the schools in membership increased from eleven to 91. Evans and his fellow enthusiasts in the teaching profession had decided that the future life-blood of Welsh rugby depended on the sensible inculcation of basic skills with special emphasis on 'letting the ball do the work'. I have to say that many school soccer players were persuaded only with great difficulty to transfer to the handling game. The sincerity and expertise of that same Eric Evans proved the turning-point in my own career and my style, which critics were kind enough to describe as classical, was due to his coaching reinforced by training and strict self-analysis. I was but one of many rugby converts who remained at school until eighteen years of age, when physical and mental development were usually adequate to face the rigours of the first-class game.

The original impact of this movement was confined to backs. Forwards who emerged, intelligent and well equipped technically, tended to be too small and it was only much later that they began to challenge the 'Rhondda-type' forwards and the many Glamorgan Police Force players for places at club and International level.

Interestingly, to complement the schools' progress, a team of Neath ex-schoolboys was started in 1922–23 by Albert Freethy, one of the more important referees and later a member of the WRU. Their standard of play was exceptionally high, and won admiration throughout South Wales. During an unbeaten run which included wins against Christ College, Brecon, and Llandovery College they ran the ball at every opportunity until losing on Cardiff Arms Park to a similar XV labelled 'Cardiff' in 1927. Freethy had shown, admittedly with a select group of young players of above-average ability, what might be accomplished by positive coaching and dedication (the exercise would be reflected many years later in the formation of the Youth Union).

The Schools organisation made such progress that in a rapid space of time it had become the single most important training ground for the Rugby Union game in Wales. The purposes of the WSSRU were set out in a programme before one of its matches:

'In short, to establish a real and abiding interest in the grand old game in the secondary schools and to serve, whenever possible, the needs of the premier clubs and the interests of the Welsh Rugby Union, which are the national interests.

'To find proof of the work being done by the Welsh Secondary Schools we need go no further back than . . . the lists of this season's Internationalists where we find the names of Windsor Lewis, Watcyn Thomas, John Roberts, J. D. Bartlett and Guy Morgan; and on looking elsewhere . . . we find the names of M. H. Evans and H. M. Bowcott who have played fairly regularly this season, the one for Oxford University, the other for Cambridge. All these players are products of the Welsh Secondary Schools Rugby Union who have passed through the portals of it to fame.

'To those enthusiastically concerned with the future welfare of Welsh rugby . . . one of the strong arguments in favour of the WSSRU is that there is little or no fear of the players produced by it ever becoming professionals. We do not mean to imply by this that those who have turned professional are to blame; but if we are to withstand the ravages of the invading League . . . the best and safest way of doing this . . . is to support the Secondary Schools Union.'

Such sentiments can be said to have had direct and indirect relevance to Cardiff Arms Park. The WSSRU's efforts to improve the skills and quality of rugby in Wales could only strengthen the governing body's hand and its capacity to plan the future sensibly – which in turn was bound to affect long-term prospects for both a national and a club ground in Cardiff.

Wales had six home wins at Cardiff Arms Park during the twenties, including one over France in which I took part. But these victories were too infrequent and people may wonder why the players of the period were not fired and inspired by the traditions of the great pre-war years when six Triple Crowns were achieved in the first twelve years of the century. It is seldom safe to compare two decades at any time, especially when looking back across most of a century; but players then, as always, thought only of 'today' and dismissed 1905 as days long ago, incapable of influencing in any way their style and standards. What did survive, and even increase, were the traditions of Cardiff Arms Park. I have always felt that the rugby ground lacked personality other than on big match days, when fervent, colourful spectators provided an experience unequalled anywhere in the world. In saying this I may be going out on a limb; but though it lacked appeal for me, its position in the city centre was certainly Utopian. The wooden pavilion was also attractive with the twin towers which flanked it.

As far as rugby was concerned the home team changed on the ground floor, their opponents in the first-floor room. Both sides shared the very adequate shower-baths, which were common by now at the bigger rugby grounds (though it was not unusual to visit more outlandish venues for charity or celebration matches and have to share a pail of cold water with fifteen team-mates to remove the mud!). There was also a gymnasium, seldom used, which was subsequently partitioned off to provide a bar and dining-room. These provisions were certainly ahead of their time, for in the amateur game players were conditioned not to expect more than the bare essentials and did not demand the comforts of later years. So in truth there could be no real complaint against the facilities which were provided, though it would have been preferable at club and International level had opposing teams been more widely divorced from each other.

To exploit such facilities Rugby Union football had hitherto denied itself the support and help of female enthusiasts. But towards the end of the twenties there came a breakthrough when the Executive Committee of Cardiff RFC appointed a certain young Miss Filer to take charge of the club's bar and catering. Maybe, given the somewhat drab surroundings of the day, not an outstanding post; but 'Babs', as she was known to players, members and visitors, became very much a part of the Cardiff Athletic Club and its history.

With the national XV's results hardly memorable it may be well worthwhile to focus now on the progress of Cardiff RFC. They had never enjoyed – if that is the word – an invincible season like some rivals, but that is desperately hard to accomplish in competitive Wales: their fixture list included not only formidable English opposition but also, if memory is not dimmed, four games every winter against Newport, Llanelli and Swansea. They had built up an exceptional reputation for 'playing the game' in every sense of the phrase.

In the first post-war season there were a number of men with pre-1914 experience who could be called upon. J. C. M. 'Clem' Lewis, at stand-off half, was a player with above-average ability who served Cardiff well between 1909 and 1924, his record including eleven Welsh caps, a couple of Blues at Cambridge University and membership of the Barbarians. Others to make a mark included a good footballing wing Wick Powell – who later turned professional and should not be confused with the other Wick Powell of London Welsh; R. A. Cornish, a speedy, attacking if at some times selfish centre three-quarter; a free-scoring wing in Charlie Bryant and an outsize Idris Richards who would later captain the club.

Games against the ancient enemy Newport drew big crowds, 20,000 coming to see the first fixture of the resumed series in October 1919. The Black and Ambers not only won the match but also ran up 29 points, their biggest total against Cardiff. Only a draw in the second game at Cardiff prevented a complete rout that season. These distasteful upsets were excusable as the Newport team of the period was selected around most of the invincible wartime Pill Harriers side, and was to trouble Cardiff for the next five winters: it won twelve out of the next 24 encounters, eight finishing in draws and only four being won by Cardiff. One of these was in 1921 when it was said that 35,000 people crammed themselves into Cardiff Arms Park, such was the drawing power of Newport.

This picture suggests an undistinguished period, but that would not be quite true. For example, the club had the unusual distinction of supplying three players to Ireland – their top scorer Charlie Bryant, Dr J. E. Finlay, and Dr Tom Wallace as captain. D. E. 'Danny' Davies – player, statistician and historian – came on strength as did Tom 'Codger' Johnson. The outstanding young Jim Sullivan's skills were paraded for the first time, too, at an admiring Cardiff Arms Park. All too soon unemployment compelled Sullivan to join Wigan Rugby League club, and his later extraordinary success in the pro-

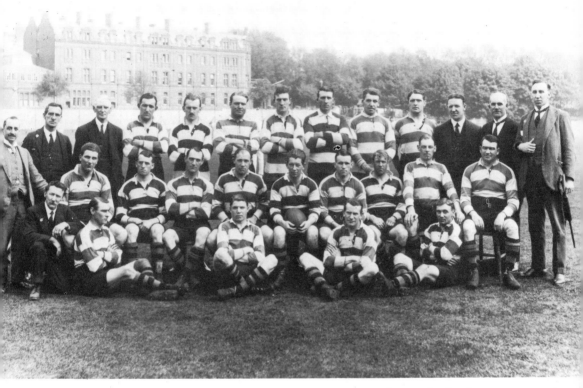

*The Cardiff side of 1920–21 captained by Clem Lewis. In the distance can be seen the Angel Hotel, one of rugby football's world-famous landmarks where players changed for International matches at Cardiff Arms Park until 1904.*

fessional game made one realise that Cardiff and Wales had probably lost the best full-back in the world.

This was doubly to be regretted since in 1924 the Second All Blacks were due in Britain and the club would clearly be seeking revenge for their narrow defeat of 1905. Hopes of a steady, incident-free period of preparation for the big match were to be dashed, however. In 1923 skipper Idris Richards, a likeable, outgoing and outsize forward who was later to win three caps, welcomed to the club B. O. Male from Cross Keys. The newcomer was selected to play for Wales against France but disciplined by the Welsh Rugby Union en route to Paddington and sent home on arrival for contravening a bye-law which stipulated that no one should play in any game within six days of an International match for which he had been chosen. The game against the French was to be played on a Thursday and Male had played, somewhat stupidly, against Birkenhead Park on the previous Saturday. In addition to the player's disappointment Cardiff RFC were deservedly censured for their lack of regard for protocol.

**UPHOLDING THE LAWS**

*The Welsh press commented excitedly on an incident which took place in October 1927 at Cardiff Arms Park during a game in which Cardiff beat Newport 10-3. Wrote 'Saracen':*

Burns was penalised for unnecessarily charging Everson after he had parted with the ball; and the players were brought back to the spot where Delahay had put in his first kick which was fielded by Everson.

This action led to repeated cries of, 'You don't know the game, Llewellyn,' and at length the referee stopped the game and took the un-usual course of jumping over the railings, going up to the spectator concerned, and warning him as to his conduct, a course which was loudly applauded in the stand.

It may not be generally known that a referee is empowered to order a spectator off the field, and if Mr W. J. Llewellyn had adopted that course few would have been surprised . . . He is a referee with a long experience of matches in this and other countries and it may be safely assumed that he is less liable to err than most us.

The other man who rocked the boat was R. A. Cornish, club captain in 1921–22. After a disagreement with the committee at the start of the 1924–25 season he went off to join Newport. In the programme for the game against the All Blacks Cardiff named 'A. N. Other' at centre, thereby fuelling furious pre-match speculation. In the event the mystery man's identity was revealed the day before the game, Cornish returning to the club for their big day.

This club match of the season, if not the decade, drew a 40,000 crowd, the gates being closed half an hour before the start. The All Blacks had won all 19 of their previous games including the first International of the tour in Dublin (and would go on to win 32 out of 32 obtaining the much-desired scalp of Wales at Swansea). Against Cardiff they were lucky to score 16 points, their opponents equally unlucky not to get more than eight. The home forwards outplayed their opponents but the New Zealand midfield defended too well to allow penetration by the Blue and Black three-quarters. There was criticism of the referee, Captain A. S. Burge, who failed, it was said, to notice two knock-ons before Andrew White's try converted by that prince of players Mark Nicholls. He also disallowed a pushover try claimed by Cardiff in the second half.

This tour gave Wales the chance to see George Nepia display his golden qualities. A first five-eighth in New Zealand, the Maori played full-back in every game throughout the tour. His quickness, anticipation, enveloping tackling and superb line-kicking were surprising in such a young man – all-round skills and athleticism which had not diminished when he played the 1930 Test series against the Lions out in New Zealand.

We have touched before on the purchase of Cardiff Arms Park from the Marquess of Bute, the formidable financial obligations this had brought in its train, and the frequent reference by the Cardiff RFC committee to the need for economies. This situation, allied to the number of players on strength considered too good to remain in second XV rugby, led to a proposal that the club should arrange fixtures for two 'first' XVs. On paper the proposal looked good, for very few Welsh players possess club loyalty unless built within a first-team foundation, and naturally it was thought that financial benefits would follow its implementation.

To help the committee determine the issue other clubs were circulated for their reaction to the scheme – an understandably inconclusive exercise: major opponents of long standing showed little enthusiasm for the project, while those in the lower order supported the approach, thinking that a Cardiff fixture with a first XV label was infinitely better than none at all. Opinion within the club, too, was divided and only by seven votes to five did the committee agree that the experiment of fielding two first XVs should run for a trial period of five seasons starting in 1926–27. But problems lay ahead.

For the first winter only one club captain was appointed, a 'floating' captain on a week-to-week basis being put in charge of what soon became known as the 'other' side. Whether disenchanted by the new system or not, some trusty servants of the club now made their departure, 'Codger' Johnson leaving for Penarth as did a useful full-back, Trevor Lee, who created a club record in September by kicking a penalty goal and converting twelve tries with only fourteen kicks at goal. New blood to compensate for these losses included myself and fellow Cambridge Blue John Roberts during our University vacations.

The performance of the two sides was not particularly encouraging either to Cardiff or their opponents. Two games were lost to the Maoris, a November contest in the mud by 18 points to 8 and a much tighter effort by the club in late December by only 5-3. The season brought eleven further reverses, three each at the hands of Swansea and Llanelli. The 'other' first XV played 34 games, winning 17 and losing 14. Next year – 1927–28 – under B. R. Turnbull the team again failed to realise its full potential and, to Cardiff members at least, it was distressing to lose four out of four matches against Llanelli. The most eagerly anticipated match was played on 3 September against New South Wales, popularly known as the Waratahs, tourists who had lost only one game (against Oxford University) and beaten Ireland and Wales. Their captain, A. C. Wallace, a wing who had won nine caps for Scotland while at Oxford, and Tommy Lawton, outstanding as a thinking stand-off half, linked smoothly with Dr W. B. J. Sheehan at centre three-quarter. These backs were given swift possession by the New South Wales forwards and the 15-9 score against the club was fair.

Some people thought that the results being obtained were reasonable, but any undue optimism was tempered by the confusion caused as the club sought

## BARREN DAYS

### Rowe Harding
*Swansea and Wales ( 17 caps at centre, 1923 to 1928 ).*

Playing as I did in an era when Welsh International rugby was at an all-time low and when Cardiff were, as they have been ever since, Swansea's bogy side, most of the events that remain in my memory of Cardiff Arms Park in the twenties are tinged with more sadness than joy.

The first concerns a game between Cardiff and Swansea when I came across from the left wing to tackle 'Codger' Johnson in full flight. Nothing in that, you might think; but when I add that 'Codger' wore a gum-shield like a professional boxer and carried that spirit on to the field you will understand why I counted myself lucky to escape unscathed from the tackle!

Then there was the final Trial of 1922 in which I played for the Probables. Not only did I misfield under my own posts – I was also outshone by Cliff Richards, a red-haired thunderbolt from Pontypool who won a place in the Welsh XV and kept it throughout the season.

So my first International match at Cardiff Arms Park was not until 1923. Before it I met the legendary Gwyn Nicholls, prince of centre three-

*Rowe Harding, holding ball, wears a determined expression befitting the captain of Wales. His team held England to 3-3 at Cardiff in 1926.*

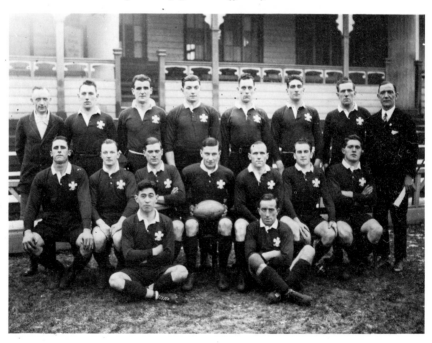

quarters and one of the gentlest and most charming of men. The game itself is famous for a Scottish try scored by A. L. Gracie which brought victory by 11 points to 8. The Harlequin played that day with demoniac energy. Once he ran straight into Albert Jenkins with such force that he knocked the thickset Llanelli centre down like a ninepin before jumping nimbly over his prostrate body. His try, too, was a glorious, spectacular effort which prompted admiring Welsh supporters to carry him shoulder-high from the field at the end of the game.

I played in only one winning Welsh XV at Cardiff – against France (whom we beat all four times during my International career from 1923 to 1928) – and I remember nothing about it. Under my captaincy we got a draw against England at Cardiff in 1926, but lost all our games to the other Home Countries (the only bright spot was a Swansea win over Ireland which robbed them of a Triple Crown).

As far as I can recollect, therefore, the sole other occasion which found me on a winning side at Cardiff Arms Park was when I led a team selected by Captain Crawshay. He had persuaded the Welsh Union to pick a representative side to oppose his XV.

Our victory meant, I need hardly add, that the fixture was never repeated.

to administer the two first XVs. Committee members had to decide each week which of their teams should play against the better opposition (if, indeed, that could be determined with certainty). Old-established opponents were not slow to complain if they received the 'other' first XV, that is, the reserve XV in all but name. Supporters were cynical, even the least perceptive realising that the two club teams must be unequal in terms of skill and experience.

To round off this particular episode, in the 1929–30 season the 'other' team won only five matches with many defeats against second-rate opposition. It was apparent that the experiment was no longer viable, and the committee decided that the club would return to the old formula of a single first XV together with a reserve team to be known in future as the Cardiff Athletic XV. The 'Rags' had been born!

Though results were not encouraging to supporters of Cardiff or Wales in the twenties, Cardiff Arms Park was fortunate to see and welcome many players of high quality from England and Scotland. To watch W. W. Wakefield in full flight, A. T. Voyce displaying his Gloucester realism, J. M. Bannerman and the Scottish pack destroying the opposition with a footrush (sadly no longer a part of the game), the complete majesty of G. P. S. Macpherson and the studied control of Tom Lawton – these were memorable privileges.

But despite disappointments Welsh players remained keen and enthusiastic. To achieve greater success and self-fulfilment they were generally prepared to embrace change. Many of my contemporaries developed outstanding skills and without thinking long I can avow that Albert Jenkins, Watcyn Thomas, Ivor Jones and others did not receive sufficient recognition during their active days – Ivor played all his peak rugby as a member of the 1930 British Isles side in New Zealand and Australia. The game, certainly, is something to be enjoyed; national honours, however much fêted in Wales, are incidental to it. But any lists of world-class players in the period must include those three names.

Mention must be made, too, of Windsor Lewis (Cambridge University, London Welsh and Wales). I have had no reason to revise my judgment since playing with and against him many years ago and appreciating his quality: he was in my opinion the best Welsh stand-off half during and after my own time. His tremendous speed off the mark, correct handling, general sense of position and concern for his centres all added up to near perfection in an imperfect world. Lewis's fellow student W. Guy Morgan (nephew of Dr Teddy Morgan) was an ideal centre. Though lacking bulk he represented his country very successfully, only to suffer the ravages of mediocre team selection. What a loss to rugby that television had not reared its head to record his immaculate all-round skills.

Wales has always been well served by full-backs, and there was none better in my day than Jack Bassett of Penarth, whose tackling and positional play defied criticism. Taken on the 1930 Lions tour he became the scourge of New Zealand – the ultimate accolade – and on his return there were few players I can think of prepared to take him on a second time in the same game. It was a great comfort to know that he was behind you. I pick out, too, W. C. 'Wick' Powell, first of the big scrum halves with a long pass – quite often an inaccurate one, too – which you could retrieve to begin an attack some thirty yards behind the advantage line.

But despite the personalities, the post-war era was one of mixed fortunes – disastrous to some, for Wales does not easily accept failure in her national sport. More sophisticated Welsh folk, however, who were prepared to examine and analyse the comparative lack of success, were able to conclude that it was simply a passing phase.

The long term future of Welsh rugby, they thought, was very healthy. The stands and terraces at Cardiff Arms Park would again send over the hills inevitable renderings of 'Sospan Fach', 'Aberystwyth', 'Cwm Rhondda' and 'Hen Wlad fy Nhadau'.

The more so with success.

# THE RETURN OF CONFIDENCE

## 1930 to 1939

### WILFRED WOOLLER

In order to understand the somewhat erratic evolution of Cardiff Arms Park into the national ground which it has now become, incorporating the full administrative headquarters of rugby football in Wales, it is necessary to understand something of the composition and constitution of the Welsh Rugby Union, and in particular its parochial concern with local politics.

At the commencement of the thirties South Wales, from Monmouthshire to Pembrokeshire, was divided into districts – there was little or no rugby played in Mid and North Wales at this time so these areas were unrepresented. The main power lay in the hands of the WRU committee, drawn from the area bounded by Newport to the east, Llanelli to the west and the Rhondda Valley to the north. This was where the strength of Welsh club rugby was contained.

The central districts of South Wales were represented by two elected members each. Monmouthshire had three representatives and the outlying western counties, Carmarthen, Pembrokeshire and Cardigan, a total of two. Voting for Union members lay in the hands of the affiliated clubs, which were those clubs accepted and approved by the WRU. These were only a percentage of the actual number of clubs playing regular rugby football.

The prestige and perks obtaining from a position on the Union's general committee inevitably led to the election of members who were prepared to work and canvass with some tenacity of purpose among the affiliated clubs in their particular voting area. Now in this period the only pre-match tickets were for the grandstands, field and enclosure being pay-at-the-gate. These International tickets were largely distributed to each Union committeeman who in turn spread them around the affiliated clubs in his area. This was a powerful inducement to encourage the right sort of vote; but it meant that too often men of little stature and even less vision commanded the WRU committees. Even less desirable still, they were intensely parochial in their outlook. This attitude made for fierce rivalry between east and west and in particular between Cardiff and Swansea – a distrust which inhibited the dispassionate planning of Welsh rugby on a national front.

The thirties started with a financial crisis in the affairs of the Cardiff Arms Park Company (formed, it will be remembered, to acquire the land from the Bute estate). No interest had been paid on the Welsh Rugby Union's debentures since 1923, and there also appeared to be some confusion in the combined accounts of the Company and the Cardiff club. The latter asked the Union to cancel its £4000 debenture holding and henceforth pay £500 rent for each International match mounted at the ground.

These were an indeterminate number each winter, since representative rugby was shared between Cardiff Arms Park and the St Helen's ground at Swansea. Now, at the turn of this decade France had been eliminated from the International scene because of interpretative confusion in their attitude to professionalism at club level (and did not return to the Championship until after the Second World War). Thus in alternate years only one home International was played, though the ground was also made available for Trials and schoolboy International games. The divided Union could not agree to any concession in the direction of Cardiff, whose request failed.

The WRU now began to explore other suitable areas for a national ground, always a dream child. Reports were called for on the development of Cardiff, Swansea, and a totally independent area at Sloper Road where Cardiff's western suburbs petered out (and near Cardiff City AFC's ground, Ninian Park). In view of the many millions of pounds subsequently spent on the national ground at Cardiff Arms Park it is interesting to note that the architects' estimate for a ground capable of holding 20,000 seated spectators and 55,000 standing – a total of 75,000 – was £45,000. The Sloper Road scheme was abandoned because the owners would not part with the freehold.

Next the Union came up with a compromise solution, a national centre midway between east and west at the Brewery Field, Bridgend. Land was acquired there and consideration given to a ground of 50,000 capacity at an estimated cost of £40,000 with a second stage costing £27,000 increasing accommodation to 79,000 in the fullness of time – that is, a project on the scale of the Scottish Rugby Union's ground at Murrayfield. There was also discussion about extending the capacity of both Cardiff Arms Park and St Helen's.

By November 1930 the Cardiff Arms Park Company, in which the Welsh Rugby Union had a major financial stake but whose broad organisation lay in the hands of the Cardiff club, withdrew its request for the cancellation of the debentures – but still asked for £500 per International match plus 10 per cent of Trial match receipts. The spectre of a national ground being established in mid-Glamorgan had, I suspect, a distinct influence on the thinking of the Cardiff club committee – just as it would again some thirty-five years later upon Cardiff City Council when there was a fresh possibility of the WRU developing a new site at Bridgend.

Rugby football like everything else at this period was suffering from the effects of the industrial Depression and the Cardiff club was experiencing severe economic pressures by 1932, so that it was vital to plan wisely. Financial guidance and help on the necessary scale might have been forthcoming from the business community in the city; but since the committee control of the

---

**A RECORD CROWD**

**Philip Trevor**
*Writing in* The Daily Telegraph, *Philip Trevor was one of many journalists to level criticism against the Cardiff administration following England's 11-3 victory over Wales at Cardiff Arms Park in 1930 :*

The match was played in the presence of what must have been for the Cardiff Arms Park ground a record crowd. Unfortunately for all present, and especially the players, it was too large and for that very considerable error of administration the authorities cannot be held blameless. Surely there was a strong moral obligation on those authorities to see that there was no possibility of such overcrowding. Welsh rugby football authorities, in particular, have had their warnings. I have a vivid recollection of the debacle at Swansea a few years ago in the Wales v Scotland match.

Now that it has been improved and enlarged the rugby ground at Cardiff holds about 60,000 people. That the gates should have been closed earlier is a certainty. When play began spectators were allowed to sit inside the ropes and within a couple of yards of the touch-line. When Black, towards the end of the match, kicked his penalty goal the crowd had reached the goal-line. A few minutes later they were actually on the field of play. I repeat that this sort of thing should be made impossible of happening. It is unfair to the early-comer and a breach of faith with those who have purchased reserved tickets.

---

club – not unlike that of the Union – was closely guarded by members, the club were unwilling to look outside the game and turned back towards the Welsh Rugby Union. After protracted negotiations the Union received 'B' shares in the Cardiff Arms Park Company which effectively gave it 76.35 per cent of the capital in exchange for a payement of £12,080 and enabled the Company to clear its most pressing liabilities. The Company then granted a lease until 2032 at a rental of £200 a year to Cardiff, and the WRU was given power to make such alterations as it required for the International accommodation at the ground.

Swansea had, in the meantime, vehemently opposed this arrangement for obvious political reasons and submitted a dissenting minority report. This hostility from the west was not finally overcome until 1954 when the last International match was played on the Swansea ground and Cardiff became the main centre for the WRU. But by a quirk of fortune Cardiff Arms Park's further development in the thirties did stem from increasing support from other western clubs. These bodies, in particular the smaller affiliated clubs, had come to realise how a larger allocation of tickets for the bigger Cardiff capacity – given the local demand – represented a valuable source of power and income to them.

Once agreement had been reached in 1932 the way was clear to develop Cardiff on a more realistic basis befitting an International venue. Thus the giant double-decker north stand to contain 5242 seats was approved at a cost of £17,500 (the eventual bill was closer to £20,000). It increased the capacity of the ground to 52,000 and was opened in January 1934 when visitors England defeated Wales 9-0, the 'take' for the Union reaching £9000 (I might have played in that particular match but had been suffering from an injury and was not picked by Wales that season).

Having broadly indicated its intention of developing Cardiff the WRU then sold the Brewery Field at Bridgend. This prompted Swansea Corporation, who controlled the St Helen's ground, to put forward a scheme scheduled to cost £60,000 to provide a capacity of 70,000 there. It is amazing how civic pride can stimulate expenditure. This pie-in-the-sky offer was unacceptable; but the Swansea club were not yet defeated and quickly advanced proposals for an expenditure of £30,000 by the WRU which would increase capacity at their ground to 48,740. These got no further than the sub-committee stage.

There was only one more hiccup in the progress of Cardiff Arms Park in this decade. It came in 1937 and involved the greyhound company which operated the unsightly track around the field's outer perimeter and also made use of grandstand accommodation. They threatened to terminate their lease unless an extension of fifty years was granted with options to break at ten, fifteen and twenty-five years, the lessors having no power to determine. Where the greyhound concern could have gone had their bluff been called is a matter of some conjecture, since they had been driven from their original home at Sloper Road by high costs.

They got their extension, with a rental of £1000 a year payable to the Cardiff Arms Park Company and £1000 per annum to the Cardiff club. They also agreed to bear part of the rates burden. This one-sided agreement was to cost the Welsh Rugby Union a great deal of money many years later when it concentrated on transforming Cardiff Arms Park into a fitting International arena because it was obliged to buy out the balance of this lease. It is my view that certain prominent individuals connected with the Cardiff club in the thirties were influenced by a profitable shareholding in the greyhound company.

By the onset of the thirties the playing pattern at Cardiff Arms Park was set. Cardiff RFC commanded the scene on all but the very few Saturdays required by the WRU. The changing quarters, gymnasium, modest bar and social facilities were situated at the north-west corner of the Rugby enclosure adjoining the River Taff. These were housed in a large, friendly, wooden structure which opened out on to the cricket·ground for which it was the main pavilion. Inside were open fires and one in particular, in the players' dressing-room, had that type of grate structure which permitted a very large kettle to be boiled for tea and had a barred front ideal for toasting the rolls and kippers

– part of the continuing story of Cardiff Arms Park! – which were made available on club training nights, Tuesdays and Thursdays. It was pleasing to find that all the players' kit was set out ready by the groundsman, with shorts and boots to the specifications required, and tidied away afterwards. Any player who has lugged his own bag to matches and carted the muddy, sodden clothes away from them to the nearest bar, as I had had to do at my Sale club in Cheshire, will know the relief of having it done for you.

The 1930–31 season was the last in which Cardiff RFC attempted to run two first teams. A club of such stature is always under pressure to accommo-date a bigger fixture list but this experiment was a failure. The results simply were not good enough. B. R. Turnbull, a Cambridge Blue, was captaining one 'first' team which lost 13 out of its 43 games. J. Rutter, a baker whose great claim to fame was his penchant for bending any pokers which happened to lie in his path – plenty in that era of coal – skippered the 'other' XV which lost 12 out of 29 games.

As in the forties, fifties and sixties the playing surface at Cardiff Arms Park was always under pressure and notorious for its mud. Had it been as

*South Africa take the field through the gate at its north-west corner on 21 November 1931 for a match in which, under Benny Osler's captaincy, they beat Cardiff 13-5. Visible at right is the terrace canopy which preceded the double-decker north stand.*

well drained and beautifully manicured as it later became the turf would still have cut up by the International season in January under the sheer weight of Cardiff's fixtures and the club's use of the playing area for training two nights a week throughout the season.

There was in addition a basic drainage problem. Cardiff's pitch, for reasons which have been made clear in this volume, lies below the higher tidal levels of the River Taff. There is – or certainly was – a large main sump at the western end of the playing area into which field drainage water flowed. Its outlet was regulated by a device which theoretically sealed the main pipe when the river water was above ground level and, once the tide had gone out, allowed field water to pour into the river. But it did not work; and whatever the technical problem it must have been insurmountable, since nobody ever seemed able to solve it – indeed, at this time there was no certain knowledge of where all the drains actually were. So, come December when Cardiff always played two or three financially valuable home fixtures over the Christmas holiday, it was inevitable that the ground became very heavy indeed. The result was that the English or Scottish International, whichever came first in the pattern of fixtures in those days, was played on an exceedingly muddy ground and in conditions which usually ensured a pretty torrid forward battle.

It was the custom of the Welsh Rugby Union in this era as always to match touring rugby nations against the leading home clubs. They provided the strongest opposition as far as playing strength went, but equally important such encounters produced the biggest financial return. In 1931 Cardiff met the Third Springboks, losing a fine contest 13-5. This was Benny Osler's tour, and with his party was Danie Craven, so prominent in South African rugby ever since. He did not play against Cardiff, though he was in the Springbok XV which beat Wales 8-3 at Swansea.

Despite occasional days of glory it has to be admitted that Cardiff RFC endured some lean seasons up to and shortly after the opening of the new north stand. In 1932–33 under the captaincy of Tom Lewis (Cambridge Blue Harry Bowcott had been elected, only to leave the Cardiff area for a post in London) seventeen games were lost. The following year Graham Jones, also an International, lost his Cardiff place and resigned as captain; while fourteen matches were lost in the next season under Archie Skym, one of the great all-round Welsh International forwards. In 1935–36 eighteen defeats were suffered under the popular little captain Tommy Stone.

They may have been very ordinary seasons by Cardiff standards, but the club was still churning out International players in considerable numbers. For example, in 1932–33 no fewer than nine of its men were selected by Wales – R. W. Boon, H. M. Bowcott, I. Isaac, A. H. Jones, Archie Skym, M. J. Turnbull, Llew Rees, R. Barrell and Graham Jones. This strong representation lasted throughout the decade, later in which both Cliff Jones and I captained our country.

## WHEN THE SPRINGBOKS PLAYED AT CARDIFF ARMS PARK

**Dr Danie Craven**
*Western Province and South Africa (16 caps, 1931–32 to 1938).*

My first Test match was against Wales, at Swansea on the 1931–32 South African tour of the British Isles. But although the International took place at St Helen's we did play against Cardiff on that tour; and because the Springboks were humiliated when they played their last match of the 1906–07 visit against the club we were highly motivated to turn the tables – which fortunately we did.

Cardiff Arms Park is all-inspiring. It is as if, to us outsiders, the whole Welsh spirit is embodied in it, and as if no one who is a Welshman is excluded from it. Just to pass through the gates which bear the name of one of the nation's famous players starts this feeling which cannot be described in rugby terms. It is one akin to trembling and/or fear; and yet one which wakes the responsibility of every player who has to feel the soft surface under his feet.

When the 1951–52 Springboks visited Cardiff we sneaked into the ground at night so that we could be by ourselves and take in that spirit in such a way that we could use it to motivate our team. Don't tell me that history does not take the past into the present; and don't tell me that history which embraces all the big names and all the big matches played on a ground does not ensure that a tradition is not built up and carried over. I know history does all that and more – for I stood with the Springboks that night, when the cold aggravated our feelings.

But reality is never the same as a hypothetical experience and Cardiff Arms Park when empty is entirely different from Cardiff Arms Park filled with a capacity crowd. In contrast to a spectatorless ground, Welsh enthusiasm bubbles over every Welsh lip, every Welsh eye carries it and every Welsh act does the same. No secret is made of Welsh optimism. Shivers throughout the visitor's body, one argues, are caused by the winter weather; but that is just a way of rationalising. The truth is that a player cannot become engrossed and forget himself in his game; and the spectator never lets down his whole weight on the seat.

It is as if the whole world – as indeed it has in the case of South Africa – turns against you, and it is useless even to try and make conversation with a neighbour in the grandstand. Those emotions which Welshmen are known to have are expressed in song, and song based on prayer. How can fifteen opponents on the field pray, and even if they could how can they pray against thousands of vociferous Welshmen? When the Springboks play at Cardiff Arms Park there is such a needle that even the Welsh players in their dressing-room before the kick-off cannot contain themselves and must also sing – adding to the isolation of fifteen strangers among thousands. Concentration is disturbed and broken – and I have often wondered how Welshmen would react when pelted by this kind of emotional flak.

> That South Africa has such a proud record at Cardiff Arms Park just shows how well prepared we have always determined to be against Wales. Our mutual experience has been cut by events beyond our wishes. But we still hope that it will be resumed, to make the rugby world a happier place for Welshmen and South Africans.

My own first visit to Cardiff Arms Park to take part in a club fixture was as a Barbarian in 1936 when Tommy Stone's team broke an unbeaten Baa-Baas' run of twenty-two games by 7-6. The following year I appeared against the tourists in the famous blue and black colours and we defeated them by the handsome margin of 16-3 – and it was not until the season before the Second World War that they could again win at Cardiff. This was, of course, the star fixture of the club's season and every year could be relied upon to attract 15,000 or 20,000 spectators who usually saw a cracking game.

I arrived to play regularly for Cardiff in September 1936 when I joined a coal-exporting firm in the city's dockland. The club captain was L. M. Spence, a very shrewd leader indeed, and playing with me was my colleague from Cambridge University days, Cliff Jones. He was a brilliant attacking outside half and it is regrettable that injury limited his Cardiff appearances.

The club went from strength to strength in the three years up to the Second World War, losing only seven, six and five games respectively and putting up the best record since the golden period before the First World War. In 1938–39 I was club captain, but war was impending at the start of my second term. We defeated a local district side; then Bridgend on the Saturday; and the next day, Sunday 3 September 1939, war was declared between Britain and Hitler's Germany. Among the advertisements in the official programme for that last day was one for 'The New Ford 8 Horse-Power saloon car. Price £115 0s 0d – £25 deposit secures!'

I joined the 77th Heavy Anti-Aircraft Regiment as a gunner and was stationed along with many of my Cardiff RFC colleagues on an old coal washery at the Docks. Our club closed its doors, balanced its books and sat back like everybody else waiting for air-raids and bombs. Nothing happened.

By coincidence our Colonel was Idris Evans, a Welsh Rugby Union committeeman and an old acquaintance in the game. He detailed Sergeant Spence and Gunner Wooller to secure use of Cardiff Arms Park for charity matches. Provided Cardiff RFC came under no financial commitment permission was given. Matches proved easy to arrange, there being various teams in existence not to mention a great many players simply dying for a game of rugby. There were newcomers too: I discovered a young mining student at University College, Cardiff, who played for us at outside half – Billy Cleaver, who after hostilities ended was to thrill crowds as he played for Cardiff and Wales.

*Wilfred Wooller's Cardiff XV of 1938–39, the last full season before the outbreak of World War II. Many pillars of the club are in the picture, including: (back row, third from right) club historian Danny Davies; (back row, right hand end), radio commentator G. V. Wynne-Jones; (middle row, fifth from left) Stan Bowes, a great-hearted prop who represented the club 184 times between 1938 and 1956; and on Wooller's left Les Spence, a dominant figure throughout the 'thirties who later became President of the WRU.*

autocratic Captain Walter Rees; thus as far as it was concerned Cardiff was no more important than Swansea, both being simply venues for matches. Hence Cardiff Arms Park was the Cardiff club – on whose ground the Welsh national team played from time to time.

The International fixture list at the outset of the thirties was in a set pattern – England were met on the third Saturday of January, Scotland two or three

Several thousand spectators turned up for each game, making it clear that the public, starved of the game they loved, were happy indeed to see their team back in action. Before long the Cardiff club realised the potential of the situation, re-opened their books, took over the organisation, and ran things from that point on a wartime basis. A year later most of us disappeared on active service to the Far East where we fell into enemy hands and became guests as prisoners of war of the Japanese Imperial Army.

I have given pride of place to Cardiff RFC in this account of the decade deliberately since the club were the dominant presence at Cardiff Arms Park. The Welsh Rugby Union divided its International activities between Cardiff and Swansea; its administrative office was at Neath and ruled over by the

*The nerve of these supporters was rewarded by a good view of the Welsh victory over Scotland in 1931 by 13-8.*

weeks later and finally, a month or so after that, Ireland. It should be re-membered that fixtures with the French had been suspended because of the professionalism issue. Unlike later years when tours by major countries became commonplace only one southern hemisphere tour party came into Wales after the 1931 Springboks, the New Zealanders of 1935. Australia travelled to play in the autumn of 1939, but war came and the tour never started.

Welsh rugby, of course, had not been strong in the twenties, and the thirties opened ominously with defeat in the traditional first game against England at Cardiff Arms Park by 11-3. In 1931 the visitors were Scotland, whom Wales beat 13-8. This was the match in which the stalwart pack leader Watcyn Thomas, later to captain Wales to their first-ever victory at Twickenham in 1933, fractured a collar-bone but refused to leave the field and indeed stayed to score the vital try of the match.

In 1932 Ireland defeated Wales at Cardiff in a match notable for some grievous errors by one of the great Welsh full-backs, Jack Bassett, which cost his country a Triple Crown victory. The Welsh and the Irish have constantly deprived each other of the mythical trophy, since for many decades they met as opponents in the final Championship match. My first year in the Welsh team came in 1933 when the home game was allocated to Swansea, an error of financial judgment. In 1934 England won comfortably under the lee of that new 82-feet-high north stand, while in 1935 I played an International match at the ground for the first time and came to understand the value to Wales of the vociferous Cardiff crowd. We beat Scotland by a dropped goal and two tries – both set up by the magical running of Cliff Jones – to two tries: 10-6.

The match of the decade took place the following December when the Third All Blacks came to Cardiff.

Wales had been the only country – indeed the only team – to defeat the 1905 New Zealanders (at Cardiff, incidentally) but had lost the 1924 encounter at Swansea by 19-0. So 1935 was to be a decider, which caught the public imagination as no other fixture had ever done – and the game certainly lived up to expectation as a match of great drama, excitement and tension. I remember that the pitch had been thickly spread with straw, a frost protection common to this era which required a great deal of labour to put on and move off – but the in-goal areas had been overlooked and were frozen solid.

New Zealand began nervously. They had lost to Swansea but had not been beaten in the next twenty games, one of which yielded them Cardiff's scalp. Nonetheless after a tough forward struggle they led at half-time through a blind-side try scored by wing Nelson Ball to nil.

*By later standards entry to Cardiff Arms Park's stands and terraces seem cheap. Even so some spectators preferred to jump over the wall along Westgate Street.*

At the interval, just before which I had moved in from my selected position at wing to centre, the decision was taken that Wales would run the ball through the back-line. This changed the course of the game entirely and some brilliant three-quarter play finished off with tries by Claude Davey and Geoffrey Rees-Jones, which Vivian Jenkins converted, allowed us to take a 10-3 lead. Victory seemed assured.

Alas, first a miskick out of defence gave opposition full-back Mike Gilbert time to drop a long-distance goal; and then came disaster: an error of fielding from a wide-angled drop at goal by that same Gilbert allowed Ball to dart in for a second try – 12-10 to New Zealand. As the mist crept in from the freezing River Taff a scrum collapsed and hooker Don Tarr was carried off with a broken neck. Ten minutes to go. Fourteen Welshmen!

*The Third All Blacks open their score against Cardiff in October 1935 with a try by Pat Caughey. Amazingly the conversion attempt failed, but New Zealand still won 20-5.*

It was now that the Welsh crowd, always a remarkable feature of this famous ground, rose as one man to encourage their gladiators. We players felt the surge of adrenalin. A Welsh heel came on the halfway line. A swift Tanner pass. Jones moved at speed. I cut through, tapped over Gilbert's head, the ball bounced high over my grasping hands.

But, as I hit the straw, I heard the roar of victory loud and jubilant. My wing Rees-Jones, following up behind, had caught the dropping ball to score in the corner. The magic of Cardiff Arms Park had again worked for Wales and we had won 13-12.

There was drama of a different kind the next season when Wales beat Ireland 3-0 to win the International Championship undefeated. Every grandstand ticket had been sold beforehand, but field and enclosure tickets were available at the turnstiles – though not in sufficient numbers for the thousands upon thousands who arrived for the game only to be shut out. However, they broke down the gates and thronged into Cardiff Arms Park – despite the pulling-in of the local fire brigade, quartered just across the road in Westgate Street, to try and establish some control. In the end they sat fifteen-deep around the touchlines and an estimated 70,000 – a record that can never be equalled – saw Wales's narrow victory through a single penalty goal. No International match was played at Cardiff in 1937, while 1938 saw Wales beat England in a gale of a wind. The last pre-war fixture at the ground in February 1939 saw a game of devastating tackling won 11-3 by Wales over Scotland.

The times were a-changing, so was Cardiff Arms Park. In late 1937 the old cricket and football pavilion had been dismantled and changing room accommodation incorporated on the first floor beneath the north stand, from which players emerged to enter the rugby enclosure from the Taff end corner. A sizeable club lounge had been provided and a committee room. At the south-east corner of the cricket field there had sprung up a pavilion and skittle alley where members of the rugby section also sat down to meals.

But as for the next decade – we could hardly contemplate survival let alone speculate on the future of our famous ground. War inhibits future planning, even in dreams.

## CRICKET AT CARDIFF ARMS PARK

**Wilfred Wooller**

Tall oaks from little acorns grow, declaimed an eighteenth-century philosopher. Not the most astute of biological insights, you may observe, but in the metaphorical sense relevant to my short history of cricket at Cardiff Arms Park. Rugby football, a burly offspring of the Industrial Revolution and bastard son of parent soccer, came initially to that open area enclosed by a meandering River Taff by courtesy of cricket, the oldest and most aristocratic of England's team games.

The Great Park, that piece of land contained by the river to the south-west of the ancient part of the town of Cardiff, was conveyed to the Marquess of Bute in 1803 by the Borough Corporation. It became the townsfolk's recreational centre for celebrating civil and military events and for sporting activities. A Cardiff Cricket Club was formed in 1845, playing first at Long Cross where the Royal Infirmary now stands. In 1848 it moved to what had now become called the Cardiff Arms Park (after the adjacent coaching inn) and played its first game against a Newport and Tredegar Combined Team consisting of players from Oxford, Clifton and Somerset. Curiously enough the Cricket Section of Cardiff Athletic Club does not claim official birth until 1867 when the Bute Estate formalised use of this area of land at the peppercorn rent of one shilling per annum. It was at this time bounded by the re-routed river and by Westgate Street, and was ringed with trees – there was even a small wood at its southern boundary.

Cricket, and indeed rugby, owed its start, its growth and its popularity to the upper classes who could afford the time and the money to play. As Cardiff grew in industrial importance in the late nineteenth century, so cricket gained ground as both a social and a spectator sport. Interest was much stimulated by the evolution of a County Championship and its junior, the Minor Counties Competition. The Glamorgan Cricket Club, which had been formed in 1888, entered the latter in 1897. Inevitably the club used Cardiff as headquarters, although matches also took place on other grounds and particularly at St Helen's in Swansea.

Meanwhile the Cardiff Club had built up an increasingly strong and regular fixture list mainly against opponents in the southern part of Wales and the extreme west of England. But a variety of other matches also took place on the Park. Many Gloucestershire players appeared in special matches, including the famous brothers Grace, W. G. and E. M.

The first touring side came to Cardiff Arms Park in 1901, South Africa, who had yet to secure Test status. In 1905, to mark the opening of a new cricket pavilion (also to be used by rugby players) beside the bank of the River Taff, a South Wales XI played Yorkshire, captained by the redoubtable F. S. Jackson and including the immortal Wilfred Rhodes.

There came, too, the first Australian touring side to visit Wales, with those great characters of the game Noble, Armstrong, Cotter and Hill all

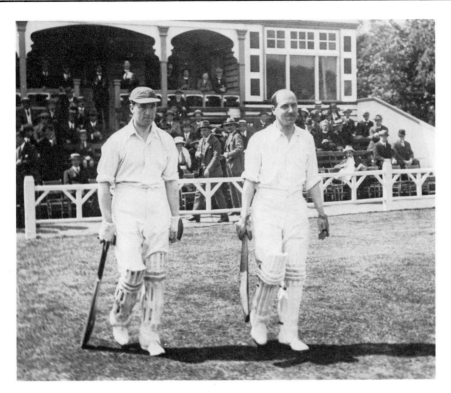

*N. V. H. Riches and T. A. L. Whittington open Glamorgan's batting against Sussex at Cardiff in the county's first-ever Championship fixture. The Welshmen shook the cricket world with their unexpected victory.*

in the XI. Among the well known Cardiff cricketers who opposed them were N. V. H. Riches, J. H. Brain, W. H. Brain (of brewery fame) and Nash, the solitary professional in the local ranks. This major fixture proved a big attraction. South Wales, put out in their first innings for 121, surprised Australia by taking seven wickets for 48 runs before the tailenders hit their way out of trouble. In the end the tourists won by six wickets (and also took the Test series, incidentally, by two games to one). Soon the First World War came along, interrupting sport and causing Cardiff Arms Park to be used as a military training camp.

By this time Cardiff had grown to be the world's largest port for the export of coal. With it grew many ambitions, not the least one realised in 1921 when Glamorgan became the seventeenth and last County to join the Championship competition. The first match played at Cardiff Arms Park – and accompanied by a lavish civic reception – saw the newcomers defeat Sussex; but the result flattered the only County to represent Wales on English soil and it was many years before its presence in first-class cricket could be justified.

Nonetheless between the Wars the Cardiff ground, so close to the heart of the city that its inhabitants could slip in to watch a couple of hours' play from their places of work a stone's throw away, provided much interesting cricket featuring many of the world's great personalities. This was particularly true at the Whitsun Bank Holiday weekend, when the other sixteen Championship counties had traditional 'derby' matches. Being the odd one out Glamorgan were favoured by a visit from whichever International touring side was playing a Test series against England (the August Bank Holiday game taking place at Swansea). The distinct flavour of Glamorgan representing Wales against a touring country certainly touched national pride – especially on occasions like the 1939 match in which I took part when the County beat the touring West Indies team.

Following the events of 1922, when a Cardiff Arms Park Company was formed to purchase the land from the Bute Estate, a Cricket Section was formally incorporated into the new Cardiff Athletic Club. Bowls and Tennis Sections were formed, then ladies' Hockey and, after the Second World War, men's Hockey.

It will be remembered that in 1934 the Welsh Rugby Union, by now principal shareholder in the Company, put up its giant new north stand. The stark sight of this massive structure, backed with a vast expanse of black corrugated iron, offended the then Marquess of Bute who had been wont to admire the southward view from his Castle estate just across the Cowbridge Road. He promptly foreclosed on the narrow strip of land alongside Westgate Street which contained courts used by the tennis club and permitted an extended block of luxury flats to be erected there in 1936 – shutting out his view of the WRU stand!

After the completion of the north stand cricket, along with rugby and the social side of Cardiff Athletic Club, moved into its mezzanine floor,

*The last county cricket match at Cardiff Arms Park – Glamorgan v Somerset, 1966.*

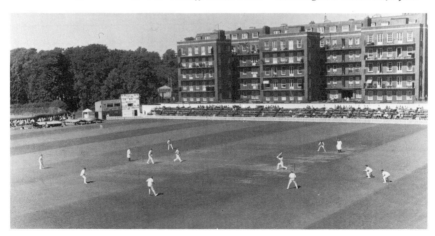

*Autumn 1966: stumps have been drawn for the last time and the cricket enclosure is ploughed up for the construction of Cardiff RFC's new stadium.*

which had windows looking out over the cricket field. The old pavilion was then abandoned and a small pavilion built in the south-east corner of the cricket field. In 1956 this gave way to a new Cardiff Athletic Club headquarters.

The pattern of usage of the cricket area of the ground remained much the same after the Second World War. It staged some thrilling games, especially in 1948 as Glamorgan, hitherto at the wrong end of the table, surprised the cricket world by winning the Championship. It was a pleasure to me, as captain, to have so much fun next to the historic pitch where I had also played rugby.

In 1968 the Cricket Section of Cardiff Athletic Club, and thus Glamorgan too, lost the historic cricket ground to the redevelopment of the complex for national and club rugby. It moved across the River Taff about half a mile as the crow flies to Sophia Gardens. This is a quite delightful rural setting, spacious and well-treed; but somehow it has never reproduced the cosy atmosphere of Cardiff Arms Park with more than a century of traditional sporting activity.

But back across old Trevor Preece's cricket square, where for long the willow held sway, Cardiff's rugby men now propel the oval ball.

# BLUE AND BLACK BRAVURA

## —— 1940 to 1949 ——

### BLEDDYN WILLIAMS

Whether the German bomb-aimer thought he had a steelworks in his sights, or a giant hangar or an arms depot I cannot tell. The fact is that the land-mine which drifted from his aircraft by parachute on the night of 2 January 1941 scored a direct hit on Cardiff Arms Park, gouging a massive crater out of the in-goal area at the river end. Parts of the south stand and west terrace were wrecked by the blast, but the damage to the north stand – opened slightly less than seven years previously and symbolising Welsh rugby's pride and confidence – amounted to nothing short of catastrophe. The great overhanging roof was shattered and for most of its length the upper deck, the standing accommodation beneath and the warren-like infrastructure which afforded storage and changing-room space lay in ruins. It would be many seasons before the great building could be restored to its pristine glory.

As a youngster of eighteen I could not know the severity of the blow which had struck home. The Welsh Rugby Union had borrowed heavily in order to pay for the north stand, and in 1939 its overdraft stood at £31,500. Not only had the war put a stop to the crowd-pulling International matches which would have ensured prompt repayment – enemy action had also removed the prime means of raising any money at all. Because of the damage none of the profitable Services Internationals could be staged at Cardiff, and the WRU debt rose steadily: by 1945 it stood at £40,700 and not until 1952 was it finally cleared (after the bank had agreed to write off £3000 of interest).

All this was far above my head. But I was still terribly upset when I first looked upon what was by any standards a desolate scene. Were things ever to be the same again, I wondered sadly. Could Cardiff Arms Park ever recapture the atmosphere I had known on 26 October 1935 when, as one of a 30,000 crowd, I cheered my eldest brother Gwyn and his Cardiff team-mates in their game but unsuccessful struggle with Jack Manchester's Third All Blacks? Would there be more occasions like the junior schools cup final the same year, when I had made my first appearance at the stadium as scrum half for the Taffs Well XV which drew 5-5 with St Albans?

Not for the first time, you see, there arises the matter of the dual personality of Cardiff Arms Park. It belongs to Wales and is a great national institution. But also it is the city ground for half a million Cardiffians, and this was even more true in my time when there was just the single rugby stadium. And

*The smiling-through philosophy of the Second World War as portrayed by* South Wales Echo *and* Evening Express *cartoonist J. C. Walker in January 1941, after a German land-mine had wrecked the north stand.*

because small boys were allowed to play special matches on it (and, if they were members of their school team, have free season ticket entry to club matches) it could not but gain a special place in their affections, a place which as far as I am concerned it has never lost.

I left Rydal School in Colwyn Bay in 1941 but was not called up immediately by the Royal Air Force as the pressing need for pilots in the Battle of Britain had now eased. I got a temporary job near home and, having represented the Athletic XV in 1939, joined Cardiff RFC. Officially the club were in a state of suspended animation, they and the Welsh Rugby Union having called off fixtures at the outbreak of war in September 1939 when the Government was in any case quick to stop people assembling to watch sports fixtures. But continuity was maintained by the 1939–40 committee which decided to stay in office for the duration, its resolve stiffened by senior members like Arthur Cornish and Danny Davies. Hubert Johnson, who had become their colleague just before the war and now held the rank of Flying Officer in a local RAF Regiment unit, was running a team – and there were games to be had.

Many familiar faces were missing. Wilfred Wooller and Les Spence had gone off to the Far East war, where they fell into the hands of the Japanese and spent the rest of the war behind barbed wire. Ken Street, a popular and able forward in the thirties, died on active service in Java. But there were compensations: the strict laws banning professional players from any form of association with Rugby Union were suspended so that I found myself lined up with and against League stars such as Jim Sullivan, Gus Risman and W. T. H. Davies in the Forces and Charity matches which took place – on the sacred turf! My game was enriched, and such men taught me the real meaning of fitness.

Hubert Johnson, still fit enough to turn out as a second row forward, brought together some promising local talent. Hooker Maldwyn James was employed at Cilfynydd colliery and, as a mining engineer, exempt from military service. The same went for W. B. 'Billy' Cleaver, then a student at University College Cardiff's School of Mining. He and I made up a lively midfield triangle with a crack schoolboy sprinter from Bridgend who was at medical school locally, Jack Matthews. The bomb hole at Cardiff Arms Park was filled in and likewise lesser craters at the city end (though to me the turf in that eastern sector of the pitch for ever after seemed to smell acrid) and as restrictions on wartime entertainments were lifted we played before some surprisingly big crowds in which navy and airforce blue and khaki were the dominant colours. At that period of the war Britain was really up against it, and it is good to think that in the broken shell that was Cardiff Arms Park we managed to entertain people and bring some cheer into the gloom.

After entering the RAF I spent some periods out of the country. There was a nine-month spell in Arizona learning to fly under American instructors. As a glider pilot I took part in the Allied push across north-west Europe, landing one of the frail craft beside the Rhine which our troops were seeking to cross in the teeth of German resistance. But in one way and another a good deal of rugby was played during those war years, especially once it became clear that the Nazis were doomed to defeat, and during my period as a serving officer I had opportunities to appear at many first-class grounds. It was still a great pleasure to end my service days at the giant St Athan station in Glamorgan from whose control tower you could almost see Cardiff Arms Park. The Blue and Blacks swiftly picked up momentum in the September following Germany's capitulation and I settled back in at centre alongside Jack Matthews and Billy Cleaver.

Our team-mates included some very gifted players. Big Bill Tamplin, a cousin incidentally, Cliff Davies, Les Manfield and Maldwyn James were all forwards who had played for Wales or soon would do so. Billy Darch was an able scrum half, and we were well served at full-back and on the wings. No wonder that Cardiff opened their post-war account with seventeen consecutive wins. This run of success provided a perfect build-up to the first big post-war spectacular at Cardiff Arms Park.

Some rugby XVs drawn from Commonwealth contingents sent to fight in Europe remained in Britain during the winter of 1945–46 and travelled the

## VIEW FROM THE USK

### Brian Jones
*Newport and Wales (2 caps at centre, 1960).*

Like every rugby-mad schoolboy I can vividly remember my first visit to Cardiff Arms Park. It was in 1945 when, as a very small schoolboy from Cwmcarn, I sat perched on the platform in front of the totalisator board dominating the east terrace to watch Wales play the New Zealand 'Kiwis'. Little did I realise that eight years later I would be privileged to step on to the hallowed turf for Newport against age-old rivals Cardiff – and mark my schoolboy hero Bleddyn Williams! That began a relationship with the most famous rugby ground in the world which would bring moments of great joy and elation as well as disappointment and despair at club and representative level.

During the immediate post-war years and throughout the fifties and sixties Cardiff Arms Park, with its heavy surface and swirling wind, saw some titanic and memorable struggles between Newport and Cardiff, including a 1951 game played before a world record crowd for a club match of 48,500. For the visitors our long walk along the dimly lit corridor to reach the field conjured up the feeling that the ghosts of all former Blue and Black players were present to remind us that we were about to have the privilege of playing somewhere special.

I am convinced, too, that the same ghosts conspired to prevent 'those Black and Amber b . . . . . . s' from achieving their one remaining ambition – to defeat the arch-enemy four times in one season. If this was not the case, why did the ball slip from Roy Burnett's grasp as he was about to score the winning try? Or why did Norman Morgan's superby-struck penalty from a morass dip at the last moment to rebound from the crossbar – leaving the scoreline blank, and denying Bryn Meredith's team of 1959 immortality? As his vice-captain I well remember the disappointment and despair in our dressing-room.

In 1969 I was Newport's coach, in harness with Ian McJennett. We felt confident that the impossible dream would be fulfilled by Brian Price's team. Sitting in the rubble of the north stand at Cardiff, which had been demolished as the first phase of the WRU's development plan, we saw the Black and Ambers go into an early lead and look well in control – but the Blue and Black ghosts were there even if the stand wasn't. Also present was a rising star named Gareth Edwards who scored nine points to equal Newport's total. The tears in Howard Norris's eyes at the final whistle showed his huge relief at avoiding the ignominy of becoming the first captain of Cardiff to lose to the enemy four times in one winter; the tears in mine were of chagrin and dejection.

The champagne corks popped at Cardiff Arms Park that evening as they did in the Barbarians' dressing-room in 1960 after that famous victory over the previously unbeaten South African tourists. Never can the tension

have been as great within the stadium as when Haydn Mainwaring made
his never-to-be-forgotten shoulder-charge on Springbok skipper Avril
Malan. The 62,000 spectators sang their encouragement to us in the way
only a Cardiff crowd can during the final quarter of the match; and then
at the close came the sheer elation of being engulfed as the crowd surged
or to the beloved turf.

All those privileged to play at Cardiff Arms Park have cherished
memories. Long may it host the very best in rugby football.

country lending colour and momentum to the game's return to normality.
Cardiff entertained and beat the Australian Air Force and a side known as
New Zealand Services. But the real challenge to our unbeaten record as the
winter wore on would clearly be mounted by the Kiwis, comprising soldiers
drawn from New Zealand units which had fought in North Africa and Italy
before staying on in Britain to undertake what was in effect a major tour. On
Boxing Day 1945 they trotted on to Cardiff Arms Park with ten wins and a
draw to their credit. The game was 'all ticket' and 27,000 spectators had come
to see this clash of giants – there would have been many more present had the
west terrace and upper north stand been available. The atmosphere was
electric.

It is safe to say that we gave the Kiwis their hardest match of the tour before
going down by a try to nil. The visitors fielded ten men who later became full
All Blacks including some of the greatest players in New Zealand's history
like Bob Scott, Johnny Smith and Fred Allen (Charlie Saxton missed this
game through injury, though was fit to turn out against Wales soon afterwards). Their score, after just eleven minutes, resulted from a superb piece of
combined play which began on the Cardiff 25-line and was rounded off with a
dramatic sprint by that agile first five-eighth Jim Kearney. For an hour we
battled away, sometimes threatening the Kiwis' line with classic back play,
sometimes having to defend for dear life – as when I floored wing Wally
Argus in the act of crossing for the visitors' second try. With time running
out a penalty awarded in front of the New Zealanders' posts could have put
us level but that most consistent of place-kickers Maldwyn James sent his
attempt wide. Afterwards it was not so much dejection, more a feeling of anti-
climax that we experienced in the changing room: as in 1905, 1924 and 1935,
so in 1945 Cardiff RFC had failed to beat a New Zealand side. Although
strictly it is not part of the history of Cardiff Arms Park, I should like to record
that in the semi-finals of the Middlesex Sevens the following April Cardiff
took revenge with a 3-0 victory over the Kiwis. It seemed almost incidental
that an exhausted VII lost the final 13-3 to St Mary's Hospital.

On 5 January 1946 the invaders were back at Cardiff Arms Park, their
opponents this time a Wales XV which I had been promoted to captain

through the unavailability of Haydn Tanner and Jack Matthews. This time the victory margin for the Kiwis was greater though all their points came in the last ten minutes of another gruelling encounter. Wales had led through a superb penalty goal kicked shortly after the interval by our full-back Hugh Lloyd Davies from just inside the opposition's half, only to be frustrated by a superb individual run when Jim Sherratt seized on a loose clearance and sprinted nearly seventy yards for a try converted by Bob Scott. The full-back also put over two penalties in the dying minutes to clinch the first-ever victory over Wales at Cardiff Arms Park by a New Zealand International team. Just how precious it was we understood when it was reported that their country-men back home had run into the streets in the middle of the night to embrace their neighbours after hearing commentator Winston McCarthy's radio description of the final scenes 12,000 miles away.

Despite the two set-backs it was clear that post-war rugby at Cardiff Arms Park was going to be as satisfying and spectacular as any that had gone before. Full International matches were resumed in January 1947 when a 'Nim' Hall dropped goal secured a 9-6 victory for England which indicated that Wales had some way to go before becoming a power in the Championship again. But the Cardiff club had hit their stride swiftly and were not only winning the vast majority of their matches but also providing matchless entertainment for their followers, who regularly packed the ground to watch us in action.

We were certainly a team of all the talents. Frank Trott at full-back was a safe line-kicker and always brave in defence. In the centre I wrong-footed opponents with my 'jink', or big side-step, and sought to perfect the timing of passes designed to put my wing into space, while next to me Jack Matthews devastated opponents with bone-crunching tackles or searing breaks. Not only was Billy Cleaver's tactical kicking expertly done, he was also a stand-off half who could make slicing breaks and then link with the centres. Bill Tamplin, Les Manfield and the other established forwards were joined by new recruits Gwyn Evans and Sid Judd, both destined to become renowned back-row players. When the great Haydn Tanner decided to switch allegiance from Swansea to Cardiff it seemed the icing on what was a well-baked cake.

That Cardiff were able to produce such consistently brilliant performances out on the pitch in the second half of the forties owed much to the feeling of camaraderie which developed behind the scenes – or perhaps one should say below the scenes, for the heart and soul of our club undoubtedly lay beneath the north stand. The rooms and facilities there formed the focus of our sport-ing lives and were the surroundings for occasions to which we looked forward immensely.

Their Saturday's sport began for Cardiff players with an expectant entry into the ground from Westgate Street, well in advance of the hoped-for crush of spectators, perhaps noting the visitors' coach from Neath or London or Coventry parked at the kerb – in those days there was no ramp down which

## THE MEDIA

### G. V. Wynne-Jones
*Peerless radio commentator post-Second World War.*

My first sight of Cardiff Arms Park was in the early twenties from a window of the Angel Hotel where my father then had his office. Since the tall Westgate Street flats had not been built one had a magnificent view of the cricket ground and of stars like Maurice Tate, Harold Larwood and Bill Voce. An early memory of watching great rugby footballers was in January 1926 when an England side captained by W. W. Wakefield, and including such great forwards as Tom Voyce of Gloucester and Sam Tucker of Bristol, gave me my first glimpse of top International forward play. I vividly remember the great 'Wakers', supported by Voyce and H. G. Periton, bearing down on the Welsh full-back of that day who was playing his first and only International. The sight of these mighty forwards so demoralised our man that he took his eye off the ball and Wakefield scored a try under the posts.

Little did I dream that I was to play on the same ground within a year when my school, Christ College Brecon, played what amounted to a challenge match against Cardiff High School which was then breeding many International players of the future such as John Roberts, Harry Bowcott, Bill Roberts and Cecil Davies. I came to know the Park even better when I joined Cardiff RFC as a player in 1930. My acquaintance was furthered in ten years' service as a Cardiff selector and committee man – and later in more than twenty-one years of broadcasting.

The condition of the pitch now is near perfect. In the old days it was so soggy if there was rain about that I personally can testify to having slid from one 25 to the other on the patches which used to develop in inclement weather on both sides of the field. On such occasions the spectators' lot might be as wretched as the players': for instance the old south stand was long, low and utterly exposed at the front to the elements. Before it was the enclosure, and those who chose to watch play from this spot paid a little more than those who stood on the terraces at each end of the ground completely at the mercy of rain or storm. The deep terrace on the north side in my early days was covered but had no seating room. It has been succeeded by two grandstands; and I well remember the elation of supporters when the first was completed in 1934. From it I watched one of the most exciting of many exciting games I've watched at Cardiff Arms Park, when Wales beat the 1935 All Blacks 13-12. The backs captured the glory that day but the forwards too deserve to be remembered, among them Arthur Rees on the flank, Eddie Watkins of Cardiff in the second row and D. J. Tarr winning a first cap as hooker. Drama focused not only on the result but also on the unfortunate Tarr – 'Jack' as he was inevitably called – who broke his neck in a scrummage and would most likely have died had it not been for the care of referee Cyril Gadney who made sure that no one touched or moved the player before the arrival on the scene of a doctor. Tarr survived but was never to play first-class football again, and thus his only game for his country was in this glorious win over New Zealand.

As a broadcaster I saw dozens of games from a little white box on top of the old south stand which was normally used as the judges' box for the greyhound races but served as a commentary box on International rugby days. And of course I saw a host of great players. From Wales they spanned an era lasting from Haydn Tanner through to that most courageous of full-backs who gained more caps than any other Welshman, J. P. R. Williams.

Many of the stars from countries visiting Cardiff, too, are unforgettable. In the fifties there was the great talent of Jeff Butterfield, usually partnered by Phil Davies of the Harlequins with whom he made a formidable mid-field duo. In the Scottish sides of that era the man who stood out to me was the wing three-quarter Arthur Smith, tremendously fast and a great all-round footballer. Of Irish teams the man for whom I had greatest regard was Jackie Kyle: all the famous Welshmen I saw in the stand-off half position will have to forgive me when I say that Kyle was the tops. The French are noted for open play and the brilliance of their backs, but it is their forwards of the early post-Second World War that I best remember – men like Mias, Basquet, Prat and, later, Domenech and Celaya. We saw overseas players at Cardiff less often but we must not forget such giants as Wilson Whineray and Colin Meads.

The capital city of Wales has a distinctive and unmistakeable accent – the 'Caardiff' accent. I first became aware of it hearing rugby supporters ask each other on Fridays 'Are you going down the Paark tomorrow?'

Since those days the question has been asked in accents from the four corners of the earth. And it will go on being asked, surely, as long as rugby football is played.

**Alun Williams**
*BBC Wales, Outside Broadcasts Producer and Commentator.*

At the rebuilt Cardiff Arms Park broadcasters have a position second to none in the world, where home and visiting commentators sit together in comfort in what I think is the ideal position – at the front of the south stand and overlooking the halfway line. Since my microphone experience covers many years and many grounds the following glossary of commentary positions may be useful for classification purposes!

*Most uncomfortable*: Twickenham – yes, Twickers! HQ itself! Sufferers from claustrophobia should find another job. Beefy former forwards like Peter Yarranton and Bill Beaumont suffer the tortures of the damned in coffin-like surroundings.

*Most comfortable*: The Racecourse, Wrexham. Shhh, a soccer ground – but it boasts two large enclosed cabins with windows, and an electric fire for winter-time broadcasting.

*Most badly positioned*: Sydney, Australia. Here the rugby players use the cricket field, and the commentators have to use the cricket position at third-man – behind the goal-posts!

*Highest*: Parc des Princes, Paris. I covered the first game here after the move from Stade Colombes and it turned out to be my first experience of commentating from a goldfish bowl at high altitude. You can only reach the commentary deck via one of those very frightening mini-lifts which the French love!

*Lowest*: The soccer ground in Athens – just a chair and a card-table on the perimeter between the touch-line and the high trellis which prevents the crowd running on to the pitch.

*Furthest from the action*: Port Elizabeth, South Africa. The front of the stand is about 100 yards from the touch-line and the commentary box another 150.

But the box which evokes the fondest memories no longer exists. It was the greyhound racing judges' box at Cardiff Arms Park (mentioned by 'Geevers' – G. V. Wynne-Jones) once called by me in an announcement, 'The little white stand on top of the South Box.' We reached it by ladder through a trap-door and had to be in position forty-five minutes before the kick-off so that the ladder could be pulled up out of spectators' way. The trap-door was then closed, isolating the commentary team until the end of the game – a situation which, in the course of ninety minutes or so, could create some physical discomfort! The story is told that in the days before the invention of the lip-microphone, which cuts out extraneous sounds, the standard BBC equipment requisition order always read '2 open microphones, 1 felt-lined bucket'!

I first stood in that box on 18 January 1947, and I shall never forget the occasion. Five great players wore the Welsh jersey for the first time – Ken Jones, Bleddyn Williams, Rees Stephens, Jack Matthews and Billy Cleaver. But England were the visitors and they won 9-6. There were only 43,000 spectators present because of the bomb damage to the north side of the ground – but they sounded like 100,000 when the Cardiff flanker Gwyn Evans broke from a line-out to score after a great run . . . Just one of enough memories of Cardiff Arms Park to last me through to the final whistle. Come on, Wales!

players could be transported right into the stadium. We ascended a flight of stairs and proceeded down the long corridor which led beneath the north terrace to our changing-room. The first arrivals might ease open the windows to take in the view over the cricket ground where, depending on the time of year, Glamorgan's batsmen could be seeing off the new ball or the Cardiff hockey XI limbering up. There would form a queue of players anxious for a loosening-up spell under the fingers of our rub-a-dub man John Powell. Jack Matthews was always worth watching as he bent himself to the task of binding up his latest bruised limb or cracked rib!

*Jack Matthews: '. . . devastated opponents with bone-crunching tackles or searing breaks.'*

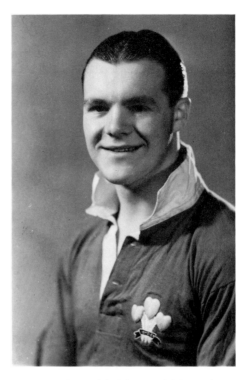

Each of us had a personal chair in the room where his kit would have been carefully placed by the ground staff: freshly laundered jersey, shorts, socks and jockstrap – great to put on. Boots, cleaned and polished, stood ready to wear complete with laces that had been in the wash. Prompted by the sight of supporters pouring into the ground via the Angel Street entrance and the shuffling, stumping sound of their feet on the terrace just above us we hastened to change, complete private pre-match rituals and pay attention to the skipper's pep talk. Then came the big moment when he led us off down another long, echoing corridor, the crunch of studs on floorboards making us sound like a platoon of soldiery on the march. Finally – out into the fresh air and on to the pitch through a gate at the river end of the ground.

Sometimes, I have to admit, the teams would be up to their ankles in mud straightaway, especially in December and January. A lot of the criticism levelled at the old pitch was more than justified. But I must make one or two points in its defence. First, two Cardiff teams used it regularly to train and play (a third once the Youth section was formed in 1949). Second, it is not generally known that the Nazi land-mine smashed some of the subterranean drains through which water was meant to seep away into the River Taff alongside. When you also bear in mind that Wales's capital is a wet city anyway on Europe's Atlantic coast, it is not really surprising that in midwinter Cardiff Arms Park was frequently unplayable. On the other hand, in early and late season I found the turf a pleasure to run on, usually firm and springy.

After the match a return journey, to satisfy thirsts with long draughts of the brimming shandies or lemonades awaiting consumption on the table in our changing-room. The ablutions were nothing to write home about, just a single bath and three or four showers. But there was no time to waste, for our next stop was the players' snug bar where we enjoyed unwinding in the company of the visitors, submitting the game to endless analysis in the days before television and action replays. Each Cardiff player's responsibility was to seek out his opposite number, make sure his glass was kept well filled with ale and generally have a care to his welfare. This seemed to me a fine custom, and I was sad that in later years – as far as I could tell – it had lapsed.

Most players stayed on long into the evenings during the forties, for the après-rugby was an important part of young men's social life. After our private hour the players were expected to branch out into the clubhouse – also at that time beneath the north stand – to meet members and hear their views and criticisms. Sometimes these were a little wearisome, prompting us to disappear briefly to the nearby City Arms pub for a change of scenery, but often there were valuable observations to hear from veterans like Rhys Gabe who had been active decades earlier and loved comparing notes with the moderns. At some stage we would want to eat, and I recall that trestle tables were laid out in the adjacent skittle alley where we tucked in to simple but delicious meals of fish and chips or faggots and peas. Inevitably there would be singing, the hymns and arias of the day plus individual turns and contributions, before

*Quay Street and the City Arms. Sometimes if criticism became wearisome Bleddyn Williams and his contemporaries might go there for a brief change of scenery.*

finally the happy company would begin to break up. The visiting team would be seen on its way, and at last it would be the Cardiff players' turn to head for home, the fortunate ones by motor car, others by bus or on the dear old trams which used to rattle and shudder their way around the city.

Now, such routine was not peculiar to Cardiff RFC. All over Britain rugby clubs socialised in a similar manner after matches. But experience suggested that the atmosphere of our evenings was well out of the ordinary. Certainly it was wonderful to see the change wrought in a basically reserved man like Haydn Tanner whose personality really blossomed in that clubhouse, surrounded by warm congenial company.

In a book published in 1956 after my retirement I wrote that Twickenham was the finest rugby stadium in the country. Because of its elegance and symmetry, because of its lavish changing-room accommodation and wealth of bath-tubs, because of its fortress-like aspect to the Welsh (who won there only once between 1910 and 1950) I hold to the opinion I expressed at the time. On the other hand England's HQ was also an austere place with an air of being kept for special occasions. Cardiff Arms Park was cosy – and lived in.

Only one feature of the place displeased me and that was Cardiff's joint tenants, the greyhound racing company. I did not like the ridiculous little lamps which lit the track for evening meetings or the big black totalisator board dominating the east terrace. Nor did I like the grubby puddles and other evidence of their presence that the dogs left behind. It seemed an affront that a game in which the amateur ethic was so important had to share premises with a somewhat doubtful kind of sport in which commercial gain was apparently the main thing. The licence the company held, however, guaranteed complete security of tenure for the foreseeable future and we complainants had to bottle up our frustration.

With that single exception Cardiff seemed to have everything going for them at their headquarters ground, and now went through the most successful period in their history. In 1946–47 just six games were lost, while in 1947–48 the number of reverses fell to two out of forty-one games played. The club's historian Danny Davies rates that winter the best of all, for although there had been a couple of seasons with only a single defeat these were around the turn of the century when far fewer games were played. Our skipper was Haydn Tanner and I was proud to serve as his vice-captain. The experienced Llanelli wing Les Williams was a new recruit whose presence outside me was very welcome. He could be relied upon to make the utmost of any chances we midfield players could set up for him, and used his great speed to cross for thirty-four tries.

He was not, however, our highest try-scorer! That honour, I am proud to say, fell to me and on the very last day of the season, 28 April, I broke the record of forty touch-downs set in 1892–93 by Colonel T. W. Pearson. Our opponents, I remember, were Gloucester and as the game began I had thirty-seven tries to my credit (from thirty appearances). The Cardiff XV knew that the record could fall and generously went to great lengths to put me over the line. As luck would have it the Gloucester team of the day were no match for us, conceding nine tries altogether, of which I got four. The applause of our knowledgeable fans rang in my ears.

Besides individual achievements there were great team efforts to look back on, one of them involving our age-old rivals Newport. In the forties there were four fixtures a year between the two clubs and the great challenge was to complete a grand slam of victories, a feat not achieved by Cardiff since 1906 (and never by Newport). On 10 April the Black and Ambers came to Cardiff Arms Park with three defeats behind them. To our great delight, inspired by superb displays from Tanner and Cleaver at half-back, we made it four. The grudging admission ought to be made, in fairness, that Cardiffians envy the several unbeaten seasons which Newport have played through, a feat never quite accomplished by ourselves.

Tanner and I were captain and vice-captain again the following winter when the record of Cardiff RFC was once more very impressive, showing only three defeats out of forty-four games. One of our reverses was at the hands of Cambridge University, who took a ground record which had survived for eighteen months, a memory which prompts me to reflect on the glittering spectrum of talent with which Cardiff supporters were entertained in those days. Glyn Davies, Clem Thomas and John Gwilliam were rising Welsh stars in the University side that day, along with Alan Dorward of Scotland and England players-in-the-making J. V. Smith and W. B. Holmes. The Barbarians brought marvellous players like Doug Elliot, Mickey Steele-Bodger, T. G. H. Jackson and D. B. Vaughan to Cardiff. Northampton's rangy flanker Don White, Coventry's Ivor Preece and Newport's Ken Jones were regular opponents who ensured that the rugby football to be seen at Cardiff Arms Park was of the very highest quality. These were vintage days, when men deprived by hostilities of many seasons in the sun were determined to exploit peacetime afternoons to the full.

The biggest challenge to Cardiff that winter, however, came from the Second Wallabies. Their 1908–09 predecessors had gone down to ours by 24 points to 8 and clearly there was more than usual at stake when they came into Wales. The Australians had adopted a physical approach which led to many opponents failing to last the full eighty minutes' play. Perhaps the only member of our team who was fully confident of seeing off the tourists in our fifth fixture of the season was Bill Tamplin. 'We'll take 'em on,' he growled. 'And we'll beat 'em!'

He was right. Though the struggle was hard, with wing 'Chugger' Eastes giving Cardiff's defenders a run-around, we took the Aussies' unbeaten record and went on to win the next twenty-two matches in a row. Another 'international' match was against the Nantes-Cognac side at Cardiff, when I picked up three tries.

*Bill Tamplin was not alarmed by the Wallabies' record. 'We'll take 'em on,' he growled, 'and we'll beat 'em!'*

Mention of the Australians brings me back to the subject of Wales and International matches. These, you will have noticed, do not feature largely in my account of the forties at Cardiff Arms Park. Part of the reason is that Swansea was still an International venue and staged one representative fixture each season. Thus in the three post-war winters Wales played only three Championship fixtures at Cardiff, losing the one against England already mentioned but beating them and the Scots in the years that followed.

There was therefore a full stadium and a high-tension atmosphere for the Test between Wales and Australia, the first against an International Board touring XV for thirteen years. Haydn Tanner pulled out with a chipped elbow and Bill Tamplin led us through a torrid confrontation which I cannot claim to have enjoyed at all. The Wallabies frequently threatened to 'sort out' our forwards, but never came near to doing so. Behind the scrum the marking of both three-quarter lines was devastating and Billy Cleaver at full-back was not called upon to make one determined tackle. Regrettably, the crowd were not to see a try but there were two magnificent penalties by 'Tamp' to admire which won the match 6-0.

For the rest, however, Welsh performances at Cardiff and elsewhere left much to be desired, with only one Championship victory in 1948 and a wooden spoon in 1949. Looking back, many people may wonder why this

## GRAND SLAM SKIPPER

### John Gwilliam
*Newport, Cambridge U, Edinburgh Wanderers and Wales (23 caps as lock or number eight, 1947 to 1954, captaining his country to Grand Slams in 1950 and 1952).*

My first visit to Cardiff Arms Park must have been about 1932 when I was nine years of age. My father, who always went down from Pontypridd to see home International matches, took me to see the Wales Under-14 side play a representative match because a boy from my school – Llan Wood, Pontypridd – had been selected and he thought there would not be too much of a crush. As it turned out there was a big crowd, which I remember vividly – though not as big as on my next visit to the ground which was not until 1947 when I came down from Cambridge to play for Wales against Australia. In the next seven years I was fortunate to play there on a number of occasions.

Memories of the games and the occasions tend to merge into a general recollection of plenty of action and excitement from which two matches stand out: one which we lost against South Africa in 1951 and the other which we just won against New Zealand in 1953. But there are also several incidents, not necessarily from actual games at all, which still loom large.

On arriving for the Friday afternoon run-about before that match against Australia I trotted onto the pitch in a fairly confident mood after eight weeks' hard training at Cambridge for the Varsity match. I joined the two prop forwards – Cliff Davies of Cardiff and Emlyn Davies of Aberavon – and we went the whole length of the field several times doing plenty of quick passing. There should have been nothing unusual in this – yet at the end of this exercise I was obliged to stagger gasping to the rails, only just detecting a wink between my companions. They had raced up and down the pitch at a remarkable speed and knew that I was saying to myself, 'Is this the speed at which all Welsh prop forwards run?' Only later did I discover that Cliff had been a sprinter in his younger days and that Emlyn had recently played in the backs for Aberavon!

An hilarious incident took place in a Trial at Cardiff Arms Park shortly after the War, and it always reminds me that people did still play the game for fun. The great 'Bunner' Travers was hooking for the Probables with, at scrum half, the almost immortal Haydn Tanner. They had been colleagues in the 1938 British Lions and were still playing brilliantly but by this time had less respect for Welsh selectors and referees than some of us in the post-war years. This Trial was being played in bad conditions, a hailstorm eventually making it very uncomfortable.

Then the whistle went for a scrum to form. Haydn called for a quick heel, Bunner struck like lightning and the ball was dispatched to the three-quarters with Tanner's machine-like precision. But Bunner, in a stentorian stage-whisper, roared: 'Stay down, boys!' – whereupon the packs remained down for several minutes in comparative safety from the hailstones. The backs carried on playing by themselves about sixty yards away to the alarm and bewilderment of the referee.

In 1949 Wales had a fine victory over England at Cardiff, but towards the end of the first half the score was equal and Glyn Davies, at stand-off half for us, made a superb break which took him to the English line. He was challenged and gave me a lovely pass for my first try for Wales on Welsh soil – except that I knocked it on and wished the ground would swallow me up. Wrote R. C. Robertson-Glasgow in *The Observer* next day, 'Gwilliam knocked on with the line at his mercy and 50,000 people groaned.' One of my friends, noting that the official crowd estimate was 52,000, concluded that the other 2000 must have had their eyes shut.

We did a little better in succeeding years!

But another afternoon I'd like to think was forgotten took place on Cardiff Arms Park in 1950 when we were preparing to meet Scotland. In my enthusiasm at being captain I decided to concentrate on improving our passing and sent Billy Cleaver and Jack Matthews up and down the field while their team-mates observed and made suggestions about how they might improve their technique. It dawned on me that even the press were looking surprised, with J. B. G. Thomas finding it hard to contain his amusement.

At last I realised that, a mere second-row forward, I was attempting to instruct two members of a Cardiff three-quarter line which had remained unbeaten for almost two years and mesmerised opponents by their skilful handling! Fortunately they were very tolerant, and we did win the match. But perhaps it was a good thing for me that Bleddyn Williams was injured on that occasion – or I might have tried teaching him how to pass!

A final memory is of the first scrum in which I packed down against Ireland, when the ball stuck in the middle of sixteen heaving giants. Suddenly a Welsh prop, who shall be nameless, twisted his body so that the referee could not see the ball and with a deft flick of the hand sent the ball through the second row for a perfect if illegitimate heel!

The only clue I am prepared to give to Welsh rugby followers is that two of our front row on that occasion spent their life on the coal face and one became a very important figure on the National Coal Board.

Our opponents' language is better left unprinted!

should be so – since the Cardiff side which was carrying all before it often supplied two-thirds of the International team. The reason, as is so often the case, lay in selection. The Big Five of the day were wedded to the inclusion of their young prodigy Glyn Davies at stand-off half. Cleaver, who occupied the position for Cardiff, thus found himself at full-back for Wales or next to me in the centre. In turn this meant that Jack Matthews was relegated to the wing. It was natural to want Cardiff's midfield triangle as the basis of the national XV, but our rhythm was wrecked by the selectors' reshuffling.

*An incident from Wales's 1948 victory over Scotland. War damage to the west terrace (left) has been repaired but the north stand is still out of commission seven years after being blasted by a German land-mine.*

This, in my opinion, gradually eroded the leadership and will to win of the great Haydn Tanner. He had touched rugby's heights with wins over New Zealand and a British Isles tour to South Africa, and dearly wanted to round off his career by bringing Wales a Triple Crown. As a captain he commanded respect and was proving week in week out with Cardiff that his tactical approach was sound. But because the selectors would neither name the team he wanted nor be influenced in any way by their senior player he gradually became disenchanted. The close of the 1948–49 season brought his decision to retire.

However, the forties also witnessed the establishing of a unique tradition which belongs to Cardiff Arms Park and which I and twenty-nine like-minded men helped to found. We took part in the first encounter between a Barbarian XV and a major touring side, the Wallabies. The fixture was added on to the end of their itinerary.

In the official history of the Baa-Baas it is stated that there were two main reasons for the extra game, both financial: inflation and mounting expenses on tour had not been adequately budgeted for; and the Australians had been persuaded to visit British Columbia on their way home to stimulate rugby football in that part of Canada, and would need more funds. The four Home Unions wanted the match to take place in Cardiff, the venue which would be most likely to provide a big crowd and a big pay-day. Their hopes were realised – and so were the expectations of the 45,000 who came to cheer. The game was truly memorable, and I can assure the television generation that in every way it was the equal of the Barbarians–New Zealand game of 1973 and its often-screened tries.

Haydn Tanner, who skippered the Barbarians, is on record as saying that there was no agreement between himself and the tourists' captain Trevor Allan to play open, crowd-pleasing rugby. That may be strictly true, but I certainly recall that the flankers – or wing forwards as they were called – had a pact to stay bound to the scrum until the ball was out. It was then up to the rest of us to throw the ball around in keeping with this spirit. The end result was described as the finest exhibition of the game that had ever been seen in Wales – quite a rating!

Mickey Steele-Bodger got a try before Tonkin equalised for the Wallabies with a penalty goal from the touch-line and also crossed in the closing stages after MacBride had made a break. But in between the Barbarians made sure of victory with a pair of cracking tries. Near the end of the first half I got through the defence at long range and ran some seventy-five yards before the cover overhauled me, S. V. Perry hitting the corner flag as he took my pass. Soon after the interval I found another gap and this time the supporting forwards were able to send Cyril Holmes across for a score wide out.

Our decisive try was another gem. Imagine how this would have looked on television: Tanner breaks from a scrum just inside Australia's half; he passes to Tommy Kemp; Kemp hands on to me and I feed Billy Cleaver, who makes ground and gives back to me; I pass to Martin Turner – and just as it appears that the attack is bound to die out, Tanner – who started it all – appears outside the wing to cross for another unconverted try! Brilliant!

For the record here are the teams which took part in this all-action spectacular:

BARBARIANS  R. F. Trott (Wales), M. F. Turner (England), B. L. Williams, W. B. Cleaver (Wales), C. B. Holmes, T. A. Kemp (England), H. Tanner (Wales, capt.), H. Walker (England), K. D. Mullen (Ireland), I. C. Henderson (Scotland), J. Mycock (England), W. E. Tamplin (Wales), W. I. D. Elliott (Scotland), S. V. Perry (England), M. R. Steele-Bodger (England).

AUSTRALIA   B. J. Piper, A. E. Tonkin, T. Allan (capt.), M. Howell, J. W. T. MacBride, E. G. Broad, C. T. Burke, E. Tweedale, W. L. Dawson, N. Shehadie, P. A. Hardcastle, G. M. Cooke, D. H. Keller, A. J. Buchan, C. J. Windon.

At the post-match dinner the Aussies announced that they had been so impressed by the whole occasion that they intended forming their own Barbarians club on their return home.

PS: They got the cash they needed to visit Canada!

On the whole the forties at Cardiff Arms Park ended on an upward curve with lots of good pointers to the future. At last the War Damage Commission were prevailed upon to pay for the repair of the north stand which was re-commissioned on 5 March 1949, Cardiff beating Newport 5-0 to celebrate the occasion. At the end of the season we played a special match against the Rest of Wales to raise funds for the installation of the Gwyn Nicholls Memorial Gates which adorn the main Quay Street entrance to Cardiff Arms Park. The start of the 1949–50 season saw the arrival of a man who was to be a dominant figure for Cardiff and Wales in the fifties, Cliff Morgan, a young stand-off half schooled at Tonyrefail.

The future looked bright, and to me particularly so when I was honoured with the captaincy of my club. Even though in the very first week of the next decade I damaged a knee and played only two games during the remainder of the domestic season my instinct was right – some great matches and moments lay in store.

At Cardiff Arms Park they always did, always do and always will!

# A LITTLE RAZZMATAZZ

## 1950 to 1959

### JOHN BILLOT

The fifties brought Britain back to life. Those who bewailed that the war had been won but the peace lost at last glimpsed the promise of better things. Petrol rationing ended in May 1950; food rationing's last restrictions were lifted in July 1954; commercial television was launched a year later; Hillary and Tenzing conquered Everest – while England regained the Ashes in 1953 for the first time since Douglas Jardine's bodyliners of 1932–33.

There was a Coronation in 1953, the scandal of the defection to Moscow of the traitors Burgess and Maclean, the launching of the radio serial *The Archers* in 1951 – while the Welsh rugby scene pulsated with activity. The familiar, wooden-structured south stand at Cardiff Arms Park was knocked down and a magnificent new edifice sprang up to bring modernity to the ancient battlefield. The Triple Crown was regained after a wait of thirty-nine years and the Grand Slam clinched with victory over France to make 1950 the greatest season of success since 1911.

Wales repeated the feat in 1952 and her teams were graced by players whose names were as familiar as any of the top entertainers of the decade. Remember Frankie Laine (*Cool Water*), Bill Haley (*Rock around the Clock*) and Dean Martin (*Memories are made of this*)? And there were Guy Mitchell (*Singing the Blues*), Tab Hunter (*Young Love*), Lonnie Donegan (*Cumberland Gap*), Paul Anka (*Diana*), Perry Como (*Catch a Falling Star*), Connie Francis (*Who's Sorry Now?*), the Everly Brothers (*All I Have to do is Dream*) and Elvis Presley with *Jailhouse Rock*. But we had Cliff Morgan – not twice nightly, but on a regular basis for Cardiff and Wales.

Cardiff Arms Park's man of the decade, Morgan really was Mr Magic. The Tonyrefail schoolboy, who had played on the ground in April 1949 to help Welsh Secondary Schools swamp England by 30 points to 3, joined Cardiff to play for the second team in partnership with another who was to become one of the all-time greats, Rex Willis, recruited from Llandaff. As a cub reporter I found it a relishable duty covering Cardiff Athletic's home matches: Cliff and Rex never let us down.

When Wales lost in Scotland in 1951 the nation was aghast. John Gwilliam's team, winners of the Grand Slam the previous season, fell apart and were humbled 19–0. The turning-point was a magnificent dropped goal by Peter Kininmonth from out near the touch-line. How many number eight forwards

## WHERE REALITY WAS GRANDER THAN FICTION

**Cliff Morgan**
*Cardiff (202 appearances) and Wales (29 caps at stand-off half, 1951 to 1958).*

I could quite easily be accused of being coltishly overfond of the fifties, and the criticism would be fair. But when I consider the famed Cardiff players who had dazzled my mind just after the Second World War – men whose very presence in the Cardiff club made it a most agreeable place in which to learn the game – I feel the warm juice of emotion.

So there is the temptation here to rave over the majesty and matchless style of Bleddyn Williams; the loyalty, strength and leadership of Jack Matthews; the awesome power yet sadly unfulfilled potential of Sid Judd; the indestructibility of Bill Tamplin; the debt I owe to my 'protector', Rex Willis. The list is long, but there is the certain knowledge that elsewhere in this book their praises are sung.

I want, therefore, to write a few personal words about mighty figures of the fifties who loved Cardiff RFC and served it well. They were very different people and yet uniquely similar in that each had a purity of purpose. That was service. The three of them went too soon to immortality.

My first contact with Cardiff came in 1949 when my 'gym' teacher (physical education had not yet been invented) Les Hayward, who played prop for the club, took me from school on a Wednesday afternoon to play for Rex Willis's XV at Porthcawl. It was there that I first met Hubert Johnson. Little did I know then what a powerful influence he would be in the years that followed. Tall and well built as any back-row forward should be, handsome and smartly dressed in a Cardiff tie and blazer, he had eyes that twinkled and a hearty laugh – but beneath all this you sensed that you were dealing with authority.

No one was naïve enough to question that authority.

Chairman of the club for countless years, it was Hubert who inspired the revival after the War. It was he who seduced Haydn Tanner to captain Cardiff. It was he who created the club museum which later became a Mecca for rugby pilgrims. I well recall the 'live' late-night eve-of-the-match television programme when Hubert first displayed his then small collection. His prize item was a cartoon showing the north stand in pieces and the crater in the pitch caused by a Nazi land-mine. The then groundsman, Jim Pursey, was telling an American visitor, 'The last game here was Wales against England.' The American replied, 'Must have been one hell of a game!'

Hubert loved the glamour and style of that night. And why not – for his very presence had given the club a polished image.

Brice Jenkins, Cardiff RFC's Secretary, had little relish for mediocrity. His standards were high and he expected the players to uphold all that was best in the game – and provided they did that, and gave their best on and off the field, nothing was too good for them: for away fixtures Brice made sure the hotel was first-class and the theatre seats the best in the house. Again, in our two home games each season against age-old rivals Newport, Cardiff always took the field in brand-new playing kit and we used new balls. The psychological advantage was amazing!

Mind you, everything had to be honest, with claims for travelling worked out to the last farthing. Kindly but firm, Brice always spoke the truth, however bitter – boldly, frankly, point blank. He was a Christian and proud of his faith. The traditions of Cardiff RFC were enriched by the influence of one who understood discipline – that delicate balance between freedom and accountability. He knew that rugby at its best does not pretend. He taught a salutary lesson.

'A woman should always challenge our respect and never move our compassion' . . . Babs Filer came to the Cardiff club in her teens and served it for four decades. For thousands of players she was its first lady. Rugby people from all corners of the earth esteemed and loved her. In the fifties, Babs's bar was the skittle alley with enormous enamel jugs of beer, and cheese, and bread and pickles, and singing, and noise, and laughter, and a piano. In a tiny corner of Cardiff Arms Park away from the sweat and embrocation, this was a haven as cosy as toast with a welcome few could outstay. Here was a unique atmosphere created by a special lady.

Its Saturday nights were memorable. Billy Cleaver would sing *Macushla*, Bleddyn *With Someone Like You*. Bill Tamplin's contribution would be *As I was Strolling One Summer's Evening Down a Lonely Magor Lane*, Maldwyn James hit marvellous tenor notes in every hymn. But I'm sure that if Babs had to choose she would opt for Cliff Davies removing his tie, standing on a chair and singing the Prologue from *I Pagliacci*. You see, the First Lady had taste and style; she gave the club a touch of class. Those privileged to know her were fortunate.

Yes, the fifties . . . after training on Tuesday and Thursday evenings there was a box of kippers in the dressing-room for us to share. You took one each and cooked it in front of the single electric fire. I can still smell that dressing-room. Nothing has ever tasted quite like those kippers since.

Come to think of it, reality, if correctly interpreted, is grander than fiction.

drop goals in International rugby? Someone with time to spare can make that calculation for our entertainment one day. For skipper Kininmonth it must be the most cherished memory of his playing career.

The Welsh selectors were in such turmoil that when they announced the team for the next match, against Ireland at Cardiff in March they included five A. N. Others. Cliff Morgan tells the tale of how his mother heard the news that he had won his first cap when the positions were finally resolved.

'She was listening to the wireless with her head down near the kitchen copper boiler,' he recalls. 'When she heard my name read out, she jumped up so excitely that she hit her head and knocked herself unconscious.'

Cliff was to prove more than a knock-out on many occasions as defences tried to prevent him wriggling through with those swinging hips and darting steps; ball held two-handed in front of him and head jerking like a demented puppet. He could be a mixture of high theatre and Punch and Judy; a ragamuffin runner one minute and a prince of precision the next. Cliff was drama and comedy; error and exactitude; inventiveness and exasperation. All this in one rugby player the like of which we have never witnessed since. He tidied up behind his three-quarter line even more nimbly than Billy Cleaver, cutting across to scoop up the grubbers or sweep onto the diagonal kicks with incredible anticipation. His reading of the game was instinctive and invariably faultless, though like us all he was fallible. Remember the time at Murrayfield when the ball rolled between his legs? God bless you, Cliff Morgan; it is reassuring to lesser men to know that you could not walk on water – or pick up every rolling ball.

Willis remembers how the Cardiff players tried to put 'this young upstart' in his place when he first joined and played for the 'Rags'; but there was no way to subdue the bouncy Rhondda Roundabout. 'He always loved to be running with the ball,' says Rex. 'And he always wanted my passes in front of him to run on to. We perfected a system whereby I often ran forward a few paces before passing and this allowed the opposing wing forward to get between us, making a bee-line for Cliff. Then I would pass out to him behind the wing forward's back. It used to surprise them! But I remember Don White turning the tables on us in one match at Northampton. He swung around and intercepted running backwards!'

Wales played eighteen games at Cardiff Arms Park during the fifties and lost only four of them. Three of those defeats were by narrow margins: there was the 6-3 success of the 1951 Springboks, who won all their International matches; an 8-3 verdict by England in 1953; and a second triumph with their 3-0 win in 1957. France's historic first victory at the Arms Park in 1958 by a 16-6 margin saw the great Cliff Morgan play his final game for his country. We could have thought of a happier way to bid farewell.

Of course, 1950 was triumph all the way. Cardiff were captained by Bleddyn Williams for the first time, succeeding the master scrum half Haydn Tanner, who retired from the game and generally was regarded as the greatest in his position among the moderns until the emergence of first Gareth Edwards and then Terry Holmes. Rex Willis stepped up from the reserve ranks – a shaky starter, but the club's selectors persevered. Their confidence was fully vindicated: Rex won his cap during his first season of top-class rugby.

Rex's début was at Twickenham, where the brilliant Lewis Jones made his first appearance and proved instrumental in securing an 11-5 victory. It was an occasion of keen disappointment for Bleddyn Williams because, having been chosen as captain, injury caused his withdrawal. John Gwilliam was appointed leader and subsequently retained. So that knee injury, suffered when Malcolm Thomas fell across him during the final trial, prevented Bleddyn captaining Wales to the Grand Slam.

Still, there were to be many moments of glory for this superlative player before he ended his playing days in 1955 and joined the pressbox contingent to report the game with perception and authority. Roy John was a first cap that 1950 January day at Twickenham and line-out jumpers are still measured by that genius of the timed spring and telescopic reach. The Neath leaper set standards of agility that have never really been surpassed and his graceful elevation was admired (and feared, depending on nationality) by rugby watchers around the world. He was to go to New Zealand and Australia with the 1950 Lions, one of fourteen Welshmen, including the five Cardiff players, Bleddyn Williams, Jack Matthews, Billy Cleaver, Rex Willis and prop Cliff Davies.

Clifton Davies scored one of the two Welsh 1950 tries at Twickers, a prop who could scoot along at a phenomenal rate of knots and whose try for Cardiff to pip the famous Kiwis in the Middlesex Sevens semi-final of 1946 as the only score, remains a classic.

Having defeated Scotland at St Helen's and Ireland at Ravenhill, Belfast, after waiting thirty-nine years to regain the Triple Crown, Wales finished the season at Cardiff Arms Park with a 21–0 victory over France. This was an occasion of sadness as well as triumph. Five uniformed buglers sounded the Last Post before the kick-off on 25 March 1950 in memory of the eighty Welsh supporters who died when their Tudor V aircraft crashed at Llandow on the return from the Belfast match. It was the worst civil air disaster in history up to that time.

Victory against France brought an International Championship title outright for the first time since 1936 and everyone was confident Wales would march on to further great deeds in 1951. Alas, ambitions were vastly inflated. Being brought down to earth with a bump is an experience not unfamiliar in Welsh rugby circles, and the Scots inflicted this fate upon John Gwilliam's unsuspecting Grand Slammers after England had been crushed at Swansea. The Murrayfield Massacre, as it is still known, was a defeat by 19–0. Glyn Davies, the classical outside half, never played for Wales again and Lewis Jones was among those dropped. Like the Llandow air disaster, this was a shadow across the fifties.

Cliff Morgan's début was in opposition to Ireland's crafty Jackie Kyle at Cardiff Arms Park in March 1951. Kyle's try, with a lovely side-stepping burst, was worth three points in those days and earned his side a draw after big Ben Edwards had kicked a 45-yard penalty goal on his only appearance for his country. The Welsh selectors, it might be noted, were not beyond unexpected experiments and switched Roy John from the second row to play at blind-side wing forward with Newport's R. T. 'Bob' Evans doing the open-side job. The ploy was not repeated. They also made errors of judgment in those days.

The newspapers were billing the Wales–South Africa clash at Cardiff Arms Park in December 1951 as a battle for the world championship, which seemed to allow for a little journalistic licence considering Wales had managed just one success in the four Championship games of the previous season. However, it must be admitted that a little razzmatazz never comes amiss. No one could deny it was going to be a helluva game.

Cardiff should have beaten the Springboks in the fourth match of the tour, but referee Cyril Joynson disallowed a try by Jack Matthews, who charged down Ryk van Schoor's punt and chased to dive on the ball. The referee ruled a knock-on, though the law had been changed for this season, permitting a knock-on in the act of charging down a kick. The referee explained he thought Dr Jack had charged down a pass, not a kick, and that would have constituted a knock-on. So the Springboks won 11-9 as Chum Ochse, the little wing with the baggy shorts, chased to the corner with Cardiff leading 9-8 and just five minutes remaining. Ochse reached Hannes Brewis's diagonal punt before full-back Frank Trott, and the Springboks had won. At the end of the season, Cardiff's 'Iron Doctor' announced his retirement. Mathews had captained the club during three seasons and played seventeen times for Wales. As a crash-tackler he had no peer. Van Schoor probably can still feel the impact. 'Don't be in the way when I'm coming through,' Ryk had warned Jack early in the game. Ryk really had picked the wrong man.

Len Blyth, the Swansea wing forward, was the only new cap in the Welsh team (his son Roger was to play at full-back for Wales between 1974 and 1980) and Cardiff had their three avengers in the line-up: Bleddyn, Cliff and Rex. Now there was to be a reckoning for being robbed. But once again Ochse swooped for a try; Brewis, the Northern Transvaal police sergeant, in the mould of the kicking expert of the thirties Bennie Osler, nudged over a drop-shot and it was 6-3 to the tourists at the final whistle. Bleddyn Williams cut in for a memorable try on a scissors with Malcolm Thomas just before the end. It was not enough. Still, there was some compensation for Cardiff: they were presented with a coveted springbok head.

The first official International match of the Welsh Youth Rugby Union in 1951 was staged at Cardiff Arms Park on 3 March with France winners by 5-0. Three of that Welsh team went on to win senior caps – Neath's Don Devereux, Aberavon wing forward Rory O'Connor and W. J. Thomas, then hooking for Newport Youth, though it was with Cardiff that he gained his senior caps. In the French team were Jackie Bouquet in the centre and André Boniface on the wing, both to play later against Wales in senior games.

'Our paths crossed through our rugby careers,' recalled Billy Thomas. 'I captained Welsh Youth in France in 1952, when they pipped us 5-3, and

*Cliff Morgan on the burst for the Baa-Baas against the 1951–52 South Africans.*

André led the French team. Jackie Bouquet was in the French team that beat Wales in Paris 8-6 when I first won a senior cap in 1961, and André Boniface was in the centre when they defeated us again in 1963 in the French capital. He remembered youth days and joked about them in his broken English.'

Wales owe a great debt to youth rugby since the Union was formed in 1949 to fill the gap between school-leaving and the senior game. It ensured continuity of development without exposure to the rigours of the game at its hardest physical level. From youth ranks have come such giants of the senior International scene as Phil Bennett, Ray Gravell, Derek Quinnell, Delme Thomas, Denzil Williams, David Watkins and Terry Holmes, as well as Billy Boston, the Cardiff dockland star who became one of the greatest players of all time in the Rugby League game.

The 1952 Championship was a second triumph for Wales in three years: the Grand Slam again with Gwilliam still as captain. It began at Twickenham with an 8-6 victory; developed at Cardiff Arms Park with an 11-0 success over Scotland to wipe away memories of the previous year's disaster; ripened in Dublin 14-3 to clinch the Triple Crown; and was climaxed at Swansea 9-5 against France, with Cardiff's Alun Thomas deputising for his injured team-mate Cliff Morgan. Alun figured in three positions for Wales that season; centre, wing and outside half, and his drop-shot helped pip the Tricolours. The mini-Golden Era of the fifties had been launched in a grand manner.

England came to Cardiff to open the 1953 programme and Welshmen will never forgive their selectors for leaving out Cliff Morgan. Willis had fractured his shoulder in Cardiff's Trials, so the selectors plumped for a club half-back unit: Newport's Billy Williams and Roy Burnett. The outcome was England's first victory over Wales for six years, 8-3 on a day when Terry Davies, the Swansea full back, Gareth Griffiths, Burnett, Geoff Beckingham, Sid Judd and Dil Johnson made their first appearances.

Yet a stimulating recovery was effected at Murrayfield with Bleddyn Williams taking over the captaincy he had relinquished three years earlier because of injury without ever leading the side. Gwilliam was dropped and Bleddyn led his team to a 12-0 win, helped by debutants Courtenay Meredith, a magnificent Neath prop, and Pontypridd's imaginative Russell Robins. Cliff Morgan operated for most of the second half at scrum half when Willis was hurt. Rex did not play again that season, so Maesteg's Trevor Lloyd came in and helped forge the victories over Ireland and France.

Then came 21 November 1953. Cardiff defeated Bob Stuart's All Blacks 8-3 with the thirty-eight-year-old Stan Bowes playing the game of his life in the front row for the club. Everyone feared the worst for the Blue-and-

*The Cardiff XV which beat the 1953 All Blacks: Standing, l-r: G. M. Griffiths, J. Llewellyn, E. Thomas, M. Collins, J. D. Nelson, J. D. Evans. Seated: C. D. Williams, A. D. S. Bowes, W. R. Willis, S. Judd, B. L. Williams, C. Morgan, A. Thomas, G. Rowlands, G. Beckingham. At 38 Stanley Bowes played the game of his life in the front row.*

Blacks' pack. Cardiff had match-winners behind the scrum; but how could they win ball from such as 'Snow' White, Ron Hemi, Kevin Skinner, 'Tiny' White, Nelson Dalzell, Des Oliver, Bill McCaw and rangy Bill Clark? Now remember these names and remember them well: Stan Bowes, Geoff Beckingham, John Evans, Eddie Thomas, Malcolm Collins, John Nelson, Sid Judd, Derek Williams. They were to become the greatest pack to play for the club – the pack who tamed the dreaded 'Blacks', with Sid Judd, a great number eight, scoring one of the two tries – and the New Zealanders had only a Ron Jarden penalty goal to show for their efforts.

Behind those heroic forwards, Willis and Morgan were magnificent. Bleddyn Williams had called on his forwards to give him just two-fifths of the ball for his backs to finish the job. He got far more than that. Yet Bleddyn was mighty thankful to hear the final whistle. 'The last three minutes were the longest in my life,' confessed the greatest centre Welsh rugby has produced since the Second World War.

A month later, Bleddyn was captain against the All Blacks again. This time it was Wales the tourists faced at Cardiff Arms Park. There was no Stan Bowes, but Wales had men of equal steel and stamina in their superb front row of Billy Williams, Dai Davies and Courtenay Meredith; with Roy John and Rees Stephens in the second row; and Judd, Gwilliam and Clem Thomas forming the back-row unit. Yet this Welsh pack could not hold the driving New Zealanders in quite the same manner as Cardiff's gallant eight.

Gareth Griffiths went off white-faced with a dislocated shoulder. He was told the game was over for him. Instead he stood up, turned to the dressing-room door and said, 'I'm going back.' There were no replacements in those days and fourteen battered Welshmen could not hope to survive. Gareth carried new defiance for the entire team with his return to the field. Wales lifted the siege and, although the towering 'Tiny' White stormed the line, four defenders dragged him down and Wales triumphed 13-8.

No one who was there can forget how Clem Thomas punted the ball flat across field when he was hemmed in. Was it desperation or uncanny perception? Who cares? Ken Jones, the flying Newport wing, went sprinting in to gather and swerve across for his famous try. Sid Judd repeated his try-scoring feat of the Cardiff victory and the All Blacks had lost for a third time to Wales in four meetings since 1905. They never forgave us – and how we have suffered ever since!

Bob Scott, perhaps the greatest full-back of all time, came with those 1953 All Blacks. This extraordinary player had been a member of the legendary Kiwis in Britain during the 1945–46 season, when the Victory International series highlighted the resumption of big-time rugby, and his return enabled us to see an attacking full-back of the kind we had never imagined. He could not save his side in those two defeats at Cardiff Arms Park, but the balding Bob left his ideas to be emulated by many in the years to come. Scott showed us that a full-back could be a devastating attacker. Somehow it seemed out of

## BANDMASTER B.E.M.

### David Parry-Jones

Just after the First World War the St Albans Military Band, formed in 1896, was invited to transfer its allegiance from Ninian Park to Cardiff Arms Park. Since most of the musicians were rugby enthusiasts the offer was promptly accepted. In 1980 the band celebrated sixty seasons playing for Cardiff RFC, the bulk of them under Bandmaster John Williams BEM.

Early in the fifties the band was invited by the then WRU secretary Eric Evans to play at a Wales v France game. For some years it alternated with other ensembles before the rivals dropped out leaving St Albans as the principal band at both club and International fixtures. It was a suggestion from the band to the WRU at the close of the 1953–54 All Blacks' tour that began a great tradition – 'singing off' the tourists after their match against the Barbarians with *Auld Lang Syne* and *Now Is the Hour*.

Bandmaster John Williams's first effort as a big match conductor was in 1951 when Cardiff met South Africa. He recalls:

'I moved away from the band to start the hymn-singing probably looking as nervous as I felt. The crowd in front of me spotted it and decided to have a bit of fun: we started *Cwm Rhondda* and they

*Bandmaster John Williams B.E.M. and the St Albans Military Band.*

started *Sospan Fach*; we started *Calon Lan* and they sang *Diadem* – I was becoming a nervous wreck.

'Halfway through the hymn I stopped the band – something unheard of. I pointed into the spectators and my musicians, versatile as ever, changed hymns and joined the crowd – and we finished the hymn with them. In the lull after it came a voice: "That's it, boyo – you stay with us and you'll be all right!" '

In the mid-seventies the WRU converted the north enclosure into a seated area. This had always been the focal point of singing at the ground, so Bandmaster Williams had to look for new positions:

'I noticed that a large crowd of Welsh and Irish supporters had crammed themselves into the area where west and north stands met – and achieved some success here. Then I felt a tap on the shoulder and heard a voice demand, "How long are you going to stay here?" The interloper pointed to the south enclosure: "Over there are crowds of blokes who've sung their hearts out for you for years. Now then, what about it?" "Fair enough," I replied. "Band! About – turn!" We marched across to the south enclosure, a storm of boos behind us and a chorus of cheers in front. We played there until ten minutes before kick-off and moved back to the north side for the anthems – this time to boos from the south side, cheers from the north.

'The lesson I've learned at Cardiff Arms Park is, you can't please everybody!'

place: like a mediaeval knight with a machine gun. After New Zealand had defeated the Barbarians at Cardiff in the final match of the tour to prevent a whitewash in the Welsh capital, the crowd chanted, 'We want Scott!' That sums up all that need be said of him.

In 1954 Wales started badly with defeat at Twickenham but Viv Evans, the dapper little Neath full-back, came in for his début against Ireland at the age of thirty-four and kicked three penalty goals in a 12-9 win to put his country back on the rails. A repeat of his penalty goal hat-trick against France at Cardiff with Willis as captain set up a 19-13 success and then it was on to St Helen's for the final International match on that historic ground. The game was postponed from 30 January because of a frozen pitch and Wales defeated Scotland there on 10 April, assisted inevitably by a Viv Evans penalty shot and with Cliff Morgan in dynamic form.

For the first time Wales played two Championship matches in Cardiff in a season, opening the 1955 campaign with a 3-0 success over England through Arthur Edwards's penalty goal in a match delayed a week because of a heavy snowfall. The pitch was at its worst: a clinging glue-pot of mud, unimaginable to those nurtured on the lush-grassed national ground of modern times. Ken Jones reached a milestone of history with his thirty-sixth consecutive cap, beating Dicky Owen's Welsh record of thirty-five that had stood for forty-six years. But this match also saw the departure of Bleddyn Williams. In victory he played the last of his twenty-two games and was never on the losing side when he captained his country in five games.

The second Cardiff match that season produced a sensational closing twenty minutes. It was 3-3 after an hour and then Ireland's defence crashed about their ears: four tries flooded in and Wales were 21-3 winners. Tony O'Reilly made his début as a nineteen-year-old wing for Ireland, and fifteen years later, following a nine-year break, he returned to International rugby at Twickenham. Ireland have a special regard for their old-timers.

On Friday, 4 February 1956 the sky above the Arms Park glowed a lurid red. It was as if a night from the Blitz had been recast over Cardiff; but it was not the famous ARP, Police Specials and Home Guard who battled against the dreaded incendiary bombs and raced to rescue those trapped in blasted buildings. This was a fight against the frost. The Cardiff pitch had been caught with its straw blanket down, so to speak. The biting cold froze the turf rock-hard and emergency measures were needed if the match against Scotland was to have any chance of taking place.

'Actually, we did not think we had much chance of playing,' admitted Bill Clement, who faced his first big headache just four days after taking up his appointment as secretary of the WRU.

'I took over officially with the Union on the Tuesday of that week and by Friday the pitch situation was critical,' he recalled. 'The frost warning came far too late for us to put our ground covering operation into action. It takes quite a time to spread more than twenty tons of straw across the pitch and protect the in-goal areas as well. It called for desperate measures, but we collected volunteers from everywhere, prepared to stay up all night on Friday and keep moving braziers from one spot to another. As soon as one patch of ground thawed out we covered it with straw and moved the brazier to the next patch. When we had inspected the ground on Friday morning there was no hope of playing; everything depended on the success of the fire treatment.

'When we raked the straw off on Saturday morning the pitch was a mess. It was blackened in patches everywhere with scorch marks and still semi-frozen in places. It was a miracle that we played – and remarkable that there were no real injuries. I never want to live through that sort of anxiety again. It was hardly the best of ways to be introduced to my new responsibilities.'

However, Bill was always a man of resilience and lasted well in the post: twenty-five years from 1956 until he retired in 1981. No more fire-devils to haunt him, but quite a few occasions that required him to flex his imagination and muster his administrative expertise – though the Welsh team took the field at Twickenham in 1958 without the Prince of Wales feathers on their

## BAPTISM OF FIRE

### W. H. Clement
*Llanelli and Wales (6 caps at wing, 1937 to 1938), Secretary of the WRU 1956 to 1982.*

Although my recollections are mainly those of an administrator I too have had the honour of representing my country at Cardiff Arms Park. My first experience there was in December 1934 when, after only a handful of games for Llanelli RFC, I was selected as left wing in the Possibles XV for the second Welsh Trial. Two aspects of it remain fresh in my mind: the first is of an afternoon spent mainly chasing and tackling Lt B. T. V. Cowey, the man in possession of the right wing berth in the Welsh XV. The other memory is of trying unsuccessfully to evade the enveloping arms of Wilfred Wooller on one of the few occasions when I found myself running with the ball.

Little did I think on that day that some thirty-two years later I would become a perennial feature of Cardiff Arms Park as Secretary of the Welsh Rugby Union.

My baptism into this high position was one I could have done without, for five days after I took office Wales were due to play Scotland at Cardiff. Without warning temperatures fell well below freezing-point and the straw cover so necessary for protecting the turf could not be spread in time. Frantic efforts were made by the ground staff to get the ground playable by the appointed time, and this was ultimately achieved by the use of many braziers liberally supplied with coal and kept burning throughout Friday night and the early hours of Saturday. So 4 February 1956 became known as 'the night of the braziers', subsequently described mischievously by Cliff Morgan as the 'night of the brassieres'!

Thus my first experience of staging an International match almost ended in failure, but fate was kind. The game went on, providentially there were no serious injuries, and Wales won.

The condition of the Cardiff Arms Park playing surface was always a matter of great concern to me during the late fifties and throughout the sixties. As the dates of International matches approached I was constantly in touch with the meteorological offices at Rhoose Airport and Gloucester. To me the weather forecasters were prophets of doom, for too often it was the same old story: 'Rain spreading in from the west, likely to be heavy in Cardiff on Saturday.'

In particular, two games come to mind. One was that against South Africa on 3 December 1960 played in continuous heavy rain. A few hours afterwards the River Taff burst its banks and flooded the ground to a depth of several feet. I shudder to think of the consequences had the flooding occurred some hours before it actually did.

The other game was that against Ireland in March 1963, once again played in continuous rain. The visitors considered the playing surface so bad that only with difficulty were they persuaded to take the field. By half-time, moreover, the referee found it so hard to distinguish Irish from Welsh players that our men changed into clean, dry jerseys. This seemed most unfair on the Irish, who did not have a spare strip; but they had the last laugh by winning the game and triumphing at Cardiff for the first time in thirty-one years.

The chain of circumstances which led to the establishing of the superb stadium we have today began two decades and more before its completion. As a result of complaints from the other three Home Unions the International Rugby Football Board took the unusual step of instructing the WRU to implement all practical measures to provide a satisfactory playing surface for International matches to be staged at Cardiff Arms Park. But problems were not confined to the pitch. Exposure to the elements was causing a rapid deterioration in the condition of the grandstands and covered areas. Moreover in the late fifties straw stored under the east terrace burst into flame and the intense heat generated seriously weakened the underside of the structure. Considerable expenditure was necessary to restore it to the safety standard required.

The move towards reconstruction gained momentum in the sixties and my personal ambition – to become custodian of Wales's national rugby ground – was ultimately fulfilled in January 1970 with the game between Wales and South Africa. True to form there was rain throughout the match, but it is a strange quirk of fate that from that day until my retirement in April 1981 every senior International match staged at Cardiff was played in dry conditions.

Now I think back to great players who have thrilled Cardiff Arms Park with their skills, to administrators who have served the game ably, and to supporters who have filled the ground match after match through triumph and adversity. These are the ingredients which have helped make Welsh rugby a great institution. It is a matter of much personal pride that I was in office throughout what was arguably the most notable quarter century in the history of the Welsh Rugby Union.

jerseys, and even Bill could not work a minor miracle and avert that embarrassment. The wrong kit had been packed and Wales played in Trial match jerseys.

From the roof of the old *Western Mail* office block in St Mary Street, I watched the glow against the top of the huge cantilever north stand, another landmark of Cardiff Arms Park history that was not to last much longer. The events of this 1956 February night re-enacted the scene on the same ground in 1893, when the fire-devils were used to thaw the pitch and enable a famous victory to give Wales the Triple Crown for the first time in combat with England. In 1956, Wales won again and this success attended the opening of the new south stand. It increased ground capacity to 60,000 with a total of 12,800 seated and brought a dramatic increase in revenue.

*Cliff Morgan (right) really was Mr Magic with 29 appearances for Wales at stand-off. Next to him Onllwyn Brace, his partner on five occasions, was another artful dodger.*

Wales had won the first match of the 1956 programme against England at Twickenham 8-3 with Onllwyn Brace, then of Newport RFC, making his début at scrum half. Brace was a bundle of tricks and, if he darted away from the scrum, defenders were never certain if he were a decoy or really had the ball hidden by his crouching stance. Subtlety was the name of his game as he whisked past tacklers; light as thistledown and an imp of mischief. Tacklers longed to wrap the little runner in grizzly-bear grips, but few managed it. Against Scotland, Ray Prosser made his first appearance: a Pontypool second-row forward who always played at prop for his country. 'Pross' was tough enough to take them all, and played twenty-two times in the Welsh jersey.

Alas, Cliff Morgan's side could not complete the Triple Crown in Dublin, but they finished the season with a 5-3 verdict over France at Cardiff with Rex Richards, of Cross Keys, playing his only game at International level. Rex, nicknamed 'Tarzan' by his team-mates at Pandy Park because of his magnificent physique and swimming and diving prowess, was to gain fame as an aqua-artist – doubtless a unique vocation for a Welsh rugby cap. The Welsh try was scored by C. D. Williams, the Cardiff wing forward, who has endured the jibe ever since that another yard and he would have scored in the River Taff. The French certainly thought the ball was over the dead-

## VIEW FROM THE WEST

**Onllwyn Brace**
*Oxford U, Llanelli and Wales ( 9 caps at scrum half, 1956 to 1961 ).*

Year in, year out, supporters of Newport Rugby Club have claimed sardonically that the only good thing to come out of Cardiff is the road to Newport. This gentle antipathy extends far beyond the border between Glamorgan and Gwent, and is even more discernible in a rugby context between East and West.

The clubs of Llanelli, Swansea, Aberavon and Neath can lay legitimate claim to being the game's heartland in Wales on one basic premise alone – that the Welsh Rugby Union was conceived in Neath. Thus adoption by the city of Cardiff, which came to house the WRU, seemed all wrong: why should the progeny be fostered and nurtured in foreign parts? Despite being Wales's capital city Cardiff lay a good stage-coach ride from the West and so estranged was the land beyond that even the Cavalry had to turn back at Briton Ferry Bridge.

So much for tongue-in-cheek. There is no doubt that in the early politicking about the venue for a national rugby ground western die-hards felt great resentment that Cardiff Arms Park should have the sole right to stage the showpiece fixtures of the International year. They argued with justification that the playing surface at St Helen's with its sandy sub-soil was infinitely better and more reliable than the Taff-menaced pitch at Cardiff; that western crowds were more knowledgeable and appreciative; and that the larger percentage of most Welsh teams were locals of the parish!

Fair enough. With the vivid recall of schoolboy entrancement I remember the tremendous atmosphere and enthusiasm that built up on International day at Swansea. Minor matters like the size of the gate could in no way compete with the magic of the Mumbles Road end where we fought for every vantage-point. The argument about insufficient seating accommodation paled beside considerations of tradition. And it seemed that Billy Trew, W. J. Bancroft, Tanner and the rest had been betrayed when the decision to axe St Helen's as an International venue was taken in 1953. The western birthright was denied for economic gain; and while the corporate expression of Welsh rugby might be in Cardiff, its soul was most definitely elsewhere.

Having said all that I must quickly add that on being invited to represent my country I had not the least objection to playing at Cardiff Arms Park – like any other youngster from any part of the Principality I would have been only too glad to turn out on a coal-tip. And for all the rain, the mud, the frost and snow I experienced there, the stadium of the fifties boasted a unique atmosphere. Its environs had a great deal of charm, while the old wooden stands breathed a warmth and colour that modern concrete cannot possibly match.

---

And there were the dressing-rooms, cosy and welcoming in the bowels of the north stand of the day. A route map was needed to find them in the first instance. Fully ten minutes before kick-off time we used to be conducted, Indian file, through a maze of corridors around and under the west terrace, finally to take the field via the south enclosure gate. Many a forward's studs were honed to points of perfection by the time this perilous journey was done – and the fond hope was that one or two of the opposing team would have been so confused and disorientated with the strange journey that their arrival on the field of play would be delayed to our advantage!

Even though to those closely involved with Cardiff Arms Park in earlier times today's concrete monolith seems cold and inanimate, it is a magnificent edifice in the modern idiom. It also has the quality of durability, suggesting that the big horse-shoe is destined to remain the headquarters of Welsh rugby football for a long, long time.

We westerners will just have to accept it as a fact of life!

---

ball line. The Commonwealth Games Marathon Gate was built at that end. 'Leave it open for me,' C. D. used to laugh.

There was something strange about the Welsh team when they took the field for the first match of 1957. The crowd at Cardiff Arms Park noticed it as all eyes turned to the player wearing number fourteen. It was Llanelli's Geoff Howells, making his début on the right wing in place of the great Ken Jones. After forty-three consecutive games during ten seasons the Newport flyer gave way and for the first time in post-war years a new face figured in that wing role. But Wales lost 3-0 and Ken was back in the side at Murrayfield for his forty-fourth and this time final cap. Scotland won 9-6. Something had to be salvaged from the season and it was, though only just, as Terry Davies kicked two penalty goals at Cardiff and Ireland were shaded 6-5. The match was unusual in that the Welsh team all went to the dressing-room after seventeen minutes of the second half, ordered to change into clean jerseys because the referee could not tell the packs apart, so muddied had they become.

Carwyn James made his début as deputy for injured Cliff Morgan when Wales defeated Australia 9-3 at Cardiff in January 1958 and no one guessed that the slightly-built academic was to become one of the game's outstanding thinkers and the motivating genius as coach to the winning British Lions team in New Zealand in 1971. He was a drifting, weaving runner; unassumingly elusive, as was the nature of the man; and a shrewd and methodical tactical kicker. Roddy Evans also made his début against the Wallabies, a fine line-out jumper for Cardiff and Bridgend. Carwyn dropped a goal, but he was to leave far more significant embroidery on the game before his tragic death in an Amsterdam hotel in the 1982–83 season while on holiday.

One of the great Welsh forwards of all time, Llanelli's R. H. Williams, wins line-out ball for Wales against Australia in 1958. Beyond, the south stand completed in time for the Empire Games at Cardiff that year.

Cliff Morgan was the tactical controller, partnered by his Cardiff clubmate, powerful Lloyd Williams, in an 8-3 victory over Scotland at Cardiff Arms Park in 1958; and Cliff played his twenty-ninth and final game for Wales in his country's 16-6 defeat at the end of March. This saw France win at Cardiff for the first time in fifty years. Two dropped goals by full-back Vannier highlighted the success of Michel Celaya's history-making team.

The fifties came to an end with two victories at the ground. England were toppled 5-0 in January 1959 as Dewi Bebb, of Swansea, marked the first of his thirty-four caps on the left wing with a spectacular try, the first against England at Cardiff for ten years. Bebb was borne from the mud-clogged pitch on the shoulders of proud Welsh fans. The luck of the Irish was far removed from Cardiff Arms Park in March when they had three 'tries' disallowed and Wales won 8-6. As ever, hooker Bryn Meredith played with inspiring verve and the rugged Ray Prosser was still a force to be reckoned with. Like Don Hayward and Billy Williams before him, 'Pross' was a second-row forward converted into a prop by the Welsh selectors as they sought to efforts to find another ground for the use of the second team and for training purposes, but the city council rejected approaches to utilise parts of the castle grounds. Suggestions were put forward to purchase suitable fields on the city's outskirts, but all brought no solution. Costs were felt to be unjustified.

However, drainage improvements were carried out after initial experiments proved failures and there was a major problem restoring the ground following increase the physical presence of their scrum. 'Pross' never forgot the thinking behind the need for physical domination and his coaching transformed Pontypool into champions and Schweppes Cup winners in the years ahead. 'Unfortunately, the game is in grave danger of becoming soft,' considered 'Pross', talking in December 1983. 'At least it is compared to the days when I played for Pontypool and Wales. More thuggery went on in one match back in my day than goes on during a whole season now.' However, rugby thrives on a great deal more than physical control. Such as Cliff Morgan showed us that.

No history of the Arms Park would be complete without reference to Hubert Johnson. His energies on the Football Committee of Cardiff Athletic Club crystallised into his election as President in succession to Norman Riches, the renowned Glamorgan batsman, who had captained the county on their admission to first-class status in 1921. 'Uncle' Hubert, suave and benevolent, gave Cardiff an extra dimension of sophistication and his legacy to the club is the magnificent trophy room with its handsome arrangement of display cabinets. There have been many men who have left their mark through committee service for Cardiff when their playing days ended; but probably none more legendary than Hubert Johnson and Stan Bowes: vastly different in every concept, but totally committed to the interests of their club.

Hubert saw his grandiose visions reach maturity with the transformation of the Arms Park and the development of the Sophia Gardens sports complex. His dream came true. It was the ultimate satisfaction for a man who was never too big for the small matters of life. The dignity of Brice Jenkins as Secretary of Cardiff RFC will always be remembered, while many will have their special memories of the formidable figure of Babs Filer, the club's longserving stewardess. Doubtless she demanded, and received, an increase in salary when the new Cardiff clubhouse was opened on 1 June, 1956 and the bar takings zoomed from £14,804 in 1956 to £25,149 in 1957. The new clubhouse was a major feature as affluence replaced the stark start to the fifties, when life was considered bleaker than in wartime, rationing was more severe than in 1945 and there was a grim shortage of housing and fuel. Cardiff's imposing new headquarters represented a symbol of prosperity and confidence in the future.

We recall with shudders the mud-heaps on which so many International matches were contested at Cardiff Arms Park: truly the pitch was the world's worst. Drainage was always a problem and, of course, the ground was heavily over-used: all Cardiff Athletic's home matches were played there, and the WRU grew concerned about the situation. Cardiff RFC made strenuous

# THE HUBERT JOHNSON ROOM

## J. B. G. Thomas

Hubert Johnson did much for the image of Cardiff RFC, not just as a good front man but also as a nostalgic keeper of its museum. It was through his enthusiasm and love for his club that the museum was officially opened on 9 March 1951 at an old players' reunion on the eve of the Wales-Ireland match.

It had started from humble beginnings before the Second World War in the old clubhouse bar, where a small showcase displayed some jerseys collected by the former Athletic Club Secretary L. C. 'Jack' Watters. By 1951 there had been presented to the club the proud possessions of many players as well as jerseys from most of the leading nations playing the game and gifts continued to pour in from former players, officials and enthusiasts all over the world.

It was Hubert Johnson who, with the aid of the administrative staff, guarded the acquisitions with pride and supervised their removal to the new clubhouse built later in the decade, where there had been reserved for them a room worthy of the rugby history contained in the souvenirs. It was designated the Trophy Room in 1969, the new title being officially bestowed by the then President of the Barbarians FC, Brigadier Glyn Hughes, before the tourists' Easter fixture against Cardiff. But nothing could have been more appropriate than for Cardiff RFC to honour the man who developed the museum by re-fitting its home and calling 'The Hubert Johnson Room'. The commemorative plaque, duly inscribed, is one of its most attractive features.

One rare item is a whale tooth from the happy island of Fiji, but many of the exhibits reflect the close rivalry between Wales and New Zealand in the game, especially happy and healthy moments of victory and defeat. There is the jersey worn by the greatest of All Blacks, W. J. 'Carbide' Wallace, in the memorable International match of 1905 when Wales became the only side to defeat the magnificent tourists. Also preserved, an interesting letter written by Dr Teddy Morgan, who scored Wales's winning try, and a description written by Rhys Gabe of the alleged 'try' for New Zealand.

Among other mementoes recalling outstanding players are the boots worn by Bill Cleaver and Barry John – the former's amazingly accurate right boot held together by sticking plaster! Then there are cigarette cases and gold watches awarded to club players after victories over pre-First World War touring teams. One set of watches was prematurely presented in 1885–86 when Frank Hancock's superb side was expected to go through the season unbeaten (a feat not yet recorded by Cardiff) only to lose the final fixture to Moseley by a try to nil! A treasured possession is a springbok head to commemorate Cardiff's victory in the mud over the First Springboks on New Year's Day 1907.

Almost every rugby-playing country is represented, and the musuem has proved a precursor of many in other leading clubs. It is fitting that Cardiff's great contribution to rugby football is symbolised in 'The Hubert Johnson Room'.

the staging of the 1958 Sixth Empire and Commonwealth Games in time for the start of the new season. Exceptionally wet weather in August hampered the job, but Cardiff RFC have always been proud that the Games were staged at their ground.

Wales was the first small country to present the event and it was a rugby man, Newport and Wales wing Ken Jones, who carried the message from the Queen in a silver-gilt baton into the Cardiff Arms Park, to be opened and read by Prince Philip. A 440-yard cinder track was built around the pitch and a temporary bridge thrown across the River Taff to provide access for the athletes arriving from the Games Village at St Athan. A giant results board was erected at the river end. It was all very impressive, but a lot of anxious Cardiff officials were unhappy until their beloved stadium was restored to familiarity.

Nevertheless the Games left the Welsh with colourful recollections of a splendid event and they remember with gratitude the three world records that were broken as well as twenty-two Games records. Who will ever forget Tom Robinson, the one-man team from the Bahamas, runner-up in the 100 yards, carrying his country's banner so proudly around the Arms Park during the opening ceremony? There was Keith Gardener, of Jamaica, the 100 yards winner; Mike Agostini, the Canadian who finished third in that tremendous photo-finish; and Herb Elliott, winning the mile for Australia by at least twenty yards. His fellow-countryman Dave Power triumphed in the six miles after a great effort by Welshman John Merriman, who finished second. Milkha Singh, the graceful Indian, was the 440 yards gold medallist; Power popped up again as Marathon champion; and Murray Halberg triumphed on the ground where his New Zealand countrymen had so often failed in rugby combat by taking the three miles.

Alas, the boom-days were to disappear all too soon. Cardiff's football gate receipts produced only £9170 in 1957–58, which was £2000 down on the previous season and the lowest since the war. However, an encouraging trend was the increase in membership with a record sale of season tickets. Spectators were prepared to pay for seats with more money in their pockets. But that situation, too, was to peak and fall into decline. The 'Sorrowful Sixties', as far as rugby was concerned, were crowding in.

# DECADE
# EXTRAORDINARY
## ——————— *1960 to 1969* ———————
### DAVID HAYWARD

I was no stranger to Cardiff Arms Park. I had witnessed the first official post-war International match there against England (and I haven't missed one since). I had been thrilled by the magnificent play of the Cardiff teams of the late forties and early fifties. I had even trodden the tattered turf for various Welsh schools sides. But this was different. I was attending my first training session since joining Cardiff RFC from Loughborough Colleges.

The journey from Newbridge by Western Welsh double-decker (return fare 2s 3d or about 11 pence) had passed serenely enough. My step through Westgate Street had been jaunty and confident, and why not for heaven's sake: hadn't I played for Fighter Command, the Combined Services, Leicestershire, Loughborough, and even in a Welsh Trial? What terrors could Cardiff hold for me?

Through the Gwyn Nicholls Gates, wide open and welcoming – now, there's a thought, must have been a special player, that one. Fancy building massive wrought-iron gates in his memory. Down the ramp into the shadow of the north stand, a slight hesitancy – which way do I go now? I walk the length of the gloomy tunnel under the stand without seeing a soul. And back again without encountering a likely-looking door, or a human voice, or even a light. Ah, well: let's try the clubhouse.

'Are you a member, sir?'

'Well, no, not yet – I've come to training.'

'With the Youth, sir?'

'No, with the first team – I think.'

'Try the office – down the corridor, sir.'

With a much less bouncy step I shuffle down the corridor, open the door at the far end – and walk straight into the members' bar. Several pairs of eyes turn from above their pints and conversation and regard me quizzically. The clack of a cue striking a snooker ball breaks the silence, the click of white hitting red crunches deeper into the broken stillness and the clunk as red plopped into the pocket appears to reverberate through the room. 'Oh my God,' I think.

'MynameisDaiHaywardandI'mlookingforthedressingroomcouldyoutellme thewayplease?'

Five years of slowing down my rate of speaking to make myself understood by people whose ears and brains were attuned to a slower, more precise mode of communication had disappeared in a moment's exposure to the apparent sophistication of the rugby club bar. A silver-haired gentleman with piercing eyes and an aristocratic nose, wearing an immaculate blazer and perfectly-knotted cravat in Royal Flying Corps colours, advanced upon me. I thought then that it was Wilfred Hyde-White but I know now it was Alex Gibson.

'Come with me, I'll show you the way. What did you say your name was?' 'Hayward. Dai.' He guided me to a door that looked minute against the vast wall of the north stand. 'There we are. Wish you all the best in the Trials – David.' And he never again called me Dai in all the years that we were friends.

Up a narrow staircase, through the skittle alley, along the corridor (again) that ran beneath the stand. Past the medical room where over the years players not only had battered limbs repaired but learned more about fundamental biology from sympathetic females than Ted Spillane, Ted Arcus or Tom Holley could ever teach them. Then to the dressing-room. Its door was wide open, and so was the window. This window was memorable in itself: a huge, flap-like thing that hung outside the back wall of the grandstand and afforded a panoramic view of the cricket pitch – which was as it should be since the Glamorgan and Cardiff teams used this same room in the summer.

Because it had taken me so long to locate the dressing-room I was not surprised to find that its occupants had all left for training – except one rugged-looking character with shoulders like a tallboy and an accent like the cut-glass that stood on it. He immediately came across to me, asked my name and said, 'Come on Dai, train with me – we'll get into this first team together!' I could hardly croak a reply, for this was the legendary Rex Willis, Cardiff's scrum half of many seasons' standing, a Welsh International and a British Lion.

We did play together the following Saturday though not for the first team. We were in Peter Nyhan's 'Rags', or second, XV at Senghenydd and only just won. Also striving for promotion to the firsts that day were Gareth Griffiths, C. D. Williams, Gordon Wells, Malcolm Collins and Stan Bowes

Later that evening, as befitted a junior member of such a prestigious outfit, I sat in a corner quietly chatting to the only other person in the team whom I vaguely knew. He was Henry Jacobs, later a talented Thespian but then a prop with whom I had played in the Welsh Secondary Schools XV. Among the general banter there were some extravagant claims being made, and some even more extravagant wagers being laid on the ability of big Malcolm Collins to lift clear of the ground any three men in the room. I gladly added my shilling to the whip-round to see if it could be done.

Of course the secret of the Lift is in the proper linkage of a properly weighted and balanced trio of men. And of course it was essential to the balance that I, with my unique shape, should be the middle man. I don't remember if Malcolm did lift us clear of the ground to the satisfaction of the judges – but it is amazing how quickly you feel 'one of the boys' after involvement in this interesting species of team experiments. I still wonder, though, how the crisps got into my underpants.

Perhaps it was inevitable that in a club containing so many graduates in the commercial, academic and industrial world the post-match activities – after the singing – would include many such interesting and lightly-competitive pastimes. Another one, introduced to me by Howard Norris and Billy Thomas, was a mathematical game of great intricacy called 'Buzz'. Basically all you did was count from one to any number substituting the word Buzz for any multiple of five. If you failed to do this you took a sip of ale. The complexities of this activity taxed my numerate ability and always gave me a headache next day.

Although my very early days at Cardiff RFC are not properly contained in the decade on which I am charged to report I have included my first impressions of Cardiff Arms Park because it is important to convey the way it struck a newcomer. My initial impression was one of awe at the fame of the Cardiff team, the great ground and the sheer size of the set-up – but I shall never forget the great kindness I was shown on my arrival. With these memories still vivid I always try to make a little more effort with recruits to Cardiff, particularly if they come from clubs in smaller communities. I would hate to think that even one player of whatever ability had taken a look, found it all too much and returned whence he came without discovering the thrill of belonging to a genuine, warm, human and happy club.

The condition of the playing surface at Cardiff Arms Park is a recurring theme in this book. Despite it, the arena has been paid some handsome compliments. New Zealand critic Terry McLean wrote in Cardiff's Centenary book, 'I would rather see the All Blacks play Wales at Cardiff Arms Park than any other game – anywhere!' Many International players from all over the world, when asked to state their favourite grounds, named the Welsh stadium for its atmosphere and the fairness and knowledge of its crowd. But it came way down the list for the quality of its pitch, invariably lamentable in midwinter. By now the reader will be familiar with the factors making for the mud-bath fixtures Cardiff and Wales were obliged to play, but a few reminiscences may not go amiss of days when it was not an uncommon occurrence for Cardiff to change jerseys at half-time, not to impress the opposition by having more than one set but purely on grounds of practicality: nobody – spectators, referees nor players – could identify participants beneath the uniform coating of sludge-brown mud. Thus the only time Brian 'B.J.' Jones of Newport ever got past me was when he was covered in mud and I thought he was team-mate Meirion Roberts doubling back to put in a relieving kick.

Another player to get the better of me in the mud was Harry Howe, a great drinking pal of mine who played prop for Glamorgan Wanderers. During a very dull, wet and muddy game on our ground he thought it would be great fun to rub a handful of mud in my face the instant before he bound himself into the front row. It took me at least three scrums to get his range and my revenge by flicking up a handful of mud from the flank position with my free hand. This led to the daubing of both front rows, my own muttering obscenities about 'stupid seagulls' on the side of the scrum loudly enough for the referee to hear. Observing the arm-action of my last and successful under-arm lob he assumed in the cynical manner that referees have that I was per-petrating some violent skulduggery and penalised me. Harry insisted that I was justly punished for 'very dirty play'.

In 1960 the Cardiff club undertook remedial measures to improve drainage but the winter weather overcame their best efforts. It was the season when the Fifth Springboks visited Britain. Avril Malan's party contained what many people regard as the greatest touring pack to have visited these islands. They were beyond doubt the best scrummagers. I will never forget the shock and feeling of sheer helplessness at being rolled back yards in the first few scrums. To this day, Cardiff prop of that vintage Colin Howe tells me he still wakes up screaming in the middle of the night at the spectre of S. P. Kuhn and P. S. Du Toit bearing down on him in the set scrums. On the day they played Cardiff, 29 October, the Springboks took no prisoners and defeated a previously unbeaten home team by 13-0. However, their grim manner won them few friends – not even in Heaven, it appeared, for by the time they returned to play Wales on 3 December the divinities who control these matters had conspired to create conditions unlike any in which rugby football is played on the High Veldt or anywhere else in South Africa. An icy wind blew stinging rain horizontally down the pitch, which had already been turned into a quagmire; but nonetheless the game went ahead and, would you believe, the teams were obliged to stand in the storm for the duration of three national anthems.

The Welsh skipper and full-back Terry Davies decided to play against the wind in the first half and when the teams changed ends at half-time with South Africa leading by just an Oxlee penalty to nil Welsh hopes were high. Now the visiting pack turned in a supreme performance to control the game and deny Wales a first win against their country. At the end the score still stood at 3-0 to the Springboks.

The conditions had been such that with a quarter of an hour to go referee Jack Taylor of Scotland asked the captains if they wished to continue playing. Their men were happy to call it a day at no-side, but the elements continued to vent their fury unabated and next day the River Taff broke its banks near the club's bowling green and within hours the whole of the famous complex was under four feet of water. Cardiff Arms Park looked as if it belonged in the Lake District.

Water swirled through the Cardiff Athletic Club offices and necessitated dramatic action by ground staff, office personnel and bar employees to save machinery and records. The club Secretary of the day, David Grant, and assistant Anne Davies were the butt of much banter about their aquatic adventures. Nobody, however, was bold enough to mention water in the beer to the great Babs Filer, stewardess of the day.

The Springboks returned for a third time to Cardiff Arms Park on 4 February 1961 to culminate their tour with a game against the Barbarians. This great South African side had swept all before them as they journeyed triumphantly through the British Isles only to fall at the last fence. In a splendid match before a huge, excited crowd they were worsted by two tries scored by young men who lived no more than a couple of miles and a small mountain apart, Haydn Morgan of Abertillery and Derek Morgan of Newbridge. Their later careers were a total contrast. Haydn continued as an archetypal destroyer on the open side of the scrum, a wing forward who represented Wales and the British Lions and won twenty-seven caps before emigrating to South Africa. Derek, who was qualifying as a dentist at Durham University, went on to play for England, gave sterling service as a player and administrator with Newbridge RFC and, while living and practising in Cwmbran, became chairman of the England selection panel.

But the game is remembered by many for a full-blooded tackle on South Africa's captain Avril Malan by Haydn Mainwaring, the Barbarians' full-back. The Springbok lock had broken away from a line-out and was thundering down the touch-line hell-bent for the corner flag when he was not only stopped but laid out by a crunching body-check to the ribs. Quite devastating, but perfectly fair. And unforgettable.

The Championship matches of that winter were full of interest, Wales winning the two Cardiff matches against England and Ireland, though losing in Edinburgh and Paris, and capping some men who were destined for long, glorious careers. Abertillery's back-row forward Alun Pask made the first of twenty-six appearances. Brian Price of Newport set off on a trail that was to last eight years and thirty-two caps. I recall too Cardiff Athletic Club's loss of a legal battle at this time. Western Ground Rents, who dealt with lessees of the old Bute lands, had claimed the strip of land on which the Crest Hotel now stands. It had been in casual use by the club over the years and was a visual amenity appreciated by members and public alike. However, the counter-action was lost and so was a shady little nook of Cardiff Arms Park.

Let us pause to take in some of Cardiff RFC's characters at the outset of this decade. Lloyd Williams captained us for two seasons from scrum half and was joined in the Cardiff colours from time to time by three younger brothers Cenydd, Elwyn and Tony. When I emphasise that their family predecessors in previous seasons had included Gwyn, Brinley and Bleddyn, and that Vaughan also played for the club, you will appreciate that this particular Williams clan was very special indeed at Cardiff Arms Park. Lloyd, a powerful scrum half, also led Wales against France.

Besides these brothers there were John – J.D. – Evans, a great rock of a prop forward from Mountain Ash whose heart was bigger than his shoulders, and his bosom pal Gordon Wells. Dannie Harris, a fine lock forward, left for the professional game and when last encountered by me was bidding fair to being the Squire of Llangefni in Anglesey – and declaring that his most cherished rugby trophy was his Cardiff first-team cap. To replace men who left or retired the club could always boast a crop of new recruits, who had often founded a reputation elsewhere. Keith Rowlands came east from Llanelli and not only gave Cardiff a much-needed boost in the second row but also, within the space of a full season, won his first cap against France and selection for the British Isles party which went to South Africa. On that tour a companion was Cardiff vice-captain Kingsley Jones who joined the club as a number-eight forward but, realising his limitations of height and athleticism, asked to be chosen as a prop with the 'Rags' – from which base, after tuition by 'Admiral' Stan Bowes and J. D. Evans, he blossomed out to gain ten caps and become a first-choice Lions prop. Howard Norris, a near-neighbour of Kingsley's in the Rhondda, followed in their footsteps with two caps and a Lions tour to New Zealand.

After a scoreless draw with England at Twickenham Wales fell to Scotland at Cardiff for the first time in a quarter of a century, Ron Glasgow scoring the first try there by a Scot for twenty-seven years. A penalty goal by Kelvin Coslett won the match against France. The game with Ireland was delayed until 17 November 1962 because of a smallpox scare in South Wales. It is often referred to as the 'hangover match' and was played as if everyone involved was suffering from one. This occasion was the last on which Wales's greatest hooker Bryn Meredith was selected, finishing with twenty-four appearances to his credit.

The 1962–63 season held many significances. It was significant for one of the worst British winters of all time. It was highly significant that England won their last match on Welsh soil for decades. It was significant that the Welsh Rugby Union, frustrated by lack of progress at Cardiff, announced their intention of acquiring land at Bridgend on which to build a national stadium. Much less significantly D. J. Hayward was appointed captain of Cardiff RFC (with Howard Norris as vice-captain). He also won the first of his Welsh caps.

The arctic weather began in late December and continued until March, seriously affecting club matches and training. It also threatened Wales's first Five Nations Championship match of the winter against England on 19 January. The pitch, however, had been protected by straw and a decision was taken that the terraces could be cleared of snow and the match should go ahead.

The team for the game was due to be announced after a Trial game at Rodney Parade, Newport, a week before the International. The selectors' deliberations were to be longer than usual because of a gas leak from a heater in the room. It rendered some of them unconscious and was thought to have affected their judgment because when the team was named it contained six

## TELEVISING CARDIFF ARMS PARK

### Dewi Griffiths
*BBC Wales Television Producer, Outside Broadcasts.*

My first visit to Cardiff Arms Park was in February 1948. I had grown up in the soccer community of Ton Pentre, had been playing rugby at secondary school for only about three months and was about to see my first International match. Three of us ended up at the top of the east terrace squinting into the sun as we watched the pride of our school, Billy Cleaver, play for Wales against Scotland. Little wonder that from that day the game was to find a huge place in my life, for by the time the referee blew for full time I had seen Haydn Tanner and Glyn Davies weave their magic at half-back and a try each from Bleddyn Williams, Jack Matthews and Ken Jones – all at our end of the ground. But I could never have imagined that for twenty-five years I would spend so much of my life at this famous place.

Within a year of joining the BBC in 1954 I was on my first professional engagement at the ground – as a probationary technical assistant with the Welsh Home Service, calling Alun Williams 'sir' and thrilled to bits that I actually plugged in G. V. Wynne-Jones's microphone cable. 'Geevers' was describing the action in a Wales-Ireland match which included tries by Courtney Meredith, Gareth Griffiths, Cliff Morgan and Haydn Morris, but I wouldn't have known it. Even wearing headphones it was impossible to hear anything with thousands of feet stamping above me. Since that day my role as a television director has meant that I still haven't seen an International at Cardiff with my own eyes.

I will always regard Wales v England 1963 as my first 'cap'; that is, my first live coverage of rugby football for BBC1's *Grandstand*. It was a day when the opening shot was of a thermometer strapped to a Taff-end goal post reading 25°F, or seven degrees of frost. Welsh Rugby Union Secretary Bill Clement did his famous imitation of Sir Vivian Fuchs crossing the Antarctic as in clouds of frozen breath and red-eyed from being up all night he slithered across the pitch bemoaning the possibility of giving 50,000 people their money back.

But our TV commentator Wilfred Wooller brought a certain colour back to Mr Clement's cheeks when, almost breaking a leg at the impact, he slammed his heel into the rock-hard surface and declared, 'It seems perfectly all right to me!' That was the last time England were to win at Cardiff for over twenty years. I've recorded it in my diary as a special day for me, too.

Then there was the problem with the greyhounds. All BBC TV crews suffered a great deal during those early years from the after-effects of these canines, who arrived in kennel vans for the racing as the rugby crowds dispersed. Those dogs had been specially trained to wait until reaching the ground before doing what comes naturally – often all over cables, cameras and crew. Our families always knew when we had been working at Cardiff Arms Park.

Soon came a sort of avalanche of development at the ground coinciding with the blossoming of quality Welsh rugby football in what became known as the 'second Golden Era'. The stadium was being redesigned and the whole world, it seemd, wanted televised rugby from Cardiff. Without hesitation the WRU accepted television as a necessary part of its new international image. For many years the Union had enjoyed a comfortable relationship with the press and radio, whose personnel had appeared in small numbers match by match. So it was a traumatic development when for the Wales-New Zealand game of 1967 I submitted a request to Bill Clement for no fewer than sixty-eight BBC TV work passes.

We were and still are a travelling circus of huge vehicles, whose cameras and commentators are just the tip of the iceberg. For the All Blacks game it was decided that David Coleman would link *Grandstand* from Cardiff; thirteen Eurovision countries would take the match; Australia and Hong Kong would take a direct satellite feed. This meant twelve broadcasters with an equal number of production support staff; all serviced by seven cameramen, eight video specialists, seven audio-technical assistants – and the posse of men who laced it all together with miles of cable, our rigger-drivers.

After that the Golden Era had arrived and there could be no let-up in broadcasting demands at Cardiff Arms Park. Welsh rugby was in demand by television networks all over the world, even in North America among whose growing clubs there flourished a pirate trade in 16mm film. I have yet to meet a rugby fan in any continent who has not seen Gareth Edwards's solo try against Scotland or the effervescent play of the 1973 Barbarians against the All Blacks of that year. Televised rugby from Wales had become hot property at a time when the quality of the game elsewhere had reached a low point. But even when the bubble burst with the devastating victory by Graham Mourie's New Zealanders over the Welsh Centenary XV, the pressure for media access to the stadium remained undiminished.

When the time came for the construction of its new south stand the WRU readily agreed that it should incorporate comprehensive facilities for broadcasting, and from original ideas and suggestions sketched by me and my engineering colleagues on lunch napkins and the backs of envelopes the architects incorporated into their final blueprint studios, control rooms and commentary positions which are considered to be the best in any European stadium.

Over the years at Cardiff Arms Park we have had programmes cancelled because of blizzards; *Grandstand* studio huts blown away in Force 10 gales; policemen pulling up floorboards between our legs during transmission because of hoax bomb alerts; diarrhoeic greyhounds; smallpox outbreaks – all sorts of disasters! But we have also focused cameras on some of the greatest players the game has ever seen. My abiding memories also include Fijians linking arms with Welsh for *Now is the Hour*; the close-up of Charlie Faulkner's total joy when he scored a try at the Taff end; the crowd's spontaneous rendering of *Hymns and Arias* when Max Boyce walked on to the pitch for his Golden Disc; the Queen's sheer delight at the spectacle of the Centenary celebration match.

And at the end of the day when the crowds have gone and Cardiff Arms Park has fallen quiet, that little glass of something special in the inner sanctum of Bill Hardiman's cwch.

new caps – the half-backs, David Watkins and Clive Rowlands, plus Denzil Williams, Brian Thomas, Roger Michaelson and myself!

If the citadels of amateur rugby football today are under siege by the massed battalions of the media, commerce and greedy International players, in 1963 they were safe, secure, impregnable, indeed unchallenged. After meeting on the Thursday before the match for a get-together (it was barely more than that), a trot around the pitch, a few scrums and lines-out, a chance for the captain to say Hello to everybody and nominate a place-kicker, we all returned whence we came to await Saturday morning, the great day. The fact that half the team lived in South Wales's snow-bound Valleys, and were liable to be buried deeper beneath drifts than a hibernating bear should there be a further fall on Friday night, did not seem to concern the powers-that-were – certainly not enough to seek information about the cost of putting their team up in a Cardiff hotel before the match.

As luck would have it, there was no more snow beforehand. Since I ran a car, albeit a battered and tatty Hillman Husky, I was detailed to pick up Dai Watkins from his home at Blaina. The journey of about ten miles and another five hundred feet up our freezing valley ranks in my mind alongside the trek of Captain Scott. Enough to say that when I arrived in Blaina, half an hour late, shattered by my experience and qualified by it to organise survival courses in Siberia, Dai had already left for Cardiff, worried that I might not reach him!

By comparison the game itself was an anti-climax. As soon as the straw was cleared the ground began to freeze and it appeared that England had picked better skaters than we had. Under Richard Sharp they won 13-6. Despite scoring the first Welsh try for five games (and offering to return to the WRU the thermal underwear which they issued to us before the game) I was dropped. I rarely mention the fact in Wales that I took part in this particular game; but in England if I ever want to bring a smile to the face of my friends, or earn a pint, or merely attract their attention, I tend to introduce the fact discreetly into the conversation.

To compound my misery, after our defeat it snowed again and I must have been the last driver that night to run the gauntlet of icy roads, massive snow-

---

**VIEW FROM THE EAST**

**Richard Sharp**
*Oxford U, Wasps, Redruth and England (14 caps at outside half, 1960 to 1967).*

My most vivid memory of Cardiff Arms Park dates back to 19 January 1963 when I led England to victory against Wales. It was not so much the score – 13-6 – as the circumstances surrounding the match which were particularly memorable.

In January that year the whole of Britain lay in the grip of the Big Freeze. Rugby matches everywhere were being called off because of iron-hard grounds, and even the final England Trial had had to be switched from Twickenham to Torquay. On the Friday before we were to meet Wales the England XV was unable to train at Porthcawl because the club pitch was frozen. Instead we went to the beach and practised a few moves as best we could on the sand. There cannot be many International teams who have trained for a big game on the beach!

The following day it was still freezing cold and only the hard work and tireless efforts of the ground-staff at Cardiff Arms Park enabled the match to be played. As it was the RFU had provided the England team with special underpants for protection against the icy conditions. After the game the dinner provided by the Welsh Rugby Union was curtailed so that the Welsh players and guests could get home safely before conditions deteriorated even further.

Some press reports make interesting reading. Wrote Tony Goodridge in *The Daily Telegraph*: 'In conditions in which even a penguin might have been excused for feeling the cold England scored an admirable win over Wales . . . by two goals and a dropped goal to a penalty goal and a try . . . The ground staff had worked heroically to make play possible but there were a number of treacherous ice patches to make matters difficult. A bitingly cold wind brought added problems of frozen hands.'

Pat Marshall in the *Daily Express* described it as 'big Rugby's first extravaganza on ice, the coldest, craziest International ever staged.'

One final thought. Reading through my scrapbook I see that my wife's stand ticket cost precisely £1 and the match programme one shilling, or five pence! Those were the days!

---

drifts and a howling blizzard that came straight from the North Pole and scoured the Ebbw Valley with the noise and force of a million-strong male voice choir. I did get back to Newbridge where, after failing to negotiate Pant Hill, I abandoned my vehicle. I did not see it again for five days.

In equally grim conditions Ireland gained their first win at Cardiff for thirty-one years. Wales ended Championship fixtures with defeat in Paris, so that the win at Murrayfield, in a game kicked to death by Clive Rowlands, was the only success of the campaign. Nor were Cardiff RFC enjoying an outstanding period, with twelve defeats out of forty-three matches played in this very fragmented season. Full-back Alun Priday had cause for satisfaction, however, scoring 176 points and beating Wilfred Wooller's club record of 163 set in 1938–39.

It is worth noting that Priday's total included nine tries. I frequently hear people assert that the running full-back became fashionable in the early seventies, especially at the London Welsh club through J. P. R. Williams. Without detracting from the magnificent team-of-all-the-talents then operating at Old Deer Park, I can assure you that Cardiff were counter-attacking and creating overlaps from full-back much earlier. Alun's tries prove the point.

Without doubt, though, the single most important domestic development that year was the creation and unfolding of Hubert Johnson's master-plan for the retention of International rugby football, side by side with Cardiff RFC matches, in the capital. Every Welshman whose heart swells with pride as he witnesses the concrete realisation of Hubert's dream – documented elsewhere in this volume – should spare a thought for the man himself. It was his driving force which saw the plan accepted by the WRU and the city of Cardiff. A great salesman – a great man.

The 1963–64 season opened with the tingling anticipation of a tour by the Fifth All Blacks under Wilson Whineray. All else became of secondary importance, at club and national level.

Well, practically everything – for the first and paramount duty of a Cardiff RFC captain was to ensure that his team did not become the first to lose four times in one season to Newport. Since I was skipper again that was my priority, and the threat of so ignominious a fate was banished on 5 October when we beat Newport 14-6 (in fact we won the first three games and were only robbed of a grand slam by a magnificent effort from a very depleted Black and Amber XV who forced a draw at Cardiff Arms Park in the final fixture the following April).

The two old rivals later bowed to changing times and pressure from other Welsh clubs and ceased playing an annual four-match series against each other. I, for one, was not at all sorry to see the end of that tradition. The pressures that built up at Cardiff Arms Park each season, particularly if Newport won the first game, were quite incredible. If they also won the second the situation became calamitous and this turned to a tragedy of disastrous dimensions if they won the third. Fortunately we always – somehow – avoided the catastrophic occurrence of a season's whitewash.

Despite the great rivalry engendered down the years and the tension of a four-match series there was great mutual respect between the clubs and their players. Although I was usually accused of skulduggery, including biting Malcolm Thomas's finger, which I did, and laying out Brian Jones in a late tackle, which I didn't, I have to state that the games were rarely if ever played in any but the fairest manner.

Newport always brought great half-backs to Cardiff Arms Park including the best of the lot, David Watkins. He was an amazing player with feet that did not stick in mud and hands that grew enormous to accept a pass. He was also an excellent kicker, extremely fit and durable, and possessed of as much guts as you would expect from a Western Valley boyo. A mighty formidable opponent.

Having played against him more than most, I would say that if he had one fault it was being unable to resist the temptation to make his opposing wing forward, or flanker, look an ass – which of course he often did. However, this would sometimes cause him to send on second-hand ball to his centres and occasionally to run across the field behind them trying to find a gap. On one such occasion I chased him from a scrum beneath the south stand at Cardiff Arms Park all the way across the pitch while he checked, accelerated, feinted and jinked, before slipping and falling with the ball near the north stand touch-line.

This saga was far from finished. Since Dai had moved behind his centres and thus out of reach of support I was presented with a golden opportunity and a clear field. However, as I dashed in to seize the ball – which he ought to have released – he snatched it back from my hands. I moved in to grab the ball once again, more emphatically, and he still clung to it.

The referee was a very popular arbiter at the time, Gwynne Walters, who had had charge of a record number of Varsity matches, and my immediate thought was that he should have stuck with the students – for when the whistle went it was to penalise not Dai Watkins but me, allegedly for evil intent. The crowd, of course, were not pleased – and every open-side wing forward who had ever been tormented by a Welsh stand-off half must have wept for me.

Welsh rugby football is such a fertile bed of talent that it grows masses of radiant blossoms and can afford to lose the odd flower without the display being spoiled. But I felt that Dai Watkins was somehow different. Barry John and Phil Bennett more than plugged the gap he left as a player when he turned professional; but I wonder what Newport RFC would look like now had he used his other talents in the cause of his old club instead of playing big-business with those strange people and importing their even stranger game to Ninian Park.

Of the myriad memories that remain about Cardiff–Newport matches I must share one other with you. It concerns Billy Thomas from Brithdir, the son of a champion boxer, who became a superb hooker for Cardiff and was a tremendous character and a clubman to the core. It was always hard work for a Cardiff hooker to hold his own against the likes of Des Greenslade and Bryn Meredith; but when the Newport scrum half chipped in by putting the ball into the second row it was time for Billy to speak out, which he did very loudly with words something like, 'For Chrissake, ref, are you blind?' Realising that his impartiality and authority were being questioned, the official broke up the scrummage, looked at Billy sternly and demanded, 'Did you say something?'

Without blinking or hesitating our man replied, 'Aye. You must be bloody deaf as well.'

The eve of Cardiff's match against the Fifth All Blacks will always be a sadly remembered day, when President John F. Kennedy of the USA was assassinated in Dallas. On the morrow the club were not to emulate their predecessors of 1953, and although my team had its chances we went down eventually by a Don Clarke penalty and a Mac Herewini dropped goal (6 points) to a Cliff Howe try converted by Alun Priday (5). Cardiff played to a tight tactical plan which allowed little flighty passing among the backs on which the New Zealanders could swoop and feed. Since the latter were of a like mind the result was determined by goal-kicking, and in that department Cardiff had an off-day.

The next months belonged also to the tourists. On 21 December 1963 New Zealand gained her first official victory at Cardiff Arms Park, having lost the Tests of 1905, 1935 and 1953. Dick Uzzell, who had immortalised himself by dropping a goal to beat Wilson Whineray's men at Newport, was a newcomer to a Welsh XV which was never able to break out of the New Zealand stranglehold. There were no heroics and no contentious issues, simply defeat for Wales by 6-0.

Apart from that solitary reverse at Newport the tourists were undefeated when they returned to Cardiff Arms Park in February 1964 to play the Barbarians in their last game. They treated a capacity crowd to a glorious exhibition of rugby and romped home by 36-3. Skipper Whineray scored the final and most popular try after selling a most outrageous dummy.

We must digress here to note that the event of the sixties which probably had the most far-reaching effect on the future of Welsh rugby took place in 1964, not however at Cardiff Arms Park but in the heat and humidity of Durban where Wales suffered a Test defeat by 24-3 at South Africa's hands in the final match of her first-ever overseas tour. Here it was that the Welsh players and management realised that our traditional haphazard approach to International rugby, based on natural skill and talent hopefully harnessed for a couple of hours under an inspiring captain, was no longer good enough to take on the well-drilled sides of the southern hemisphere. In the space of six months Wales had lost to New Zealand for the first time at Cardiff and been crushed by the Springboks.

It was a cry from that Welsh touring team for the kind of organisation and team-work at national level which had enabled our clubs to perform well against touring sides that was heard back in the corridors of power at Cardiff. There were many long and serious discussions deep into the night, and to the eternal credit of the tour management, Dai Phillips and Alun Thomas, they

*Three great New Zealand forwards at Cardiff: Colin Meads (left) and Kel Tremain chair
Wilson Whineray from the field after the All Blacks' 1964 victory over the Barbarians.
Whineray got his team's final try after selling an outrageous dummy.*

listened and marked; and in their subsequent report to the parent body must
have added their weight and wisdom to the urgings of their players. The
Welsh Rugby Union in turn reacted with vitality, speedily setting up a working party to investigate the state of the game in Wales. This 'think tank',
the WRU coaching sub-committee and its brainchild advisory committee,
eventually isolated the problems and made recommendations for their
solution. The groundwork was prepared for the appointment in 1967 of a
full-time coaching organiser and a scheme which led eventually to the
flowering of the Welsh team of the seventies into one of acknowledged world
class which played winning rugby of quality.

Back at home, despite the installation of floodlighting at Cardiff Arms
Park, it was the Fijian touring team who really lit up the Welsh scene and

145

added another colourful chapter to the story of the great stadium. In a scintillating game under September sunshine Wales and Fiji contrived to score thirteen tries between them, the south sea islanders thrilling a big crowd with thirteen points in the last twelve minutes of play to set a final score-line of 28-22 to the home team. The invitation to Fiji was a risky financial venture in that the visitors were a completely unknown quantity. But in the end it proved successful, underlining the forward-thinking and vision of the men running the Welsh game. It also broke through the protective wall of comfortable insularity that the International Board threw around its members. The game was growing, the world was getting smaller, and the Welsh wanted to be in with the leaders of innovation and adventure.

Against England at Cardiff Arms Park Wales won her opening Championship game for the first time in six years. The final tally was 14-3 and the 14-12 victory which followed at Murrayfield meant that the stage was set for a confrontation with Ireland, also twice victors, which would determine the wearers of the Triple Crown, last won by Wales in 1952 and by Ireland in 1949. It sparked off much good rugby. A typical Dai Watkins outside break brought a try converted by big full-back Terry Price which enabled Wales

*Wales wing Dewi Bebb wears a pained expression as he is collared by a Fijian. The south sea islanders thrilled a big Cardiff crowd in 1964.*

to lead at the break despite the absence from the field with injury of John Dawes, Alun Pask moving into the back division to cover temporarily. In the second half Dewi Bebb scored from a tap-down at the front of the line-out, Tom Kiernan kicked a penalty for Ireland and Price dropped an incredible 45-yard goal. But the visitors were not done for and a midfield scissors move resulted in Flynn scoring a try which Kiernan converted. Then Clive Rowlands, displaying all the craftiness of a West Wales scrum half, stole away from a scrum without the ball to be tackled by Noel Murphy, against whom a decisive penalty was awarded. In the nightmare visit to Paris which followed, the Triple Crown winners could not go on to a Grand Slam, falling at Colombes by 22–13 and having to settle for a flawed Championship title.

From then until the final season of the decade it is mainly milestones and great moments that must be recorded rather than masterpieces of history or grand Championship feats. New arrivals at Cardiff RFC included D. Ken Jones, a wonderfully gifted centre once described by Barry John as the last of the great amateurs, and Gerald Davies, destined to become one of the finest of all wing three-quarters and a player whose running thrilled and amazed me as no one else before or since. The playing record was an improvement over previous years; and in accordance with the current thinking of the Welsh Rugby Union the club appointed a coach, Roy Bish.

The International season was successful for Wales, even if individual games lacked outstanding quality. The only defeat was at the hands of an Irish side which was probably fired by having been hooted off the pitch by its own supporters after an abysmal display in the previous fixture. But England and Scotland were overcome, and finally France in a match which produced perhaps the try of the decade at Cardiff Arms Park. After trailing 8-0 Wales climbed back into the game with two Keith Bradshaw penalties and won it through a marvellous solo effort by Stuart Watkins. The Newport right wing intercepted a pass from Gachassin within the Welsh 25 and thundered away towards the Taff-end goal-line into the strong wind that swirled round the end of the north stand. France's full-back challenged him, only to be handed off fiercely, and Watkins was still going strongly when he touched down at the corner flag after a seventy-five-yard dash which effectively gave his country the Five Nations title for the second year running.

In 1966–67 Cardiff RFC were destined to record their fourth straight win over Australia. Billy Hullin played brilliantly at scrum half, John Hickey ruthlessly hunted down the Wallaby halves and the line-outs were controlled by Lyn Baxter and Keith Rowlands. The last-named was the elected captain for the year, but before Christmas was lost to the game as a player. After a game against London Welsh Keith was in pain from a leg injury and limped as he left the pitch to begin the long journey to the changing-rooms high in the north stand. It was as he was negotiating the steps leading up from ground level that his cracked leg – for this was the unknown injury – snapped with the sound of a dry branch being broken, thus giving those close at hand an unforgettable and unwanted memory of those premises. Keith never played again, but of course went on to serve the club as an administrator and the Welsh Rugby Union and British Isles as a selector.

Although the Wallabies beat Wales to start a sequence of defeats at the hands of Scotland, Ireland and France (the latter game marking the début of two 'greats' in Gareth Edwards and Dai Morris), everything changed on 15 April 1967 when not only did the sun pour down on Cardiff Arms Park but also a brilliant new star was born. England were the visitors and they ran up against Keith Jarrett, an eighteen-year-old centre from Newport chosen out of position at full-back. This was his match: not content with kicking five conversions and two penalties, he also sprinted sixty yards down the north stand touch-line for an unforgettable try and a total of 19 points in a 34-21 triumph.

As far as Cardiff RFC were concerned the milestone of the 1967–68 season was the arrival of Gareth Edwards to team up with Barry John in a partnership that has rarely if ever been equalled. But it is nice to find room for mention of the most successful 'Rags' season in the club's history under the captaincy of John Price. They lost only one game out of thirty-three played and ran up 760 points against 149. A true Cardiffian and Blue and Black, Price maintained his links with the club in later years by becoming Athletic Club steward.

That winter the All Blacks were back for a short tour and 11 November 1967 saw them beat Wales 13-6 on what had become the customary mud-heap. They were handed the result through a defensive blunder, and as it turned out the only blemish on an otherwise untarnished record was made by an East Wales XV who held the tourists to a draw in their final game and whom I had been given the honour and the task of coaching. A lot of thought and discussion with people of original ideas such as Dai Harries of Newbridge went into preparations for the game.

There appeared to me no point in taking on an All Black pack with what was virtually a scratch selection, so I decided the game should be played away from their strength using brisk, long drop-outs to the open field whenever possible. At the scrummages we would use quick put-ins and rapid heeling to minimise long-drawn-out, strength-sapping confrontations, and once possession was secured spread it to the wings mainly by kicking. Line-out ball was to be run, with the full-back coming in at all times, and likewise any free possession they offered us by miss-kicks. In this way it was intended to move their pack wide and prevent the build-up of their awesome and un-stoppable driving rucks. It would also give East Wales the opportunity to put the ball behind the defence where, through their total commitment to first-time tackling, All Black sides tend to be vulnerable.

It worked! Whether by design or because Cardiff Arms Park was given a preview of a hitherto untried combination – Gareth Edwards, Barry John, John Dawes, Gerald Davies and Keri Jones – which was to achieve huge

## LEAVING ONE'S MARK

### Air-Vice-Marshal G. C. 'Larry' Lamb

I am almost ashamed to admit that the first time I ever set foot inside Cardiff Arms Park was when I went there to referee my first home International match, Wales v Scotland, on 8 February 1968. A letter beginning 'Dear Sir' and signed very formally 'W. H. Clement' had asked me some ten days earlier to confirm whether or not I could 'accept this appointment'. Can a duck swim? I gave the matter great thought – about five seconds' worth to be precise; and back went, 'Dear Mr Clement, I am available . . .' Needless to say my thoughts were never far away from Cardiff Arms Park for most of the intervening waking days. What would it feel like? What was the Welsh for 'foot up' or 'barging in the line-out'?

So on Friday 7 February off I went across the Severn Bridge and Offa's Dyke down the M4 to the Angel Hotel. An early night – obviously – but not to sleep, or at least only very little. To go down to the dining-room next morning and be acknowledged by Richard Burton and Spike Milligan breakfasting together, both of whom expressed the hope that I would have a good game, was a sign that one had passed from the humdrum existence of a normal referee to, if not exactly fame, then at least personality status and I liked it! However, the waiter who told me, 'Kippers are extra' was clearly less impressed.

The morning passed slowly: a gentle jog around the grounds of Cardiff Castle, a light – very light – lunch; and then it was time for the walk to the ground, every step taken as if on air. As part of the match build-up my features had appeared on Welsh television the week before as I piloted an RAF Comet and this did little to preserve one's anonymity. Thus casual glances from the milling throng occasionally focused into stares of recognition. 'It's the ref.' 'Look, Dai, there's Larry Lamb.' I kept wishing that I could think of an excuse to go back to the Angel and start the trek all over again; but I couldn't, and pressed on.

A pass marked 'Referee' got one past the eagle-eyed stewards, but almost as one entered Number Five gate the sad realisation dawned that at least one dream had now ended. Never again would that 200-yard journey have the same delectable, exhilarating feeling – for the first anything is always special. Even if I were ever to travel this short road again, never would I experience the sublime ecstasy shared with the first solo flight, first love and the many other 'firsts' with which one's life has been so bounteously dotted. There was, of course, the match still to come and to be savoured; so this daydream died and gave way to consideration of the serious business which lay ahead.

And not before time, for clearly I had not been paying attention to where I was going. Suddenly I found myself putting my bag down in a dirty old broom-cupboard through whose broken window half a gale seemed to be blowing. It was silly of me and my escort could easily redirect me, I felt sure, to the referee's dressing-room which presumably would be like the one used by all officials at Twickenham – beautifully polished floor with one's own bath, shower, toilet, mirrors, table, and even coat hangers.

His response was an uncompromising, 'This is it.'

Dark thoughts about Welshmen playing their usual tricks on the unsuspecting English sped through my mind.

'You're joking, Dai,' I said. 'Does Mr Clement know you're putting me in here?' After further questions and blunt answers there seemed no option but to accept circumstances and make the best of them. If it had been good enough for Messrs Gadney, Vile, Lambert, David, Taylor, Kelleher and their like, who was I to complain on this my very first visit? Before changing, however, I did hint – let it be said in a very quiet voice to the Cardiff rooftops – that if this was the best the locals could do, I might not come again even if they went down on their bended knees to invite me.

I need not have worried, for no one had reckoned on the status I was eventually to achieve as resident guest speaker at the annual rugby dinner of the Swansea Valley Rotary Club, and on the offence that would be taken at this cavalier treatment by the good folk of Ystradgynlais. These latter must have heard my whispered threat through the broken window for the thought that Larry Lamb might never be seen again in Cardiff was enough to stir them into action.

Once the Rotary Secretary, the Reverend Geraint Evans, aided by stalwarts like Claude Davey from this hotbed of Welsh rugby, heard what had been suffered by this favourite referee they began pressing the Welsh Rugby Union for a new dressing-room to be provided in future for the man who had once 'commandeered' (their word) the Royal Yacht to ferry out to the Bahamas some text-books collected by the Rotary Club for needy schools there.

Dear reader, believe it or not, the response to the appeal for this new referees' dressing-room was so enormous that my allies in Ystradgynlais eventually had to get hold of a chap called Ken Harris and suggest to him that with the money left over the Welsh Rugby Union should surround it with a new stand so that it did not look out of place.

And, as the world now knows, they did just that. I withdrew my threat never to come again and, as a result, was invited to referee the first International match, Wales v Fiji, at which this new north stand was utilised. They had even taken my complaint about the broken window to heart, for the new room doesn't have any windows at all.

It would appear, therefore, that I have left my mark for all time at Cardiff Arms Park and for that generations of referees yet unborn should be very thankful.

PS Wales won 5-0, the singing was marvellous, the rugby less so – but Gareth Edwards actually called me 'sir' just as 586 Leading Aircraftsman Clive Rowlands always does – or did!

success at higher levels, we do not know. What is certain is that the East Wales pack held its own and the All Blacks were given the run-around. The draw that resulted, with a try by Steel cancelling out one by Frank Wilson to save the tourists' unbeaten record, did scant justice to an East Wales team which had shown that native Welsh flair, given a chance within a balanced approach, can overcome the physical presence and organisation of New Zealand. I was proud of the team I had prepared.

*In March 1969 – the year of his Investiture – the Prince of Wales visited Cardiff Arms Park, witnessing a 24-11 victory by the home team over Ireland in a tempestuous game. Here he is introduced by WRU President Ivor Jones to Welsh team captain Brian Price. Reconstruction of the north stand had begun, limiting spectator capacity to 29,000.*

Give or take a Lions tour, well stocked with Welshmen, a 'B' level visit to Argentina by Wales and a first-ever Grand Slam by France (completed at Cardiff) the rest of my story is about the brilliant new generation who lit up Welsh Rugby, and Cardiff Arms Park in particular, as the sixties drew to a close. Gareth Edwards became the youngest man, at twenty years of age, to lead his country as Scotland were beaten 5-0 in February 1968. J. P. R. Williams and Mervyn Davies made International débuts the following January, both essentially products of London Welsh and the exciting, inventive and effective style perfected under the charismatic leadership of John Dawes (soon to assert his authority on Wales and British Isles XVs). Maurice Richards scored four tries in March as Wales beat England 30-9 to clinch a Triple Crown and Championship title – the reconstruction of the great stadium limited spectator capacity to 29,000 but even the new, enlarged ground is scarcely big enough to contain all those who wish to claim 'I was there' when the Cardiff wing equalled a record held jointly by Reggie Gibbs and Willie Llewellyn since the start of the century.

Many of the rising stars were in the Welsh party which lost a two-match Test series heavily in New Zealand that summer. Tour victories were recorded over Australia and Fiji, and there were respectable outcomes to provincial matches against Taranaki, Otago and Wellington; but nothing could alter the fact that the All Blacks had won by 19-0 at Canterbury and 33-12 in Auckland. However, there is no doubt that in the white heat of Test rugby was forged and tempered the Welsh team that swept all before it in the seventies.

What an extraordinary decade was the sixties! It opened with Wales being plunged to defeat in the mud of a ground then owned by the Cardiff Arms Park Company and used by all the teams of Cardiff RFC, which not only had a sub-standard pitch but was showing ominous signs of wear and tear in the fabric of its superstructure. It opened with Wales having won two Triple Crowns in forty-one years; with highly-talented players whose individual skills were infinitely greater than those of the corporate whole; with a team that was unlikely to play rugby football further from home than Paris, yet bought its own boots and was grateful for the chance to order a hotel dinner à la carte.

It closed with a team who were already European champions and were to win seven Triple Crowns in fourteen years. A team that grew out of the strength of an organised coaching framework, polishing its skills at squad sessions and practising them on tours to the southern hemisphere and the Far East. A team whose outstanding players became household names in Britain and the rugby-playing world.

And it ended with the mushrooming growth of a magnificent new national ground, with a pitch worthy of the setting.

# THE SUPERSTARS
## 1970 to 1979

### DAVID PARRY-JONES

Throughout the twentieth century Cardiff's skyline had been good to look at. Though not exactly a dreaming spire the tower of St John's Church was a liturgical centrepoint dating back to 1483. Tall crenellated walls surrounded the castle restored for the Butes by William Burges. A short distance away lay Cathays Park with extravagant buildings bearing witness to the nationhood of Wales and the vitality of her principal city.

And now, as the seventies opened, fresh profiles competed for approbation. The knuckled canopies of two new stadia at Cardiff Arms Park had sprouted beside the River Taff – pale in colour, angular in aspect, clearly identifiable as theatres for gladiatorial combat. Some passers-by saw them as exclusive and belligerently masculine; others, pausing to gaze from Canton Bridge, perceived a massive gentleness in the architecture which seemed to support and cradle something precious.

Within these man-made ramparts nature could now flourish. Usage of the turf whose resilience had formerly been ground out by unending batterings beneath metalled boots was about to fall dramatically. The Welsh Rugby Union contemplated no more than ten games a year on the national ground; Cardiff RFC's pitch would perforce have to do duty more regularly but, when the weather was wet and stormy, training and lesser matches could take place across river at Sophia Gardens. The grass at Cardiff Arms Park at last had a chance to grow and be verdant.

Its ground staffs, too, could display their expertise. On big-match days spectators grew accustomed to the sight of playing surfaces wonderfully cosmeticised by gang-mower and roller. The great All Black captain and flanker Graham Mourie was once asked how the turf at Cardiff compared with grounds back in New Zealand. 'Oh, we have plenty of pitches like this at home,' he replied with a twinkle in his eye. 'The difference is, we use them for tennis and bowls!'

So the characteristics and configuration of the mighty new complex were revealed: Cardiff RFC's ground complete, a compact enclosure admirably suited to the needs of the club; the U-shape of the WRU stadium one-third finished – and for the time being looking distinctly lop-sided.

The grandstands and terraces stood ready and expectant. People wondered if the quality of the rugby football to be played before them could possibly complement the vision of the architects and the skill of the builders. They need not have worried. The promise was to be fulfilled.

*Wales 5, England 0, 17 January 1959 – on what might have been 'the nastiest, foulest day of them all'. A picture epitomising the quagmire conditions in which midwinter rugby often took place at Cardiff before the 1970s.*

But not straightaway. The weather had a final spiteful blow to strike at Cardiff Arms Park where the decade's representative rugby opened with a visit by South Africa to the national ground on 24 January 1970. Some 4000 seats at the eastern, or city, end of the unfinished north stand were made available, raising the ground capacity to 40,000. Most of this gathering felt that the home team could win the match and end a sequence of six Test defeats at the hands of Springbok teams dating back to 1906. The tourists seemed there for the taking, with Newport and Gwent two of the five teams which had defeated them.

Certainly their pack was strong, the great Frik du Preez being among the tight forwards, with a magnificent back row in Piet Greyling, Tommy Bedford and Jan Ellis. But South Africa were short of outstanding players behind the scrum, where much rested on the shoulders of the scrum half and captain Dawie de Villiers. Off the field their preparations had been upset by demonstrations against apartheid. Nails and glass were scattered on pitches where they were due to appear, bomb threats were delivered to their hotels, chanting and banner-waving greeted them at every turn. There had been particularly ugly exchanges at Swansea where stewards had clashed angrily with protesters attempting to occupy the St Helen's pitch. Barbed wire, erected at the national ground for the December game against Cardiff, still bristled as the Springboks took the field for the Test.

But heavy rain had been falling ceaselessly for two days and it was clear from the kick-off that the result was bound to be a lottery. Squelching through ankle-deep mud Wales's rapidly maturing half-back partnership of Gareth Edwards and Barry John was unable to assert the tactical mastery which might have been possible on a dry day. South Africa led by two penalties to one until the game's final moments when Edwards slithered over the mire for a try he just failed to convert. The match was drawn.

That might just have been the nastiest, foulest day of them all. Those who had been at the ground on 17 January 1959, when a brown-camouflaged Dewi Bebb skated through liquid mud for a try to beat England, considered that a worse occasion. South Africans who had been in Wales before recalled that the last Test between the two nations on 3 December 1960 also took place in conditions more suited to reptiles than rugby players. The truth was that for years the 'atmosphere' of Cardiff Arms Park and its Celtic *hwyl* had pre-empted popular criticism of its desperate shortcomings. To expect rugby football to be played in such conditions was meaningless, an insult to well-prepared teams – and obscene.

*The slum-like rear of the south stand in the forties: '. . . for years the "atmosphere" of Cardiff Arms Park and its Celtic* hwyl *had pre-empted criticism of its desperate shortcomings.*

But as 1970 wore on and as celebration matches mentioned elsewhere in this book were played to mark completion of the master-plan's first stage it became clear that the problem had been banished. Welsh Rugby Union members had demanded a pitch 'fit for our young men to play International matches on'. The reborn Cardiff Arms Park had it.

But the pitch was only one of several factors contributing to the splendour of the rugby football which graced the ground in the seventies.

In 1968 the Australian Dispensation rule, which 'dispensed' with kicking to touch on the full between the 25-yard lines, was introduced as an experiment. It straightaway encouraged a more fluent game, with players frequently electing to run loose possession rather than take the safe but negative option of kicking the ball out of play. The new generation of full-backs – Villepreux of France, Irvine of Scotland, Ensor of Ireland and above all the Welshman J. P. R. Williams – applied itself enthusiastically to seizing the opportunities that arose to cast aside dull care and join the attack. 'Coming into the line' was a popular option. Before long the experiment was incorporated into the laws of the game.

Then, in time for the 1971–72 season, the try was upgraded to four points. This also proved an incentive to attack. Kicks at goal were still taken after infringements (though crowds took to hooting their displeasure) but since, for example, three tries were now worth four penalties teams which had fallen behind often preferred to act positively and run a free ball yielded by a penalty.

A very important development was the series of invitations extended by the Welsh to the world's newer rugby nations. In the past, teams from New South Wales – the 'Waratahs' – Fiji and the Maori community of New Zealand had played matches in Cardiff. But such occasions had been the exception rather than the rule, squeezed between Test matches in which overseas opposition was limited to International Board countries. Now, with plenty of spare dates available at WRU headquarters, and fast jet travel shrinking the distances involved, tourists from North America, the Far East and the Pacific came eagerly to display exotic skills in the Welsh capital.

What is more, to the great satisfaction of the WRU, they proved dynamic crowd-pullers. Although Fiji's match against a Welsh Under-25 side was a late addition to their 1970 tour itinerary the south sea islanders still drew to Cardiff Arms Park 48,000 spectators who saw a tremendously close game. A try by Visei and a Batibasaga penalty goal gave the tourists an interval lead, only for tries by Barry Llewelyn and Ian Hall, plus a J. P. R. Williams conversion, to capture the spoils for Wales.

Canada came next, a side mainly drawn from the British Columbian fraternity but also containing men from Quebec, Ontario, Newfoundland and Alberta. The final Trial in Vancouver, so it was said, obliged the easterners to travel further across North America than the distance between Toronto and Cardiff. The wearers of the Maple Leaf were not a good side, but 20,000

---

### THE VISITORS' DRESSING-ROOM

**George Morgan**
*Elected to WRU 1967, WRU Liaison Officer for touring sides from 1971.*

Without any doubt the animation and atmosphere of the city of Cardiff and of its great rugby ground in particular is greatly appreciated by overseas tourists in Wales.

The mood in the visitors' dressing-room immediately after an International match naturally reflects the result. With the exception of most New Zealand sides of recent years – and the Japanese XV of 1983, who experienced a sense of victory in their narrow defeat – other touring teams have had to choke down initial disappointment at having lost to Wales. But then they reflect that, despite defeat, they have enjoyed the privilege of playing on a ground renowned throughout the world.

Emotion was most evident among the Argentinians of 1976: tears of elation at a seemingly victorious position in the final quarter of the Test against Wales were transformed to tears of despair after Phil Bennett kicked a winning penalty goal against them in the final moments.

The Tongans of 1974 forgot the unfamiliar cold temperature in their eighty minutes of unsuccessful endeavour. Immediately after the final whistle, however, they rushed to their dressing-room and dived into their plunge-bath without even the preamble of discarding their kit.

The 1973 Wallabies genuinely sought to utilise the singing of the Welsh National Anthem before the kick-off as motivation for themselves, the tactical philosophy being that the crowd would not have been singing with such hwyl but for their presence as tourists. However, as various players confessed later, on hearing the first few bars sung in the traditionally emotional manner by a capacity crowd they realised that it was for the scarlet-clad Welsh XV that every voice was raised.

Cardiff Arms Park represents a threefold challenge to every rugby nation of the world: to beat Wales, achieve a rare feeling of euphoria in the visitors' dressing-room, and win a place in rugby football history.

---

spectators still turned up to see them whipped 56-10 in the Test by a Welsh team with six full caps. These were times when men wore their hair long, and there can have been few more dramatic sights beside the Taff than the flaxen-maned Spence McTavish speeding beyond the defenders for his two tries. The crowd harmonised, 'We'll keep a Welcome in the Hillsides!'

Because these fixtures took place in early autumn before grim application to Championship rugby became the priority the abiding memories are of bright, sun-kissed afternoons on turf that was firm for men who wanted to swerve and side-step. Japan came, and Tonga – the former too small to set real problems for beefy opponents, the latter too scatter-brained. On their own soil Argentina, the visitors in 1976, had beaten a below-strength Welsh touring side in 1968 and now came close to winning at Cardiff Arms Park.

## A SCOTTISH VIEW

**Andy Irvine**
*Scotland's full-back between 1972 and 1982.*

My first recollections of Cardiff Arms Park – restricted, of course, to International matches relayed on television by the BBC – are of days when David Watkins skimmed over the glue-pot surface evading tackle after tackle and when players leaving the pitch at the end of a match resembled Neanderthal Man. I often wondered how it came to pass that Wales of all countries, with an incredible passion for the game of rugby, ever managed to have such a dump as their national stadium.

I got a closer view of it in 1969 when the stadium was being re-built and I was a member of the visiting Scottish Schools side. A certain John Bevan, later to play for the British Lions before turning League, scored two tries.

Things have changed much since those days and I believe that Wales can now, with France, boast the finest national stadium of them all. There are two fundamental factors which determine the quality of any ground: its atmosphere and just as important, for backs at least, its playing surface. The pitch within the reconstructed Cardiff Arms Park is first-class. Moreover because of the design and shape of the majestic stands matches there are rarely spoiled by wind.

As far as atmosphere is concerned, the ground has always been my favourite. The Scottish Press in previewing any International match against Wales there always describe the place as a wailing cauldron where the Welsh enjoy a free lead of at least six points. I never felt that way about it. The location of the stadium is something special, right in the heart of the city centre, and I enjoyed mingling with spectators during the short walk to the ground from the hotel. I loved the singing, and the crowd's knowledgeable applause and appreciation. In fact, I just loved playing there, even though success was rather rare.

Part of the reason was that the games were so enjoyable. Welsh teams I met invariably played 'Rugby'. That is, they preferred playing a 15-man game to booting the ball as far downfield as possible and exerting pressure within the other team's territory.

Scotland's win in 1982 by 34 points to 18 will always remain one of the highlights of my career, since it was our first in Cardiff for 20 years. But for sheer pleasure the 1980 Welsh Rugby Union Centenary spectacular in which a Scotland-Ireland XV played Wales-England will always rank with me as the most exciting match I ever played in. I was convinced we had it won, but in the very last minute Terry Holmes manufactured one of his Houdini tricks from his own 22 – and the net result was a winning try beneath the posts for his half-back partner Gareth Davies.

Their stand-off half Hugo Porta, ranked among the two or three best men in his position during the seventies, marshalled the Pumas magnificently and only a high tackle by Travaglini which a Phil Bennett penalty goal punished

*The pluperfection of the WRU pitch brought the best out of visitors like Michael Gibson of Ireland, with ball.*

robbed them of the spoils. In 1979 Romania showed with a defeat by just 13 points to 12 that they had become a rugby power to reckon with (and were to take terrible revenge upon Wales in Bucharest four years later).

Such matches served innumerable purposes. They gave great pleasure to the visitors, who had become accustomed to viewing telecasts by satellite of happenings at Cardiff Arms Park and relished the experience of treading on the famous and by now gorgeously manicured turf. They established criteria of entertainment by which the Welsh could judge the quality of other games. They helped the WRU to keep its bank overdraft within manageable limits. And, since the crowd was usually sizeable, they provided a useful blooding for young Welsh players in big-match conditions.

There emerged, also, the superstars. In Barry John, Gareth Edwards, John – J. P. R. – Williams, Mervyn Davies, Gerald Davies and later Phil Bennett,

## SENSING HISTORY

### Gareth Edwards

I imagine that Test cricketers get the same feeling when they step into Old Trafford or Lord's. When I visit Cardiff Arms Park I feel an overwhelming sense of history, the more compelling for having been part of what happened there.

When I first played at Cardiff there was just the one rugby stadium. Although it was packed for club games twenty years before my time, by 1967 when television had eroded the crowds it was too big for Cardiff RFC. So from 1970 onwards I came to love the new arena to which we moved, surely Britain's best club ground. It was just the right size, a 15,000 gate giving it a wonderfully intimate, theatrical feel. I never tired of club appearances for Cardiff, whose supporters have always been so sensible and sane: they desperately want their team to win, but defeat does not mean the end of the world.

Next door, the national ground, so close to the beating heart of Cardiff that we almost take it for granted. I remember it as a quagmire in the sixties, and I recall my acute embarrassment that expert opponents like Mike Gibson, Roger Young, Ian Robertson, David Duckham, Jacques Cantoni and others of their ilk had to play on that abomination of a pitch.

*A typical Gareth Edwards try for Wales at Cardiff Arms Park. He scored 20 for his country in the course of winning 53 caps.*

Imagine my pride at the Great Transformation and the way a later generation of players would make a point of telling me, 'To play here is the
greatest experience rugby has to offer!'

You will understand my personal feelings about the national ground.
In 1972 I got a try there against Scotland which came all the way from the
Welsh 25-line and which is still my favourite of all. In 1973 I touched down
the magnificent opening try of the Barbarians-New Zealand classic. In
1978 I dropped a goal to beat France and clinch a Grand Slam at Cardiff
in my final International game. Such moments are unforgettable. They are
associated with Welsh success, which cements them even more firmly in
my memory.

They are the reasons why every now and then, when I am in Cardiff, I
park my car and stroll down the tunnel from which I often raced as a
player. I stand on the halfway line and look around.

And to myself I smile a private, contented smile.

Wales produced a crop of exceedingly gifted men who could bring a crowd to
its feet with the brilliance of their play – sometimes pre-planned, sometimes
impromptu, always good to watch. The pluperfection of the WRU pitch also
brought the best out of visitors like Jo Maso, David Duckham, Andy Irvine,
Michael Gibson, Jim Renwick and others. Coincidentally the arrival of
colour television and satellite transmissions paraded such men and their
skills before world-wide audiences who warmed to them not just as stern
competitors but also as marvellous entertainers. So after decades when it
modestly claimed to be no more than a players' game which some people
enjoyed watching, rugby football suddenly became a gigantic spectator sport,
its TV audience measured in scores of millions. By comparison association
football had entered a period of decline characterised by mediocrity on the
field and waning popular enthusiasm. Rugby was macho, masculine and very
modern.

And at Cardiff Arms Park more than anywhere else high drama seemed
guaranteed by the all-star cast.

Take Gareth Edwards. Born and bred in West Glamorgan he had joined
Cardiff in 1967 while a student at the local training college. By the time he
retired in 1978 he had laid just claim to being the finest all-round player ever
produced by his country. Certainly a try scored by him against Scotland in
1972 remains in the minds of many onlookers as the best individual score they
ever saw. Breaking past the opposing back row near his team's 25-line the
scrum half surged powerfully along the south stand touch-line, reaching the
halfway mark before the visiting full-back's challenge obliged him to chip on
towards the eastern end of the ground. By now Scotland's right wing was alive
to the danger and corner-flagging for dear life, only for Edwards to respond
by hacking the ball a further twenty-five yards over the opposition's goal-line.

---

**THAT CERTAIN FEELING**

## Barry John

Unlike Gareth and Gerald, who could decide when it was convenient for them to score, I have only one try to talk about at the national ground, Cardiff Arms Park (even then, in 1969, Maurice Richards had to steal all the glory by scoring four!). It was touched down on a day when the 'posh' north stand of today was in embryo. My Mum and Dad were sitting in the old south stand.

I scored my Try in the left-hand corner at the city end. Perhaps from line-out, perhaps from a scrum, Wales moved left about forty yards from the goal-line of our opponents, England. Keith Jarrett put in a little chip.

Following the rules that all stand-off halves abide by, I had lingered behind my three-quarters with very little intent. Suddenly the ball jack-knifed back, sideways – and straight into my arms. Five or six seconds later, a try.

Obviously, a very precious moment, for every Welshman wants to score at Cardiff. But, I promise you, as much as the try itself I recall the happy faces, full of jubilation, and the wobbly yellow construction hats of the site-workers, 'on duty' in that corner of Cardiff Arms Park.

And it was a lovely feeling.

---

Amazingly he had enough energy left to win the race for the touch-down – and a try that surely no one else in the world could have scored.

Though he played twice for Wales in 1967 with David Watkins of Newport, Edwards's first extended half-back partnership for club and country was with the cool, insouciant Barry John who had begun his International career a year earlier. Another westerner, John brought elegance and grace to Cardiff Arms Park, enjoying his high noon during 1971 as a key member of the Wales Grand Slam XV and the successful British Lions party in New Zealand before a 1972 retirement which seemed premature to his admirers. As a runner he was audacious and exciting, but in the Welsh capital he is as vividly remembered for the goals he dropped. His game against England in 1971 contained two, while another against Ireland contributed to a Triple Crown victory.

John did not confine his feats to the bigger WRU ground. In ninety-six appearances for Cardiff RFC, many on the new club pitch, he struck thirty dropped goals. Four came in a burst one November afternoon against Llanelli. The historian Danny Davies writes that John 'appeared to shape up for a fifth in quite a favourable position, but changed his mind and passed the ball out'. Presumably he was satisfied at having set a new club record (equalled in 1983 by a successor at stand-off half, Gareth Davies). He scored twenty-four tries for Cardiff and his half-back association with Edwards must rank among the most feared and potent the game has known.

The difference between these two and the rest is that the main rugby home they knew was Cardiff Arms Park. Both played club and International football in the old and new arenas. For years their names in the Blue and Black XV listed for a match could put thousands on the gate. A loudspeaker announcement to the effect that one or the other had been forced to withdraw would be greeted with loud and prolonged groans from spectators, who felt deprived of the extra excitement their presence injected into a game. Although they were not natives of the capital their loyalty to its rugby club was intense. And the feeling was mutual: the jerseys and boots of Barry John and Gareth Edwards occupy prominent positions in the Hubert Johnson Room; their portraits adorn its walls.

Gerald Davies, too, brought lustre and distinction to Cardiff Arms Park. In 1974, after a six-year break spent in the ranks of Cambridge University and

*J. P. R. Williams: the final obstacle would-be try-scorers had to surmount – and seldom did.*

*Phil Bennett: by 1978 probably the world's most exciting midfield player.*

London Welsh, he returned to a post in Wales and rejoined Cardiff RFC, serving as club captain for three seasons during the late seventies. The side he moulded and led did not win a major trophy but in retrospect many people considered that the XV which John Scott later took with great style to Cup and Championship triumphs bore the Gerald Davies stamp and philosophy. All too often, however, when playing on the national ground for his country this peerless wing, a match-winning runner, got less than his share of the ball, spending many matches on lonely touch-line patrols. For a slight man he was a determined defender who made tackles that saved certain tries.

But what with Trials, Internationals, celebration matches, regular club fixtures and tours by the Barbarians, the other superstars were frequently in action at Cardiff too. Like Gerald Davies, J. P. R. Williams and Mervyn Davies had been members of the magnificent London Welsh side of the early seventies before returning to Wales and joining Bridgend and Swansea respectively. If Edwards, John and Gerald Davies are remembered primarily as attackers, the great contribution of the latter two lay in defence, and in particular in the courage they displayed when tackling and falling on the ball.

JPR was Wales's last line of defence, often the final obstacle would-be try-scorers had to surmount – and seldom did. A brave, all-enveloping tackle of Scotland's Steele in 1974, in which his teeth were heavily struck by the wing's knee, meant that Cardiff Arms Park was the only ground in the world where he failed to finish a Test match, for oddly enough history repeated itself in 1979 when a severely-gashed shin forced his withdrawal from the fray to applaud his team's victory over England from the sidelines.

Whereas JPR also loved to attack, number-eight forward Mervyn Davies was a last-ditch man: 'One good tackle gives me more pleasure than ten tries,' he would declare. Never was the point better illustrated than in the 1975 Wales–Australia Test when a fiercely full-blooded tackle on the dangerous young Wallaby back-row player Mark Loane sent him hobbling to the touch-line and out of the match.

Later that season 'Merv the Swerve' was the central character in the saddest episode Cardiff Arms Park has known. Playing for Swansea in a Cup-tie on the club ground he suffered a sub-arachnoid brain haemorrhage which nearly took his life, and forced his retirement from the game at the age of twenty-nine. His bristling aggression and commanding presence were sorely missed by both his club and his country.

Davies was succeeded as Welsh captain by Phil Bennett of Llanelli, sixth and last of the superstars. A jinking, bewildering runner – especially from broken play – in direct line of descent from Glyn Davies and David Watkins, he took over the Wales stand-off half position from Barry John only to experience an unfortunate period in his career when private problems and a general rugby ennui beset him. Such was the effect on his form that robust John

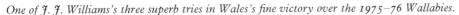

*One of J. J. Williams's three superb tries in Wales's fine victory over the 1975–76 Wallabies.*

Bevan of Aberavon ousted him from the Wales XV. But Bennett, who frequently led his club in stirring encounters with Cardiff RFC on the club ground, fought his way back to favour and won many more caps before his retirement from International play in 1978. By that time he was probably the most exciting midfield player in the world.

There were others: great-hearted Ray Gravell, the viking-lookalike Derek Quinnell, speedy John 'J. J.' Williams who graced the wing thirty times for Wales, phlegmatic Steve Fenwick, big Geoff Wheel and Allan Martin, that host unto itself the Pontypool front row – Graham Price, Bobby Windsor and Tony Faulkner – and their abrasive and inspiring clubmate Terry Cobner. The supporting cast could hardly have been more vital and vibrant.

It was to play against and talk with such men that Fijians, Tongans, Japanese, Canadians and so on were more than ready to cross the world. They came not so much on a tour as a pilgrimage to Cardiff Arms Park – where the Welsh were quick to appreciate the lessons to be learned, for pilgrims are folk who have been around and have much to contribute. Supporters and hero-worshippers found to their delight that because of the stadia's design the players were accessible, albeit briefly. Before the short walk to nearby hotels or bars for post-match socialising it was necessary to pass through the public concourse. Autographs could be obtained, and shoulders rubbed.

One paradox of the seventies concerned the Challenge Cup competition introduced by the Welsh Rugby Union and its final staged at the 'new' Cardiff Arms Park.

Tournament play between the top clubs had lapsed after 1914 when Aberavon became the last winners of the old South Wales Challenge Cup, beating Blaina 10-0 in a final disfigured by violence on the pitch and scuffles on the terraces. In 1971–72 the revived competition immediately indicated that it could capture public imagination. Even with the televised FA Cup final as a counter-attraction the first final on the WRU ground drew 12,000 spectators who paid £6000 and saw Neath defeat Llanelli 15-9. By the end of the decade the occasion regularly attracted crowds of 40,000 and takings in the region of £100,000. The Schweppes Cup final, as it became known after 1976, brought domestic seasons to a suitably competitive climax.

Usually, at the end of April, the weather was good. So, now, was the playing surface. Having fought their way through five rounds, and months, of gruelling encounters the teams involved were worthy finalists. All the more extraordinary, therefore, that with the exception of Llanelli's 30-7 victory over Cardiff in 1973 finals were dour, uninspired affairs rather than the hoped-for extravaganzas in which the highest qualities of Welsh club rugby would be paraded. One after the other Newport, Swansea, Cardiff again, Pontypridd and even effervescent Bridgend came to the national ground during the seventies, only to be deserted by their normal richly entertaining touch.

Why? It is hard to pronounce with certainty. The Welsh rugby winter is long and arduous, and possibly at the end of its thirty-fourth week players could be forgiven for feeling stale and devoid of enterprise. On the other hand, onlookers grumbled, surely the occasion and the trophy at stake should have been capable of motivating them to one last 'high'.

There were people who said that big-match nerves were to blame, stifling initiative and undermining skill. The gap between playing before 4000 spectators, say, at Pontypridd and 40,000 at Cardiff Arms Park was too great for club players to bridge in eighty minutes. That was why, it was argued, the side with the greater number of 'big-match' players usually came out on top. But there was another side to this coin. In a period when the Wales XV contained men who were accumulating vast numbers of caps and closing the representative door to a host of gifted rivals, the Cup final shed welcome limelight on also-rans who would surely have been capped in other eras. The 1972 final, for example, threw together Martyn Davies of Neath and Llanelli's Selwyn Williams whose paths to the top were sealed off by Gareth Edwards.

Williams, Hefin Jenkins and Andy Hill, however, had the satisfaction of appearing in the astonishing series of four victories gained by the Scarlets in the succeeding years. Armadas of Llanelli coaches – caparisoned with dragons, saucepans, leeks and signs like 'Gravell eats Soft Centres' – swinging into Westgate Street behind the team bus became a feature of Cup-final

*A try to clinch the 1978 Schweppes Cup Final by hooker Jeff Herdman – another uncapped player to impress the gallery.*

morning between 1972 and 1976. It thus seemed as if Welsh rugby had been stood on its head when in January 1977, after trailing 12-0 before a capacity crowd on their club ground, Cardiff rallied to dismiss the Scarlets 25-15. The Blue and Blacks dearly wanted to win the Cup in their Centenary Year, but went down by a point to an unfancied Newport XV on the WRU ground in the final.

Newport's defence of the trophy twelve months later was foiled by Swansea hooker Jeff Herdman with the sole try of the final, he being another uncapped player to impress a 40,000 gallery. Though the last final of the decade was won by Bridgend, Pontypridd veteran Bob Penberthy gave a virtuoso line-out display to hint at the service he might have given to his country had he not remained loyal to a club which but rarely caught the eye of the Welsh selectors.

The other puzzle of the decade was over the decline of seven-a-side rugby in Wales and spectator interest in it. For many post-war seasons sixteen of the top Welsh clubs had taken part in the 'Snelling Sevens' tournament (named after its Newport founder) bringing a Maytime flourish to Cardiff Arms Park. The event drew 20,000 or so spectators to see a knock-out competition which began at noon and reached its climax at teatime. The stands and terraces were well populated with shirt-sleeved fans refreshing themselves with flagons of ale and meat pies who went home sated with fluent, uninhibited play. Clubs like Newport, Cardiff and Bridgend took the Snellings seriously and entered well prepared teams. A special breed of seven stars emerged like Ian Lewis of Bridgend and Cardiff's John Davies and Tony Williams.

Yet by the end of the seventies the Snellings attracted fewer than 10,000, and despite experiments with seeding and complex 'pool' systems the organisers were having no luck with efforts to bring back the departed thousands. The Welsh Rugby Union's own competition, open to all member clubs, fared no better and at Stradey Park barely 2000 were present to see Swansea take the title with a big win over Llanelli in 1979.

There are several probable reasons for the decline. A series of cold springs with chill winds whistling around Cardiff Arms Park helped to dampen enthusiasm. Even for fans swathed in sheepskin coats and long-john underclothing six-hour stints on chilly terraces were scarcely a good way of spending Saturday afternoons. Nor could it be guaranteed that clubs would field their strongest teams. With the advent of May star players whose presence would have brought in many uncommitted onlookers were away on holiday, involved in cricket, or simply relaxing in front of their TV sets after a surfeit of rugby football.

Also the nature of the fifteen-a-side game had undergone a transformation. In the old days it had compared poorly with the non-stop action of sevens, whereas now its emphasis was all upon running, handling and attack. Perceptibly the appeal of the smaller game shrank. Always an anaemic form of exercise, it could no longer offer a sufficiently distinctive appeal compared with the red-blooded fifteen-a-side football now to be seen in both Cardiff Arms Park stadia.

Statistics show that Wales had always been hard to beat at the famous ground. But as the seventies went by her teams excelled themselves, winning every home Championship match but one. Only the French side of 1974 returned home undefeated, thanks to a late dropped goal by Jean-Pierre Romeu which tied the scores at 16-16. Three Grand Slams were achieved and five Triple Crowns, many of the decisive matches taking place at the new headquarters ground. South Africa were held to a draw, the Wallabies vanquished twice.

Spectators came to Cardiff Arms Park, it seemed, not so much to view rugby football as to celebrate another victory by the national XV. They lionised the great players. They complained if their team scored less than 20 points. All Wales walked tall as victories in the new stadium came thick and fast.

Then, in perverse Celtic fashion, came the time when people started to accuse the rugby fraternity of arrogance and complacency. People who in less illustrious eras trembled with rage if a Welsh player made an error handing victory to the opposition now declared with conviction that 'it would be a good thing if we lost a game or two'. Critics said that the Welsh needed cutting down to size. They need not have worried. For nearly a quarter of a century one nation had always been able to achieve what was usually beyond England, Scotland and the rest. Twice in the seventies New Zealand came to Cardiff Arms Park for scheduled Test matches. Twice they won. Twice, moreover, the encounters were marred by controversy and acrimony.

The All Blacks of 1972 led by Ian Kirkpatrick and managed by Ernie Todd contained a hard core of seasoned campaigners who might have been expected to show maturity during the tour but instead chose to remain surly and uncommunicative. Their resolve for the Test had been stiffened by an early-tour reverse at Llanelli, and the pressure they exerted in the first quarter at Cardiff Arms Park drew fatal errors from a Welsh XV which was a vastly more experienced side on paper but fell victim to a bad attack of nerves.

The mistakes were ruthlessly punished by Joe Karam's expert goal-kicking, so that the tourists held a lead of 19-16 when the game entered its final ten minutes. But as the Welsh, top dogs in Europe for the last four seasons, threw everything into attack their victory bid was foiled by illegal body-checks and late tackles, Phil Bennett missing a last-minute penalty attempt which could have tied the scores. That night after the post-match dinner an incident at the adjacent Angel Hotel resulted in the sending home of Keith Murdoch, the All Black prop who had scored his team's try. There was an uneasy feeling in Cardiff that somehow New Zealanders would find a way of blaming Welsh rugby for what had happened.

## THE BARBARIANS

*The Barbarian Football Club first appeared at Cardiff Arms Park in 1891, going down to their hosts by seven points to three. Since that time they have figured there in some of the most exciting and dramatic games of rugby football ever to take place.*

*Two such matches are remembered here. John Dawes, a successful skipper of London Welsh, Wales and the British Isles, led the Baa-Baas in their encounter with the Seventh All Blacks, while Gerald Davies was Cardiff's captain on a day when the club won what was certainly its most remarkable, if not its greatest, victory.*

### John Dawes

*27 January 1973.* In this most classical of rugby matches there were two tries – one in the game's early moments and the other late on – which have been talked about and shown on television probably more times than any others. To be part of them was a privilege and a thrill and has produced everlasting memories of a great game.

The match was, as usual, the final fixture of the current New Zealand tour of the United Kingdom. The All Blacks had not been beaten in any of the four Test matches and as a result there was an unusual amount at stake. What was more important, however, was the manner in which the game was to be played. Consequently the Baa-Baas selected a team based on the successful 1971 Lions. Fortunately two late enforced changes, introducing John Bevan for Gerald Davies on the wing and Tommy David for Mervyn Davies in the pack (Derek Quinnell switching to number eight) did not weaken the team or change its attitude. To complement all this there was a final team-talk from Carwyn James. We were ready to take the field and attack and counter-attack but – let no one think otherwise – also totally determined to win.

In the first two minutes almost everyone in the Barbarians' side had touched the ball, and this of course was a good confidence booster. It was in the third minute that from a typical All Black drive the ball emerged to Ian Kirkpatrick who transferred it to Bryan Williams. This happened near the halfway line where, true to New Zealand fashion, 'B.G.' hoisted a high kick towards the Baa-Baas' posts and behind all their players – at the moment of the bounce there was no one between the ball and the defenders' goal-line. However, as a result of knowing each other and the type of game the Lions had had to play in New Zealand, within one or two seconds there were many black and white jerseys in a position to receive the ball.

For a counter-attack to begin it was necessary for the collector of the kick ahead to have the confidence to run. That player was, of course, Phil Bennett, heir-apparent to the retired Barry John in the Wales XV and nurtured by Carwyn James at Llanelli. Once Phil had decided to run I am sure we all felt we could run ourselves out of trouble although no try was in our minds at that stage.

In what followed there were many crucial moments, at any of which the movement could have broken down. First came Phil's magnificent side-stepping which started the flow of the ball; then J. P. R. Williams's strength in withstanding a high tackle from Bryan Williams (not usual for 'B.G.', who was a good defensive player); the transfer and quick pass to me by John Pullin (who later stated that if he had been playing for England he would have kicked for touch). At this stage we had come laterally across the field but nevertheless placed the All Blacks in some disarray.

It was obvious to me that my course of action should be to put John Bevan away by drawing the All Black in front of me. What actually happened is still a mystery. I was not aware of doing anything unusual – and yet suddenly the defenders had gone. I looked inside to see nearly all our forwards in support and my reaction was to keep the movement going. I passed to Tommy David who in typical fashion added his own brand of momentum to the movement. His pass was not the best in the world and Derek Quinnell still revels in what he calls the best catch he ever made.

My pass to David had taken play away from the touch-line, but Tommy's pass to Derek Quinnell reversed that direction. The significance of this

*The Barbarians' XV v New Zealand in 1973.*
*Back row, l–r: E. M. Lewis (touch judge), G. Windsor Lewis (secretary), J. V. Pullin, W. J. McBride, R. M. Wilkinson, D. L. Quinnell, A. B. Carmichael, D. J. Duckham, G. Domercq (referee), D. Spyer (touch judge).*
*Middle row: G. O. Edwards, C. M. H. Gibson, H. L. Glyn Hughes, S. J. Dawes (captain), H. Waddell, J. Bevan, R. J. McLoughlin.*
*On ground: J. F. Slattery, T. David, P. Bennett, J. P. R. Williams.*

was that John Bevan had not been utilised and it was to him that Quinnell passed. But now a player who, when the forward momentum of this movement began, was still retiring towards our goal-line appeared out of nowhere. Gareth Edwards, like the superb athlete he was, intercepted the intended pass to Bevan and scored a most memorable try.

A point worthy of emphasis is that every player involved made a contribution – and also had the opportunity to have done something else. Fortunately for us each man chose to do the right thing. A great try was the result, and also a pattern set for the remainder of the match.

The second extra-special try (and sixth of the game) was memorable for different reasons. The Barbarians had reached half-time 17-0 up only to be pulled back to 17-11 by some stirring All Black play. Play had continued to be full of attack and counter-attack and hard tackling, with no quarter being asked or given up front. Sid Going had been replaced at scrum half by Lindsay Colling who played an entirely different type of game. The next score, therefore, was crucial – and fortunately it came from the Baa-Baas.

It was their attitude and willingness to keep the ball moving that finally produced the try. From the line-out which secured possession to the actual touch-down by JPR there was a ninety-second period of unbroken play, in itself most unusual in rugby football. There were in this spell some missed tackles by the All Blacks – not unexpected; after all it was late in the game and continuous movement of this duration demands a great deal of running. There were also some excellent individual sallies by David Duckham, Mike Gibson and finally JPR. But it was the determination of the Baa-Baas to keep play flowing and, in obedience to the old maxim, 'let the ball do the work' which finally cracked the New Zealanders' defence. That try and the superb conversion by Phil Bennett was the final blow to end a marvellous game of rugby.

The All Blacks' contribution was a truly splendid one, and the two tries by Grant Batty were also gems. As in the game itself, if I had any breath left it would be a pleasure to describe them too.

## Gerald Davies

*Easter Saturday 1976.* No one game of rugby football can be treated the same as any other. With delicate, doubtful steps a player tentatively, albeit enthusiastically, takes the field in September in a different mood from that of April when he is awash with complacency and full of thoughts of a summer break. The traditional Boxing Day fixture after spirited festivities is unlikely to arouse the same response as a Cup semi-final tie in March.

And on Easter Saturday, when terraces are flooded with primary colours and a jaunty humour settles once more in the stands, the fixture between Cardiff RFC and the Barbarians at Cardiff Arms Park is uniquely and refreshingly different. It is an occasion which the three-quarters may relish

*If the Barbarians' Gerald Davies (with ball) is checked by a covering Australian, Ray Gravell is at hand to take up the running.*

but which forwards can only approach with misgivings since the rest of the season is so inadequate a preparation for what is to come. A member of the front five, once brash and brazen in contemplating an uncomplicated match in the mud, is reduced to guilty introversion and frowning wariness when he views the prospect of the unequivocal style of the Baa-Baas. Like it or not the very name imposes its will on the opposition.

The ninety-third game between Cardiff and the Barbarians, played on Easter Saturday 1976, was an extraordinary affair in every way. For if sport is about any one thing, it is about Chance: the matter of good and bad fortune, the fickle bounce of the ball, and the rub of the green. Between the threat of failure and the sweet promise of success hang the peculiar favours of that saucy Lady Luck who will amuse and tease according to her whims. At her wink and random nod great reputations come to grief or are raised in triumph. She flatters only to betray and not content with mowing a man down sends him spinning head over heels.

She was, this lady, in a giddy and capricious mood on this particular Easter Saturday, a bright, sunny spring day. The Barbarians for their part seemed at the outset irresistibly handsome, dashing and cavalier as only they know how to be. But at the finish every player in each team had been made aware that Lady Luck's favours are characterised usually by the shortness of their duration.

However, by the time half-time arrived she had smiled consistently on the tourists, who led 24-0. Tries had been scored by Andy Irvine – from a devastating counter-attack; by Mike Biggar, following good work from Alan Lawson at scrum half; and by Tony Neary, Biggar in turn having paved the way. Not content with his superb try Irvine had put over three conversions and a couple of penalties. When Cardiff made a gesture of response, Gareth Edwards scoring a try, the tourists immediately restored the margin by sending Mackay over for 28-4.

On such embarrassing occasions a captain's appeal, mine in this case, had to be a basic one – to pride and concentration on individual performance. Added to this was only one spur – that if the Barbarians could score so many points in the first half, then so could we in the second.

While we were burning in the sun and reeling beneath the onslaught, the pulse began to beat. And as its tempo quickened John Davies, Chris Camilleri, Alan Phillips and I added tries to the one scored by our scrum half. With Gareth Davies converting three we were still adrift 26-28.

The climax was devastating and ecstatic, Gareth Edwards dropping a winning goal from rucked ball. Twenty-three points had come in fifteen minutes.

Lady Luck, independent piece of skirt that she is, bestows few of her favours on the faint-hearted.

---

Tension between the two nations could still be sensed when Graham Mourie's accomplished 1978 side was confronted by a Welsh XV which may have been less sophisticated than their predecessors of 1972 but made up for this with fire in their bellies. This time Wales led until the fortieth minute, at which point two All Black locks took dives at a line-out with the aim of deceiving referee R. C. Quittenton into awarding their side a penalty. This he did – though for an offence by a Welshman – whereupon Brian McKechnie kicked a goal to win the match by 13-12.

If a pair of Welsh forwards had possessed the effrontery to pull such a ruse against a New Zealand team then, perhaps, their countrymen too would have smirked their way to the end of the decade. As it was the 'big cheat' scarcely mended the severely strained bonds between Cardiff and Wellington. That had to wait until the opening of the next decade.

In the light of these episodes it is pleasurable to record that New Zealand were one of the sides involved in the most magnificent match ever to take place at Cardiff Arms Park. Though it contained seven Welshmen the other team was neither Wales nor Cardiff but the Barbarian Football Club.

The 1972–73 All Blacks had beaten three of the Home Countries and drawn with the fourth, Ireland. But despite the presence in their party of brilliant runners like Grant Batty, Bryan Williams, Bruce Robertson and Bob Burgess their successes had been achieved with a dour nine-man approach in which scrum half Sid Going was the dominant figure. Moreover it has been noted

## BLACK AND AMBER VIEWS

### Gareth Davies

'Let's play towards the clubhouse in the second half' is a comment always heard when Cardiff win the toss. It is downhill (though groundsman Albert Francis will not admit to that) and there is the advantage of the prevailing wind.

The same cannot be said of the adjacent national ground, now surrounded by towering concrete structures. Swirling winds present the greatest of problems for kickers. A perfectly struck ball can be blown just the wrong side of an upright, or drift that yard too far into touch on the full.

Receiving from a line-out I lean back and the ball sails away, wind-assisted, fifty yards downfield. At the re-start, seconds later, a good old-fashioned Garryowen is held up by the same wind and indeed blown back behind me. This brings groans of anguish from the fervent crowd and, worse, threatening stares from the eight forwards who have toiled away for the last five minutes trying to deny possession to the opposing pack – and now one of the Prima Donnas has give it away again.

Tremendous atmosphere is common to club and national grounds, but there are contrasts too. Cardiff RFC's audiences are sporting, appreciative – not partisan enough on occasion some players feel. Their great longing is for attractive and entertaining rugby; obviously they prefer to see the Blue and Blacks win but do not demand it.

Next door the national ground can contain sixty thousand Welshmen, all desperate to see the Red Jersey victorious. After all, imagine losing at home to the old enemy.

Two great arenas, so near yet so far apart.

## MATCH DAY

### Alun Priday
*Capped twice for Wales, Alun Priday made 410 appearances as a full-back for Cardiff RFC and became Honorary Secretary in 1973.*

Saturday morning: peer out of bedroom window. Eye rain with distaste. Over breakfast ponder club commitments: first XV and Youth at Cardiff Arms Park, seconds – 'Rags' – at Sophia Gardens.

A significant day – the Youth due to play a touring South African high school side. On way to ground pass demonstrators outside Angel Hotel. Not many of them, and a calming police presence as well. Don't banner-wavers realise we are against apartheid too? We differ simply over the means of changing South Africans' attitudes.

Meet Grounds Manager Albert Francis. Agree that if the Youth play their match at 1.00 p.m. the pitch will resemble a paddy field for the first XV game at 3.00. Decide that the Youth game will take place up-river at

Sophia Gardens, kicking off at noon, so that players can return in good time to watch Cardiff play Cambridge University. Double-check their meal arrangements, scheduled for 2.30.

Glance at cars beneath grandstand. Are they from last night or have they entered illegally this morning? Wish people wouldn't park here on Saturdays when the firsts are at home.

Pitch seems to be standing up to the rain well – in October the dominant colour is still green, light for the pitch, darker where the row of cypresses stands along the river bank – the wind is certainly bending them, hope they don't blow down! The trees were Hubert Johnson's idea, like the double stadium complex: what a pity he never saw his great dream fulfilled.

No panic messages in the office. For once, no withdrawals from our teams. All committee men available for duties.

Check match programmes, attendance of gatemen and stewards, reception arrangements for visiting team, accommodation and tickets for sponsors and guests, readiness of privately booked suites. Confirm arrival of referee and arrangements for running the line. Deal with last-minute media problems. Allocate complimentary tickets to guests of the club. Final check on team lists.

After all that, loudspeaker announcements about team changes and forthcoming events are positively relaxing!

## Cardiff RFC Secretaries

| | |
|---|---|
| 1876 E. C. Fry | 1892 C. S. Arthur |
| 1877 R. H. Foa | 1925 L. C. Watters |
| 1878 J. A. Jones | 1946 R. A. Cornish & B. H. Jenkins |
| 1879 E. D. Thomas | 1947 R. A. Cornish |
| 1880 W. H. Treatt & J. S. Smith | 1948 B. H. Jenkins |
| 1884 W. H. Treatt | 1955 R. F. Trott |
| 1889 W. H. Treatt & A. F. Bland | 1969 W. H. Wilkins |
| | 1973 A. J. Priday |

### THE WEST COUNTRY CONNECTION

## John Scott

*The West Country connection with Cardiff RFC has traditionally been very strong. F. E. Hancock – pioneer of the four three-quarter system – was an early club captain. Later there were Gwyn Nicholls (born across the Severn) and Barry Nelmes. Like them John Scott, a Devonian, was honoured with the captaincy (1980 to 1984) of the club. He writes:*

Our ground at Cardiff Arms Park must be one of the best club stadia in the world, if not the best. I always feel that Cardiff should take full advantage early in a game while the opposition are still sight-seeing and a bit over-whelmed by its excellence which takes in the changing facilities and the playing surface.

*John Scott, a Devonian, led Cardiff RFC for four seasons from 1980 to 1984. Under him the club won the Schweppes Cup three times and were unofficial champions in 1982.*

There is more to it than that, in particular the unrivalled atmosphere. What does this amount to?

Firstly, Cardiff are always on their mettle, because everyone wants our scalp. To win at Cardiff is an ambition of all teams.

Then there is the man on the terrace, knowledgeable and witty. I remember referee Clive Norling taking the field wearing his newly-cultivated beard. Came the voice from the sidelines, 'All right, Norling, we know it's you.'

Thirdly there is the team's awareness of a great tradition. Cardiff's members love to see the wings score tries. This is the style of rugby the club expects. Very high standards of play and conduct have been set. They must and will be maintained.

that these were not the most charismatic of tourists off the field, so that by the time they came to Cardiff for the farewell game against the Barbarians on 27 January 1973 there was an unusually deep desire in Britain at large to see these saturnine visitors put in their place.

There were other dimensions to the match. John Dawes, who had led the 1971 British Isles side to a first-ever Test series victory in New Zealand but was now playing only club rugby, accepted the captaincy of a Baa-Baas XV which contained eleven of his Lions. Two of them, Sandy Carmichael and Ray McLoughlin, had been punched out of Test contention in a notorious match at Canterbury and were clearly keen to experience victory. Lions coach Carwyn James came to deliver the changing-room pep-talk.

Beyond doubt the try Gareth Edwards scored for the Barbarians after three minutes, and described elsewhere, was quite outstanding. Avid viewers of TV programmes came to know every stride taken by Phil Bennett and his team-mates after the Llanelli man put the Baa-Baas into attacking gear with prodigious side-steps. The sole pity is that the climactic quality of the move has tended to blunt recollection of the superlative rugby played throughout the remainder of a glittering afternoon with five more tries of exceptional quality.

In the end the Barbarians crushed a determined New Zealand rally for a 23-12 victory achieved in traditional style. But it takes two to play the kind of permissive rugby football which thrilled onlookers that day, and no praise is too high for the All Blacks. They discarded safety-first tactics in favour of a running approach foreign to their nature at the time. They lost, but are not forgotten.

In the years that followed nothing quite matched the splendour of 27 January 1973. But if men from opposite ends of the earth shared such a vision of the way rugby football was meant to be played, then Wales's new colosseum had much to look forward to. Demonstrably it was worth spending millions of pounds on this particular Field of Praise.

# BEYOND
# THE CENTENARY

## RAY WILLIAMS

They came out of a sunny, clear blue sky and landed with traditional precision on Cardiff Arms Park. They were the Red Devils, the British Army's parachute team, not rehearsing some SAS-style invasion but making an important contribution to the Welsh Rugby Union's Centenary Gala Opening. Staged on 26 July 1980 the event heralded the beginning of a season of special events to mark a hundred years of organised rugby football in Wales.

And what a day it was, one to rival any Commonwealth or Olympic Games opening ceremony. Cardiff Arms Park had never known an occasion like it before and was unlikely to again – at least until the bicentenary!

The whole of Welsh rugby was represented, from the Welsh Schools Rugby Union's junior group right up to the national squad. There was a parade of nearly fifty male-voice choirs comprising close on two thousand voices, headed by the St Alban's Military Band. Another procession featured rugby organisations and a host of personalities, headed by bands from the Royal Welch Fusiliers, the Royal Regiment of Wales, the Band and Corps of Drums of the Junior Soldiers, the Prince of Wales Division, and the Corps of Drums of the Welsh Guards. There were also a detachment of Guardsmen to assist with the raising of the flag bearing the Union's new coat of arms and a group from the Royal Air Force station at St Athan.

The Red Devils parachuted in towards the end of the afternoon bearing messages from the Presidents of the Rugby Unions of England, Scotland, Ireland and France. Their appearance presaged the climax of the occasion, when a mystery runner was to enter the ground carrying a message from the Queen, patron of the Welsh Rugby Union.

In order that as many people as possible should be aware of the honour granted by Her Majesty to the Union it had been agreed that the message should be taken from Buckingham Palace to Shropshire and then carried throughout the Principality by a relay of rugby runners. It would travel within a special ball designed and presented to the WRU by the Welsh division of the British Steel Corporation.

The Queen's Message began its journey at 9.45 on 15 July at Buckingham Palace where HRH the Prince of Wales handed over the ball and its contents to the captain of London Welsh RFC. From there it went with the assistance of the Rugby, Coventry and Birmingham Welsh clubs to the Shropshire border, at which point the North Wales Union took over. The relay continued throughout the whole of Wales and involved every WRU club. By the time the Message entered Cardiff Arms Park it had covered more than 1300 miles and been borne by hundreds of players.

The ball's arrival at the ground was the highlight of an afternoon already crammed with highlights. Welsh rugby is not known for keeping its secrets, but the identity of the mystery runner was certainly well disguised. When the runner entered the ground, however, few could have failed to recognise him. It was the Welsh International and captain at the time, Jeff Squire – flanked by the captains of Wales at all levels.

The ball was opened and the Message – signed 'Elizabeth R' – read out by Centenary President Cliff Jones. The Queen had written: 'Rugby Football occupies a special place in the life of Wales, and Welshmen have played a

*Kenneth Harris, Ray Williams, Cliff Jones and Bill Clement with the 'ball' in which the Queen's centenary Message travelled to Cardiff Arms Park.*

major part in spreading the game throughout the Commonwealth and beyond. I am delighted that the Welsh Rugby Union have decided to mark this with such a grand programme and wish you every success in the coming season.'

With this final act on a memorable afternoon Cardiff Arms Park witnessed a splendid launching to the WRU's centenary. There was, however, an interesting sequel which is not generally known.

The specially designed ball carrying the Message was excellent in every respect. It took, however, some ten days for the relay to progress from Buckingham Palace to the gala opening, and in the British summer of 1980 there was a fair amount of rain. Unfortunately water leaked into the ball and the Message became rather tattered at the edges. As the intention was to frame it and place it among the Union's treasured memorabilia, the tattered parchment was returned to the Palace with a request for another, fair copy.

Such was Her Majesty's interest, however, that she declared the original document to be much more historic. So it now hangs, tatters and all, in the Union's headquarters at Cardiff Arms Park.

The work of preparing for the celebrations of the Welsh Rugby Union's centenary, centred on its headquarters at Cardiff Arms Park, had begun as early as 1973. In 1979 I was appointed as Centenary Officer, charged with three main tasks. First, to ensure that the occasion was celebrated in a manner worthy of the place that rugby football has occupied in the sporting and social life of Wales. A second need was the raising of substantial funds to assist in the final stages of the rebuilding of Cardiff Arms Park and at the same time to launch an appeal for the funds of our charitable trust, whose broad aim was to support players incapacitated as a result of playing rugby and their dependants. Finally, in 1980–81 it was Wales's wish to make a contribution to the development of the game throughout the world.

Naturally the first objective was pursued through special events, mainly matches. The outcome lived up to all expectations – except perhaps the result against New Zealand, who played at Cardiff on 1 November 1980 and left Wales far behind with victory by 23-3. The All Blacks had reached Cardiff Arms Park with wins already registered over Cardiff, Llanelli, Swansea and Newport; but their short tour achieved much more than the mere winning of games. It restored friendly realtionships between two great rugby rivals where, for a number of reasons, the rapport was in danger of becoming totally sour. The New Zealanders' visit, so important to Wales, changed all that. The Welsh Rugby Union will be forever grateful.

The other special matches in the programme began with Wales pitted at Cardiff Arms Park against an Overseas XV drawn from Argentina, Canada, Fiji, Japan, Romania, Tonga and the USA. That match took place on 20 September, while on 29 November the traditional game was mounted between Wales and England against Scotland and Ireland in the presence of Her Majesty the Queen and Prince Philip – what a welcome they received!

*A radiant Queen Elizabeth II, Patron of the WRU, paid her first visit to Cardiff Arms Park for the Centenary game between a Wales-England XV and Scotland-Ireland. She was introduced to players and ground staff by the Union's President, Cliff Jones.*

On 25 April 1981 Wales played and beat a President's XV selected by Cliff Jones from the stars of England, Scotland, Ireland, Australia, New Zealand, South Africa and France.

The contribution towards the development of the game throughout the world was achieved by organising an international conference of coaches and referees. Representatives from some forty-seven countries assembled in Cardiff for an event which had immense significance – so much so that the International Board decided to establish similar events on a regular basis.

It was, however, the WRU's objective of raising funds which created most controversy. The Union found itself accused of being too mercenary and

---

**BECKONING AND FORBIDDING**

**Graham Mourie**
*A great New Zealand captain who played five times at Cardiff Arms Park in 1978 and 1980.*

For the mountaineer, Everest. For the tennis star, Wimbledon. In each field of endeavour is a goal not quite, but almost, unobtainable.

To rugby players Cardiff Arms Park on Test-match day is that goal, beckoning and forbidding. Its mystique – as much a part of the challenge as its extraordinary atmosphere – sends shivers down your spine as you stand, nearly alone, and let the massed voices sweep across your soul. Knowing that in a few minutes you will be required to display not only your rugby skills but also your ability to absorb the mental stress of playing a Test. Knowing that those gentle Welsh folk who sing so sweetly in the Valleys metamorphose as they pass through the hallowed portals into a one-minded, one-bodied mass, willing the destruction of anything not garbed in red. The 'Arms' is their monument, which comes alive with the spring of boots on turf, the thud of leather on leather, and a roar from its tribunes.

I was fortunate never to lose a game in Cardiff. Fortunate to be part of a team which realised the unique potential of the place to hone our motivation to its finest edge. For rather than be intimidated by the impact of its ambience we utilised it, following Bryan Williams's advice to 'imagine that they are singing for us and not against us!' rather than be dwarfed by the mystique – for how many times would we be privileged to play there? Surely not so many that we could afford to play badly even once.

Twickenham with those Rolls Royces and bottles of champagne. Lansdowne Road and its terraces, Murrayfield and the Scottish Gloom, even Parc des Princes. All have their charms and quirks. But if you're an All Black and you're looking for rugby and especially a Test, then Cardiff Arms Park is the place.

And does it really matter now whether Deans scored, or Haden dived? For these are the things that legends are made of.

---

adopting too professional an approach. No one, however, came up with alternative ideas as to how the enormous amounts of money should be raised, not just to continue the redevelopment of Cardiff Arms Park but merely to repay borrowing for work already done.

At the beginning of its centenary year the Union was overdrawn at the bank to the extent of a million pounds. Further, the redevelopment of the stadium's southern side would require on the most conservative estimate another four million pounds. Until this work had been completed and the debt largely repaid there was little opportunity for funds to be made available for the game's grass roots development. Thus the centenary was seen as an oppor-

*A coterie of Welsh captains graces the Centenary Suite in 1982 for the presentation by Wilkinson Ltd of a stainless steel sword to the WRU. Back row, l-r: John Dawes, Rex Willis, Steve Fenwick, Lloyd Williams, Terry Davies, Onllwyn Brace, Gareth Edwards, David Watkins, John Williams. Middle: Ken Jones, Bryn Meredith, Rhys Williams, Brian Price, Alun Pask, Mervyn Davies, Clem Thomas, Clive Rowlands, John Lloyd. Front: Bleddyn Williams, Jack Matthews, Idwal Rees, Harry Bowcott, Cliff Jones, Wilfred Wooller and Bill Tamplin.*

tunity to mount a large-scale commercial and marketing operation with the object of laying a firm financial foundation for the next hundred years.

Much speculation took place before the centenary began. How much money would be generated by this mammoth enterprise, people wondered? If some of the more optimistic figments of the imagination had been realised then the Union's financial problems would have disappeared without trace. But regrettably life is not like that and many people – some who should have known better – came to realise that there was not a queue of companies and individuals lining up to give money to Welsh rugby. Every transaction that took place was a commercial one, with people looking for a return on their investment – a perfectly proper expectation.

The WRU did break new ground, in British rugby at least, by seeking and obtaining major match sponsors, among whom were Barclays Bank, Crown Paints, Rediffusion and International Computers Ltd. Once more the critics were hard at work bemoaning such action; but again none could give any indication as to how rugby, not just in Wales, was to make progress and develop in a harshly competitive world when legitimate methods of fund-raising received such adverse criticism. No Union, anywhere, is immune from the effects of inflation. Funds have to be generated through the game

## THE GROUND STAFF

They are a charismatic pair: the Head Groundsman of the Welsh Rugby Union and the Grounds Manager of Cardiff Athletic Club – Bill Hardiman and Albert Francis. They lead the XV of experts who tend the world's most celebrated spread of turf reserved for amateur sport, the fifteen acres of Cardiff Arms Park's rugby arenas with their associated cricket and hockey pitches up-river on the opposite bank at Sophia Gardens.

Give or take a sudden heavy frost, nothing causes a frown to cross their brows. Even in the great drought of 1976, when the use of mains water for non-essential purposes like sprinkling grass was forbidden, there was no panic: the underground stream which flows into the Taff beneath the south stand was tapped and enough water bubbled up to give the pitches a regular soaking. The experience gained was useful again in 1984's dry summer.

The two men smile readily, converse cheerfully. Often it falls to them to greet the pilgrims who visit the Welsh Mecca in their hundreds each week: Europeans and North Africans, New Zealanders, South Africans, Australians, Americans, Canadians, Japanese, South Sea islanders. All of them are shown the smiling face of Welsh rugby – while for a few minutes the mowers, rollers, clippers, sacks of fertiliser and weed-killer, line-markers, sawdust, lime, paint-pots, hammers, nails, putty, lead-piping, corner flags, abandoned boots and black plastic bags are left to their own devices in the ample storage vaults beneath the stands and terraces.

*Pictured in 1984, the ground staff who tend Cardiff Arms Park and its surrounds. Seated with their teams, fourth and fifth from the left, are Albert Francis (Cardiff Athletic Club) and Bill Hardiman (WRU).*

### GROUNDSMEN'S LORE

*Bird-life* at Cardiff Arms Park includes many varieties – ducks, robins, swallows, peacocks (winging their way intrepidly from Cardiff Castle grounds), a pair of kestrels who nest from time to time above the north stand, as well as the common or garden population of crows, blackbirds, thrushes and sparrows who hunt for worms and crumbs. Seagulls drifting up the Taff from the Severn estuary constitute the biggest nuisance, choosing to nest high in the safe no-man's land on the grandstand canopies. Staff climbing aloft to clean and sweep away detritus are at risk as the birds fiercely defend their nestlings.

*Mowing* takes place three times a week between March and October, but not at all during the winter months when spiking only is carried out. Cutting the whole area of turf with a 36-inch mower involves a walk of some 4500 metres. On big-match morning the pitch is given a final cosmetic touch and rolled with a mower whose blades have been lifted.

*Pick-pockets* are a fact of life inevitable where large crowds of people assemble. After filching a wallet and removing its contents they frequently dump the incriminating evidence inside toilet cisterns. One Monday morning no fewer than fourteen wallets were recovered from these watery hiding-places.

Of the *33,000 seats* at the national ground, up to 1000 may have to be replaced before a major match. But do not imagine that debenture holders are vandals – sustained strong sunshine is capable of cracking the brittle plastic of which some seats are made.

The average *cat* population is seven. Considering how close it stands to the river, Cardiff Arms Park is surprisingly free of rats, only two having been sighted during the years when the ground was being reconstructed.

Protection against *frost* is effected by covering the turf with thirty-two plastic sheets each measuring 42 metres by 8 metres. After a weather alert these can be spread by the ground staff in about eight hours. Usually they are left in position until the morning of a big match when volunteer helpers from all over the Cardiff area arrive to begin their removal. Work starts at 7.30 a.m. and goes on intensively until 11.30.

The *grass* is the S23 rye variety planted in the thirties. Its texture has been improved with sowings of new dwarf perennial ryes imported from Holland.

Thorough *cleaning* and sprucing-up of the national ground, Cardiff Arms Park, before a big match takes three weeks.

The ground staffs are quick to clear away *snow* from their territories, and at times of persistent heavy falls cast occasional anxious glances at the huge grandstand canopies. But these have been made strong enough to bear snow packed to a height of five feet.

New Zealanders visiting the ground often want to be shown the point at which *Bob Deans* claimed to have scored an equalising try against Wales in the All Blacks' single defeat of the 1905 tour. Since the playing area was shifted westwards and northwards during the seventies to accord with the stadium's new contours the spot is no longer on the pitch. However, it can be seen just behind the dead-ball line at the city end, and is marked by a metal disc – coloured red and black.

*Favourite remark* by tourist: 'You guys must have planted your dark-green and light-green grass seed mighty carefully to get that wonderful striped effect!'

itself and, provided there are appropriate safeguards, the use of sponsors is a sensible way of attracting cash. In no way, it has to be underlined, could it be argued that sponsorship, as exploited in the WRU centenary year, has changed the game in any way. Rather, it has become the norm – for Unions who can secure it.

It should not be thought for an instant that the WRU was solely concerned in its centenary year with making money. In keeping with its objective of celebrating the historic season fittingly the Union showed generosity in involving the many facets of the game in Wales during this period. In addition to its usual hospitality it spent some £30,000 on the Conference for Coaches and Referees. There were two after-match functions in Cardiff's City Hall which each attracted more than four hundred guests.

The major entertaining event was undoubtedly the Centenary Dinner when, on 12 March 1981 – exactly a hundred years from the formation of the WRU – some 1040 people attended a splendid occasion in the National Sports Centre for Wales, just upstream and across-river from Cardiff Arms Park. The Sports Council for Wales had agreed that the Centre could be closed for three days so that this function, one of the biggest ever mounted in the Principality, could be organised.

The cost was enormous: the hire of the Centre, making good the loss of income during closure, transforming the main hall, catering in a suitably grand manner – all these items produced a bill of monumental proportions. The end, however, more than justified the means and was a most fitting way to celebrate a hundred years of Welsh rugby in all its light and shade.

In the final analysis it is difficult to make a precise judgment on the outcome of the centenary year. Certainly from an overall viewpoint it was a marvellous success, but there were also many grey areas, especially in some of the marketing operations. Some of the disappointments could be directly related to the economic situation in Britain at the time. If only the Union had been formed in 1870 instead of 1880! – in those circumstances a centenary balance sheet would have been very different.

Perhaps the greatest disappointment came from the sale of centenary souvenirs. This market was grossly overestimated not only by the WRU but by some major manufacturers as well, sales turning out nowhere near as high as was originally expected. Some overambitious assumptions were made about the support expected from member clubs but the clubs' function, primarily, is to organise rugby football for their players; and honorary secretaries, hard-pressed men at the best of times, simply did not have the time to become honorary shopkeepers as well.

In spite of the set-backs there were many successes as well and it is a fact that the Union, beginning the season with a million-pound overdraft, not only cleared it but achieved a healthy credit balance as well. The centenary year, therefore, provided a launching-pad for the successful completion of the Cardiff Arms Park national ground project. Without it, the WRU would not have been able to give instructions for the final stages to begin.

But it did more than that, pointing the way to the future as far as the Union's finances are concerned. The game, while adhering strongly to its amateur principles, must be marketed and promoted with the best of professional techniques. Whether at school or senior level it is in the market-place. Unless it is attractive and gives value for money people will be seduced elsewhere.

Cardiff Arms Park, of course, is the absolute core of the Union's financial viability. Funds are almost entirely raised around the use of the national ground through gate money, television and advertising. These sources exist only in the context of an International rugby match or some other rugby event almost equal in magnitude.

All the efforts of the Union in recent years have been concerned with giving Welsh rugby a stage, one worthy of the epic sporting struggles which have taken place there in the past and will take place, one hopes, in an equally glorious future. It has been recorded elsewhere in this book that but for the Union's decisiveness in the mid-sixties and subsequent action there probably would now be no International rugby in the Welsh capital, certainly not at Cardiff Arms Park.

The Safety of Sports Grounds Act of 1974 put stringent controls on bodies operating large sports grounds. It has necessitated the spending of hundreds of thousands of pounds at Cardiff Arms Park alone in order to bring it up to the required safety standards. The total cost of the whole development was near nine million pounds.

That poses, quite understandably, the question whether sufficient use is made of Cardiff Arms Park. Should it not be used much more than it is?

A very fair question, which deserves detailed examination. First of all we must establish and clearly understand that the national ground was developed originally for one purpose only, as the headquarters of the Welsh Rugby Union. The project was financed almost wholly from funds raised by the

Union itself. In these terms, therefore, no other body has a legitimate claim on its use.

The next point is that the ground is used on far more occasions than people realise. To take an example, in 1984 the following matches were scheduled to take place at the national ground: Wales v Scotland; Wales v France; Wales v WRU President's XV; Schweppes Cup Final; Cardiff v Australia; Wales v Australia; Barbarians v Australia. These were all major occasions calculated to attract very large crowds. In addition there were other games like the Welsh Brewers Cup Final (for junior clubs); Wales v Italy at under-15 level; the South Wales Echo/Welsh Schools Rugby Union Mini-Rugby Festival; and the British Fire Service against the French Fire Service. Cardiff Arms Park, then, is not as under-used as many people imagine.

There are two further very important facts to be borne in mind. An increase in use of the ground would undoubtedly lead to a deterioration in the condition of the playing surface. Some years ago it was, rightly, regarded as the world's worst International pitch. Now, as a result of a lot of expense and effort it is arguably the best. This is an accolade the WRU will guard most jealously and be extremely reluctant to jeopardise. There is another limitation on the use of the national ground: the proximity and rights of the Cardiff Rugby Football Club. Remember that the campus comprises two grounds, the national and club grounds. The only way two stadia could be built in the area available was to combine the WRU's north stand with the south stand of Cardiff RFC. In that complex the two bodies share joint facilities – which totally precludes the staging of two major events on the same day.

Having said that one has to admit, of course, that there is a period during May, June, July and August when neither body has any major event to put on. Could not the national ground be used at this time for other activities?

In principle, and bearing in mind the need for ground maintenance and remedial work, the short answer is, 'Yes'. One must then ask the questions: For what? By whom?

It is very doubtful whether any Welsh sports governing body could justify the use of a ground which holds nearly 63,000 people. Association Football? Perhaps – but recent attendances at Welsh soccer International matches would hardly justify hiring Cardiff Arms Park. The ground's 33,000 seats might be an attractive proposition, but it seems likely that the Football Association of Wales would have internal battles to fight with its League clubs before International soccer could be moved from Ninian Park, the Vetch Field and the Racecourse, Wrexham, to Cardiff Arms Park. Even if it wanted to, that is.

A limiting factor is the absence of a facility for evening games. Provision of floodlights, together with secondary back-up lighting for stands and terraces, would cost at 1984 levels nearly £500,000, an expenditure which the WRU's financial state at the present time has made it impossible to contemplate. Moreover the ground cannot be used for international athletics

## THE RELIGIOUS CONNECTION

**Russell Bennett**
*Team member Cardiff District Convention.*

Thursday 24 July 1975 – the day Jezebel was fed to the dogs on the turf of the national rugby ground, Cardiff Arms Park.

Well, not really! In fact the person playing the part was carefully lowered on to a strategically placed padded mattress just behind the stage set. It was all part of the well rehearsed Bible Drama staged by Jehovah's Witnesses on the opening day of the first District Assembly to be held in the stadium. Twickenham and Murrayfield had already been regular hosts to such conventions, so it was a happy day when Cardiff made it a hat-trick – as I should know, because I was there!

More than 14,000 people were present on the final day of the Assembly, Sunday, which pointed the way towards successive summers in which thousands of happy conventioners would converge upon the burgeoning stadium. Only 1978 broke the continuity, when a series of International Assemblies were held at other venues in the British Isles; but the desire to be in Cardiff again was so strong that back they came in 1979. Although the Convention caters largely for visitors from South Wales and part of the West Country it would be true to say that delegates from all parts of the globe love to come and enjoy the family atmosphere there.

Naturally there is a big difference between attending a rugby match at Cardiff Arms Park for a couple of hours and spending four whole days there in a programme of sacred service. A large team of willing volunteers first gives the ground a spring clean before setting out to provide for the bodily needs of those present. Food is prepared on site – cooked meals, snacks, hot drinks and when the sun shines plenty of cool refreshing fruit juices.

Rugby is a male-orientated pursuit in which conversions play a part; while an Assembly of Jehovah's Witnesses has a big proportion of the fair sex present who are grateful for conversions of another kind – namely many of the toilet facilities being made suitable for them and also for invalids so that all can enjoy the proceedings in comfort.

All this is possible with the warm, friendly co-operation of the WRU ground staff. With their stadium now rated as Europe's best, our conventions can only get better and better!

**David Williams**

May 31 1980 is a date that will long be remembered by many members of the Church in Wales. It was on that day that some 30,000 of them gathered at Cardiff Arms Park for an open-air Communion Service after walking through the streets of Cardiff in a procession that took two hours to pass into the stadium.

Needless to say planning for the event had taken several years. It had all started when a number of small adult study groups had expressed their desire to take part in something which would show that being a member of the Church meant belonging to something that was bigger than just one small group or even just one parish. This came just at the time when the sixtieth anniversary of the disestablishment of the Church in Wales was coming up; and it seemed a good idea to have an event which would show to the world (and to its own members) the fact that the Church in Wales was very much alive. To show, in fact, that sixty years of disestablishment had done it a power of good.

Having taken the decision to mount an event the next question was, 'Where to hold it?' Such questions are not answered lightly in the Church in Wales. Very often we end up having meetings at places that have the dubious value of being inaccessible to all in a desire to be fair to the North, South, East and West of a Principality not renowned for its ease of communication. In the case of 'Celebration '80' there was little debate: all

*Bishops of the Church in Wales step from the players' tunnel on to the Cardiff Arms Park turf for 'Celebration '80', the open-air communion service which marked the sixtieth anniversary of Disestablishment.*

*'Oggie, Oggie, Oggie!'* South Wales Echo *cartoonist Gren's irreverent view of the ceremony.*

wanted to come to Cardiff and, to cater for the numbers wishing to be involved, all wanted to come to the national ground, Cardiff Arms Park.

Those present thrilled to an act of worship on the scale that the stadium allowed. That all problems of organisation were soon overcome was due in no small measure to the then Lay Training Officer of the Church in Wales, Captain Derek Jones of the Church Army and his band of helpers. Their efforts ensured that all those at Cardiff Arms Park on that last day of May 1980 found it a day to remember.

because it is now too constricted to accommodate an eight-lane track to a sufficiently high standard.

It would appear, therefore, that Cardiff Arms Park would grossly over-provide spectator accommodation if used by other sports bodies and would thus be a very expensive facility to hire. To put things in perspective, a charity collection at Cardiff Arms Park on an International day probably yields more money than most other governing bodies (apart from soccer) ever take from spectators at their representative matches. To draw the threads together, the WRU's headquarters stadium is not particularly suitable for most other sports because it either lacks the appropriate facilities or is too large a ground for the potential gate. That is not to say, however, that the Union would not give very serious consideration to requests to use the ground coming from any other sports bodies.

As we look into the future, however, it becomes clear that the Welsh Rugby Union has built itself a facility which is very expensive to run and, as we have seen, beyond the means of other sporting bodies in Wales to hire. At the time of writing it seems that the only recourse is to look to more commercial interests for extended use of the national ground in order to reduce the drain it places on the Union's resources – as the eighties got under way the rates paid were amounting to £52,000 a year and it was expected that when the new south stand assessment was made the annual bill would be around £75,000. It is true that Twickenham and Murrayfield are in the same position; but the rating levels are much lower in England and Scotland as far as those grounds are concerned than they are in Wales. All sport in Ireland is exempt from taxes of any kind. What a difference a concession like that would make to the Welsh Rugby Union!

Incidentally, the French Rugby Federation does not even own Parc des Princes where it stages major International games. The stadium is rented from a Paris municipality which merely gets a percentage of the gate. This is reflected in the considerable sums which the Federation has at its disposal. As a matter of fact in rugby football it is only the four Home Unions which actually own grounds. All other International Board countries use premises owned either by local authorities or by provincial or state Unions.

What sort of events, then, can be mounted at Cardiff Arms Park which will utilise its facilities more fully and at the same time make some contribution to the heavy capital and running costs? It will be obvious that they must be capable of attracting large crowds.

A world-title boxing match, featuring an outstanding Welsh fighter like Colin Jones, might be an answer. Nowadays, however, boxing rarely generates a large amount of money via spectators. Inevitably the bulk of the 'take' comes from television contracts, an area in which Britain hardly starts to compete with the American market. The result is that the big boxing match never gets here anyway.

Another attraction could be a pop concert. Many entrepreneurs with experience in this sphere regard Cardiff Arms Park in its completed form as probably the best venue for such concerts in Britain, and in fact plans were made in 1982 for the Rolling Stones to hold a concert in the stadium. Terms had been agreed with the promoter, Harvey Goldsmith, and Cardiff City Council had granted a licence. The concert was to take place on a Sunday from 12.30 pm until 6.30. There were some objections from nearby residents, but on balance it was thought that the event could take place with the minimum of inconvenience.

Unfortunately, however, because of the developments then taking place at the ground the promoter was not able to organise matters in the way he wished and the concert, accordingly, was transferred elsewhere. But undoubtedly he or other promoters will be back in the future – when there will be no rebuilding to hinder any arrangements.

Perhaps it can be seen that the future use of the national ground as a revenue earner is no simple matter. But remember: its primary purpose is to provide the Welsh rugby team and those who come in the future with the best possible facilities in which to play; and at the same time to afford the thousands of supporters (from both sides) an opportunity of watching their heroes in conditions that are safe and comfortable. Nothing should be allowed to detract from that.

The redevelopment of Cardiff Arms Park was a great act of faith. Few people appreciate the magnitude of the achievement, which is probably unequalled throughout the world.

There will be pressures to change the place's image; the name 'National Stadium' is an example. But to rugby men everywhere it will forever be 'Cardiff Arms Park'. A precious heritage which should be – and will be – jealously guarded.

# EPILOGUE

On 7 April 1984, a hundred years to the week since it first staged International rugby football, Cardiff Arms Park was the venue for an invitation match in which Wales played a select World XV to celebrate the completion of the National Ground project initiated with the ploughing-up of the cricket field seventeen years earlier. Selected by WRU President E. B. Davies, the guest side was managed and coached by Denzil Lloyd and Leighton Davies and had played a mid-week warm-up game in Llanelli.

The Red XV kicked off under Mike Watkins of Newport, his country's ninety-second captain, with a 35,000 crowd very much aware of the giant irony surrounding the rebuilt stadium. As the Five Nations' Championship season had proceeded, with visits to Cardiff by Scotland and France, it became apparent that Wales now possessed the finest purpose-built premises for rugby football in the northern hemisphere, possibly in the world.

The trouble was that after two decades of near-impregnability the citadel was no longer immune from capture. Scotland, later to celebrate their first Grand Slam since 1925, won a second successive victory in Cardiff. France went home with the spoils for the first time since 1968. It was not as if there was anything profoundly amiss with Welsh rugby, for gritty wins were achieved at Twickenham and in Dublin. But in their own spanking new super-stadium, with its unsurpassed comforts for players, administrators and spectators (give or take some south terrace teething troubles), the Welsh seemed unable to assert themselves.

And after an early penalty goal through which they took the lead the home XV looked unlikely to shake off this unprecedented Cardiff malaise. A miscued clearing kick was caught by Jerome Gallion who drew defenders and passed to John Rutherford. The Scot, wrong-footing Welsh defenders who had come frantically upfield to nip any attack in the bud, sent a sweet pass to Maori centre Steve Pokere who was by now at full speed and used only the suggestion of a dummy to clear his path to the line for an unconverted try. All Wales could manage in reply was a Bleddyn Bowen penalty.

The crowd roared appreciation as men sprinted, side-stepped, counter-attacked daringly from their own line and generally gave the ball a lot of air. Star backs Pokere, Wilf Cupido, Bleddyn Bowen and Rob Ackerman all tried to create space in the midfield only to be cut down by relentless tackling; and the next score needed the assistance of back-row forwards. England's Mike Rafter and Springbok skipper Rob Louw, with a brilliant dummy, were the men whose support play created space for David Leslie of Scotland to cross unopposed for a try converted by John Rutherford. Things looked black for the host nation as half-time arrived with the deficit 13-6.

---

### THEATRE OF PASSIONS

**Eddie Butler**
*Captain of Wales in the first match at the rebuilt national ground on
21 January 1984.*

It is when Cardiff Arms Park is full that the mid-city concrete bowl ceases
to be merely an architectural curiosity and becomes a real theatre of passions.
The lifeless rows of turned-up seats are suddenly a moving mass of cans
and hip-flasks and, above all, open mouths blasting sound up and over the
ground to descend on the poor unfortunates outside who redouble their
efforts to find a wall to scale or a steward to bribe.

The drama extends beyond this pure form of public frenzy to the more
secretive world down in the bowels beneath the stand – the changing-
rooms. Behind portable iron fences the crowds of children armed with
pens and paper and requests for 'Any more programmes, mister?' are
distanced from the pre-match waves escaping from these quarters: waves
of heat from the plunge-bath already running, from the tubes of embrocation discarded and crushed by endlessly checked studs, from the exercises
that each player goes through in an attempt to forget how slowly time is
passing. Waves of last-minute, apparently forgotten messages passed on
for the twentieth time, waves of nerves that are plainly visible but vigor-
ously denied afterwards.

Then – it is out of the shelter into the area under the stand; where the
air is cold but still dark; and where the noise from above arrives only
as a vague murmur, drowned by clacking studs as the restrained shuffle
to the final tunnel begins. That brings light, and there is suddenly colour –
but all senses give way to the ear as it collides with the wall of noise one
step away from the turf.

To run on to that pitch, to be greeted by that sound, is one of the few
acts that lives up to and exceeds all personal anticipation; it is the act of
one second whose memory will keep the blood surging for a lifetime.

---

Immediately on the resumption, however, centre Bleddyn Bowen prised
open the World XV's defence with an angled run which sent four would-be
tacklers scampering to cut off Mark Titley away to the right. Deftly the young
policeman switched his pass back to the burly Ackerman who went under-
neath the crossbar for a try converted by Howel' Davies. The full-back, fresh
from breaking the Welsh points-scoring record for a Championship season,
was now nominated twice by his captain to kick penalties when a large sector
of the crowd clearly wanted Wales to run free balls. But the wisdom of his
decisions was underlined when Pokere, put into space twenty metres out,
sprinted in for a second try.

The day's highlight had yet to come. It was presaged by an Ackerman chip
to the President's XV goal-line where the Wallaby wing Peter Grigg jinked

his way arrogantly forward to link with Maurice Colclough. The big Englishman transferred to his fellow lock, All Black Gary Whetton, who tucked the
ball under his left arm and ran as no lock forward could have run in a hundred
years of rugby at Cardiff Arms Park. Flankers, halves and three-quarters
floundered in his wake and even Howell Davies did no more than buffet him
into switching the ball to Patrick Esteve. The speedy Frenchman was hauled
to earth with an inspired cover tackle from Mark Titley as the Welsh line
seemed bound to be crossed for a fourth time.

But now the all-star XV, bravely and intelligently led by Louw, had shot
its bolt. The Welsh forwards tightened the screw; the World XV and its

*At the outset of the eighties Terry Holmes became Gareth Edwards's successor at scrum half for
Cardiff and Wales.*

out-of-season southern hemisphere complement gasped for breath; and Terry Holmes struck like a cobra behind a goal-line scrummage. Howell Davies converted his try to send the crowd home happy – and dispel any malign spirit that might be hovering over Cardiff Arms Park's new ramparts and towers.

Mike Watkins and Rob Louw were clearly exhilarated as they complimented each other before the television cameras after the final whistle. Louw brought a rare South African perspective to bear on the quality of the forward play of the home team, whose mauling and scrummaging technique he described as magnificent. Wales's captain struck an apposite chord when he talked of the vigour and commitment of the exchanges.

'That's how it has been this afternoon,' he summed up. 'And that's how it will be at Cardiff Arms Park for hundreds more seasons.'

WALES   H. Davies (Bridgend), M. H. Titley (Bridgend), R. A. Ackerman (London Welsh), B. Bowen (South Wales Police), A. M. Hadley (Cardiff), M. Dacey (Swansea), T. D. Holmes (Cardiff), I. Stephens (Bridgend), M. J. Watkins (Newport, capt.), I. H. Eidman (Cardiff), S. J. Perkins (Pontypool), R. L. Norster (Cardiff), R. D. Moriarty (Swansea), E. T. Butler (Pontypool), D. F. Pickering (Llanelli).

WRU PRESIDENT'S XV   R. Gould (Australia), P. C. Grigg (Australia), W. Cupido (South Africa), S. Pokere (New Zealand), P. Esteve (France), J. Rutherford (Scotland), J. Gallion (France), H. J. Van Eswegen (South Africa), C. T. Deans (Scotland), M. A. Harding (Australia), G. W. Whetton (New Zealand), M. Colclough (England), D. G. Leslie (Scotland), R. J. Louw (South Africa, capt.), M. Rafter (England).

Referee: C. Norling (WRU); Touch judges: A. Richards, W. Jones (WRU).